NEOLITHIC

How did people move from caves to condos? When did the rich become different from everyone? Who built Stonehenge? And who invented the hoe?

The answer to all these questions lies in the Neolithic era, when people's lives were irrevocably altered by the invention of agriculture.

This book is a lively and engaging introduction to this momentous period during which our ancestors stopped hunting and gathering and built permanent, settled villages where they developed farming, herding, new technologies and new social systems: in short, when all the patterns of modern life first appeared.

After familiarizing the reader with essential archaeological and genetic terms and concepts, McCarter explores the latest evidence from scientific analyses as varied as pollen identification, radiometric dating and DNA research, condensing them into an up-to-date academic account which stays accessible to even the novice reader.

Focusing primarily on sites in southwest Asia, *Neolithic* addresses questions such as:

- Which plants and animals were the first to be domesticated, and how?
- How did life change when people began farming?
- What were the first villages like?
- What do we know about the social, political and religious life of Neolithic people? And
- What happened to human health as a result of the Neolithic transition?

Lavishly illustrated with almost a hundred images, this enjoyable book is an ideal introduction both for students of archaeology and for general readers interested in our past.

Susan Foster McCarter holds a degree in Mediterranean Prehistory from Brandeis University. For almost twenty years she has been a member of the Department of Near Eastern Studies at Johns Hopkins University. She also teaches art history and archaeology at York College of Pennsylvania.

NEOLITHIC

Susan Foster McCarter

Illustrations by Catherine E. Weaver

Routledge
Taylor & Francis Group

NEW YORK AND LONDON

First published 2007
by Routledge
711 First Ave, New York, NY 10017

Simultaneously published in the UK
by Routledge
2 Park Square, Milton Park, Abingdon, Oxon OX14 4RN

Routledge is an imprint of the Taylor & Francis Group, an informa business

© 2007 Susan Foster McCarter

Reprinted 2008 (twice)

Typeset in Goudy by
RefineCatch Limited, Bungay, Suffolk

British Library Cataloguing in Publication Data
A catalogue record for this book is available from the British Library

Library of Congress Cataloging in Publication Data
A catalog record for this book has been requested

ISBN10: 0–415–36413–2 (hbk)
ISBN10: 0–415–36414–0 (pbk)
ISBN10: 0–203–01532–0 (ebk)

ISBN13: 978–0–415–36413–3 (hbk)
ISBN13: 978–0–415–36414–0 (pbk)
ISBN13: 978–0–203–01532–2 (ebk)

CONTENTS

CONTENTS

ILLUSTRATIONS

PREFACE

In his 1956 memoir, *Still Digging*, Sir Mortimer Wheeler wrote that when he began his studies before the First World War, few people wanted to become professional archaeologists. At that time, he notes, the past "had no future in it."[1] Wheeler went on to say that by the mid-twentieth century things were much better because "[t]he distant past is being combined . . . with the complexities of the present in a lengthening perspective which at least provides a sort of working substitute for philosophy and at best a reassuring context for our own antics and absurdities."[2] Fifty years have passed since Wheeler's book, and today archaeology is flourishing. Thousands of archaeologists explore everything from modern landfills to ancient caves as they attempt to provide a context for the antics and absurdities of modern life. Their conclusions appear in dozens of scientific journals devoted to archaeology. At the same time, web sites, popular magazines, newspapers, movies, and television series offer the general public entertaining – if not always accurate – reconstructions of ancient life. They invite you to hold your breath as Egyptian tombs are opened for the "first time in millennia," choose sides in the controversies surrounding the Shroud of Turin, and imagine the chaos as Pompeii and Herculaneum are destroyed by the eruption of Vesuvius.

Like the three examples I've just mentioned, almost all the popular presentations are about well-known periods. Only a few deal with prehistory – the roughly two-million year period during which all the important aspects of human culture first appeared – and that's too bad, because if you really want to understand the present, prehistory is the place to start. In the past half-century, specialists in more than a dozen different areas of research have turned their attention to prehistoric life: some study our earliest human ancestors, others explore the cultural achievements of the first modern humans, and still others, like me, focus on a period called the Neolithic. We want to know why people domesticated plants and animals, why they began living in villages, and why the political, social, economic, and religious systems that they developed continue to define our lives.

Almost every time I meet people and tell them that I study archaeology,

xi

the response is the same: "Oh! Aren't you lucky! I wanted to be an archae-ologist when I was little." I'm always slightly surprised, because when I was a child I never thought about being an archaeologist. I'm not even sure I knew what an archaeologist was. In fact, until I was in graduate school I'd never considered archaeology as a career. But the minute I took my first course about the Neolithic I was hooked, and my first excavation experience more than met my expectations. Ayios Epiktitos Vrysi is a small Neolithic village on the north coast of Cyprus. It lies a few feet above the Mediterranean, on a small bay where racehorses from a nearby breeding farm swim at dawn (at least they did in those days). Behind the site are the romantic peaks of the Kyrenia Mountain range and on clear days, the Taurus Mountains in Turkey are visible across the water. It's one of the most beautiful places I've ever seen – Neolithic Cypriots certainly knew where to build. I was assigned to the pottery shed, and as soon as I began processing the ceramic remains, I began to ask questions. Why did Neolithic people prefer ceramic vessels to stone, wood and skin containers? Why did the bold geometric patterns on the bowls and jugs look a lot like Navaho blankets and Turkish rugs? Who were the potters? What did they use the pottery for? Did they sell it? To whom? How was it paid for? Thirty years later prehistorians still don't have answers to all of these questions, but we have some reasonable theories.

This book is intended to share what I've learned about the Neolithic. In it, I provide an overview of the period, and then discuss the various aspects of modern life that appeared during this most interesting (and significant) stage of human cultural development. The Neolithic arose all over the world, and I draw examples from cultures from Asia to the Americas, but because the earliest Neolithic sites are found in an area stretching roughly from Greece on the west to Iran on the east, and from the Black Sea on the north to the Sinai Peninsula on the south, I focus on this region.

ACKNOWLEDGMENTS

Many people helped make this the project a reality. Kate Weaver, from the Department of Art as Applied to Medicine at the Johns Hopkins University School of Medicine, agreed to create a few illustrations, and ended up as a full partner. The book is much better, and much more entertaining, because of her efforts. My academic colleagues, especially Pam Hemzik, reworked class schedules to give me uninterrupted time to write. Specialists from many fields provided support: Mel Atkins suggested bibliographical sources for the Jōmon culture and permitted me to adapt a photograph from *Prehistory of Japan*; Van Dixon explained the complex astronomical concepts associated with Stonehenge; Rev. Mary Louise Ellenberger gave me a copy of Wheeler's *Still Digging*; Yossi Garfinkel allowed me to adapt two photographs from Sha'ar Hagolan; Charles George lent me out-of-print architectural history books; Peter Kuninholm provided a drawing of dendrochronological sequences; John McCarter fact-checked the chapter on disease; P.K. McCarter, Jr. allowed me to adapt several of his drawings; my former student, Brandon McFadden drew the burials; James Mellaart allowed me to adapt illustrations from his books *Çatal Hüyük* and *Hacilar II*; Gary Rollefson agreed to my request to adapt photographs of the 'Ain Ghazal statues, and sent me clear images to use; Ian Todd (who introduced me to prehistoric archaeology so many years ago) sent two drawings of the architecture of Kalavassos-Tenta; and David Zohary allowed me to redraw several maps from *Domestication of Plants in the Old World*. I greatly appreciate their generosity. The Council for British Research in the Levant, Yale University Press, and Routledge very kindly gave permission to reproduce illustrations from their publications. Bill Regier of the University of Illinois Press gave me much-needed advice and helped me refine both the concept and the format, as did my anonymous reviewers. My editor at Routledge, Richard Stoneman, his assistant Amy Laurens, and Richard Willis of Swales & Willis provided invaluable guidance. Along the way, my friends also helped. Dot and Carl Schneider, the book's godparents, provided technical advice and constant encouragement. Paul Robie read an early chapter and kept me going by asking "is it done *yet?*" Grace Wright read and copy-edited draft chapters, and Margaret Wright read the manuscript intelligently and thoroughly, and told me what was good (and what wasn't). The book owes its world-wide emphasis to my students, who always want to know more about how Neolithic people everywhere were "just like us," and I'm especially indebted to my friends and students at the Johns Hopkins Evergreen Society: they not only ask wonderful questions, they tell me where to look for the answers. And finally, this book would never have been written without Kyle.

ILLUSTRATION CREDITS

Every attempt has been made to secure permission for the reproduction of copyright material; author and publisher would be glad to hear from any copyright holder not here acknowledged. Unless otherwise noted, all illustrations are by Catherine E. Weaver.

Chapter 1

Figure 1.1 From the author's photograph.
Figure 1.2 From Kenyon, K. (1981) *Excavations at Jericho*, Vol. III, PL. 295. Reproduced by permission of the Council for British Research in the Levant.
Figure 1.3 From the author's photograph.
Figure 1.4 From Keller, F. (1898) *The Lake Dwellings of Switzerland and Other Parts of Europe*, Vol. 2, PL. XII.
Figure 1.5 Reproduced courtesy of Peter Ian Kuninholm, the Aegean Dendrochronology Project, Cornell University.
Figure 1.6 From Keller, F. (1898) *The Lake Dwellings of Switzerland and Other Parts of Europe*, Vol. 2, PL. VII.
Figure 1.7 From Keller, F. (1898) *The Lake Dwellings of Switzerland and Other Parts of Europe*, Vol. 2, PL. XIII.
Figure 1.8 Adapted from Keller, F. (1898) *The Lake Dwellings of Switzerland and Other Parts of Europe*, Vol. 2, PL. CLXI: 65a and b.

Chapter 2

Figures 2.1–2.7 Catherine E. Weaver.

Chapter 3

Figure 3.1 Catherine E. Weaver.
Figure 3.2 From the author's photograph.
Figure 3.3 After Kenyon, K. (1957) *Digging Up Jerusalem*, PL. 13.

Figure 3.4 After a photograph courtesy of Yosef Garfinkel, Hebrew University of Jerusalem.

Figure 3.5 From Davis, S.J.M. (1987) *The Archaeology of Animals*, Figure 1.8. Reproduced by permission of Yale University Press, and Routledge. Original drawing by Judith Ogdan.

Figure 3.6 From the author's photograph.

Figure 3.7 Catherine E. Weaver.

Chapter 4

Figures 4.1–4.2 Catherine E. Weaver.

Figure 4.3 Adapted from Zohary, D. and Hopf, M. (2000) *Domestication of Plants in the Old World*, Maps 1, 3, and 5. Permission courtesy of Daniel Zohary and Maria Hopf.

Figure 4.4 Catherine E. Weaver.

Figure 4.5 Adapted from Zohary, D. and Hopf, M. (2000) *Domestication of Plants in the Old World*, Map 7. Permission courtesy of Daniel Zohary and Maria Hopf.

Figure 4.6 Catherine E. Weaver.

Chapter 5

Figures 5.1–5.7 Catherine E. Weaver.

Figure 5.8 After photographs by M. Wright and the author, courtesy M. Wright.

Chapter 6

Figure 6.1 Catherine E. Weaver.

Figures 6.2–6.3 From the author's photographs.

Figure 6.4 Reproduced courtesy of I.A. Todd.

Figures 6.5–6.6 Catherine E. Weaver.

Figure 6.7 From the author's photograph.

Figure 6.8 Catherine E. Weaver.

Figure 6.9 From the author's photograph.

Figure 6.10 Catherine E. Weaver.

Figure 6.11 From Kenyon, K. (1981) *Excavations at Jericho*, Vol. III, PL. 244. Reproduced by permission of the Council for British Research in the Levant.

Figure 6.12 After Kenyon, K. (1957) *Digging Up Jerusalem*, PL. 25.

Figure 6.13 After a photograph courtesy of P.K. McCarter Jr.

Chapter 7

Figure 7.1 Adapted from a drawing by P.K. McCarter Jr. Permission courtesy of the artist.

Figures 7.2–7.5 Catherine E. Weaver.

Figure 7.6 From the author's photograph.

Figure 7.7 Adapted from Kenyon, K. (1957) *Digging Up Jerusalem*, PL. 11B

Figure 7.8 After Aikens C.M. and Higuchi, T. (1982) *Prehistory of Japan*, Figure 3.30. Permission courtesy of C.M. Aikens and T. Higuchi.

Figure 7.9 Catherine E. Weaver.

Chapter 8

Figure 8.1 Brandon Travis McFadden.

Figures 8.2–8.7 Catherine E. Weaver.

Chapter 9

Figure 9.1 Catherine E. Weaver.

Figure 9.2 After a photograph courtesy of Yosef Garfinkel, Hebrew University of Jerusalem.

Figure 9.3 From the author's photograph.

Figures 9.4–9.5 Brandon Travis McFadden.

Figure 9.6 From Keller, F. (1898) *The Lake Dwellings of Switzerland and Other Parts of Europe*, Vol. 2, PL. XI.

Chapter 10

Figure 10.1 Catherine E. Weaver.

Figure 10.2 After Kenyon, K. (1957) *Digging Up Jerusalem*. PL. 15b.

Figure 10.3 Adapted from a drawing by P.K. McCarter Jr. Permission courtesy of the artist.

Figures 10.4–10.5 After photographs courtesy of I.A. Todd.

Figure 10.6 From Keller, F. (1898) *The Lake Dwellings of Switzerland and Other Parts of Europe*, Vol. 2, p. 516.

Figure 10.7 From Keller, F. (1898) *The Lake Dwellings of Switzerland and Other Parts of Europe*, Vol. 1, PL. CXXXV.

Figure 10.8 From Keller, F. (1898) *The Lake Dwellings of Switzerland and Other Parts of Europe*, Vol. 2, PL. CXXXIX.

Figure 10.9 From the author's photograph.

Chapter 11

Figures 11.1–11.2 Catherine E. Weaver.

Figure 11.3 After Schmandt-Besserat, D. (ed.) (no date), Monumental Statuary Figure 1a, Symbols at 'Ain Ghazal: 'Ain Ghazal Excavation Reports Vol. 1. Permission courtesy of Dr Gary Rollefson and Professor Dr Zeidan Kafafi and the 'Ain Ghazal Archaeological Project. Original photograph by Peter Dorrell and Stuart Laidlaw.

Figure 11.4 After Mellaart, J. (1970) Hacilar II, Figure 57.1. Permission courtesy of James Mellaart.

Figure 11.5 Adapted from Mellaart (1967) Çatal Hüyük: A Neolithic Town in Anatolia, PL. 67–68, and Figure 52. Permission courtesy of James Mellaart.

Figure 11.6 After Mellaart (1967) Çatal Hüyük: A Neolithic Town in Anatolia, Figure 33. Permission courtesy of James Mellaart.

Figure 11.7 After Mellaart (1967) Çatal Hüyük: A Neolithic Town in Anatolia, Figure 15. Permission courtesy of James Mellaart.

Figure 11.8 Brandon Travis McFadden.

Figure 11.9 After Kenyon, K. (1957) Digging Up Jerusalem, PL. 21.

Figure 11.10 After Mellaart, J. (1970) Hacilar II, Figure 233. Permission courtesy of James Mellaart.

Figure 11.11 After Schmandt-Besserat, D. (ed.) (no date), Catalog of Statue Cache 2, Figure 41, Symbols at 'Ain Ghazal: 'Ain Ghazal Excavation Reports Vol. 1. Permission courtesy of Dr Gary Rollefson and Professor Dr Zeidan Kafafi and the 'Ain Ghazal Archaeological Project. Original photograph by John Tsantes.

Figure 11.12 After Schmandt-Besserat, D. (ed.) (no date) Monumental Statuary Figure 3, Symbols at 'Ain Ghazal: 'Ain Ghazal Excavation Reports Vol. 1. Permission courtesy of Dr Gary Rollefson and Professor Dr Zeidan Kafafi and the 'Ain Ghazal Archaeological Project. Original photograph by Peter Dorrell and Stuart Laidlaw.

Chapter 12

Figure 12.1 Gebauer, A.B. and Price T.D. (1992a), "Foragers to Farmers: An Introduction," Table 1.

1

INTRODUCTION TO
THE NEOLITHIC

If you ask a group of people when the modern period began, some will point to the invention of digital communications. Others, with a slightly longer view of things, may mention the end of the Second World War or the beginning of the first one. Those who've studied western history usually answer that the Industrial Revolution, or the Enlightenment, or maybe the Italian Renaissance marks the beginning of modernity. But the truth is, the basic patterns of modern life developed more than 10,000 years ago, in a period called the Neolithic, when people's lives were irrevocably altered by the single most profound change in human cultural history – the invention of agriculture.

This book describes what happened to our ancestors as they changed from hunting and gathering to farming. I begin by defining some basic terms and concepts, including a brief description of archaeology, the main source of information about Neolithic culture. After a summary of the natural mechanisms that underlie domestication, I address the following questions: When and where did the shift from hunting and gathering to farming first take place? What plants and animals were the first ones to be domesticated? Why did early agriculturalists concentrate on those particular species? How did life change when people began farming? What did the first villages look like and why was their development significant? Who were the first craft specialists and what did they do? What happened to human health as a result of the Neolithic Revolution? What do archaeologists know about the social, political and religious life of Neolithic people? And finally, why did the transition to farming occur?

Prehistory

As you will see, in a surprising number of ways the lives of the first Neolithic people were not much different from yours. They lived in houses; ate bread, vegetables, fruit, meat, and cheese; used fired clay dishes; wove cloth for clothes; liked luxury goods; and buried their dead in special places. But in one way, Neolithic life wasn't at all like the twenty-first century:

1

Neolithic people didn't write. Cultures that haven't invented writing are referred to as prehistoric, and for more than two million years (until about 5,000 years ago when writing was invented in Mesopotamia and Egypt) everyone on earth was prehistoric. Once writing appeared most people moved into history, but in some parts of the world prehistoric cultures survived well into the twentieth century.

Scholarly interest in prehistory in general, and the Neolithic in particular, is a fairly recent phenomenon. It arose in the mid-nineteenth century, when Europeans studying pre-Roman cultures divided them into three stages based on the materials used for their tools: the Stone Age, the Bronze Age, and the Iron Age. John Lubbock, an English nobleman who wrote popular science books, noticed that some Stone Age tools had been shaped by grinding or polishing instead of by the more common chipping techniques, so he subdivided the Stone Age into two phases: an earlier Paleolithic (or Old Stone Age) phase, when only chipped stone tools were made; and a later, Neolithic (or New Stone Age) phase during which ground stone tools were invented. Although methods of tool manufacture aren't the only distinctions between Paleolithic and Neolithic cultures, Lubbock's division, which he published in a 1865 book on archaeology called *Prehistoric Times*, is still used today. During the twentieth century, particularly since the 1950s, new excavations and new scientific ways of processing data have produced a flood of information about everything from Neolithic marriage customs to prehistoric tooth decay. Today, we can no longer think of Neolithic people as Stone Age savages. Instead, we must view them as the founders of modern life, and among the most creative problem-solvers the world has ever known.

Archaeological assumptions

Because it lies in prehistory, almost everything that we know about the Neolithic was discovered archaeologically. Archaeologists study the physical – or material – remains produced by human activity. Any place with material remains is by definition an archaeological site: a meadow is simply a meadow, but a meadow with a broken bottle on it is a site because the bottle is a physical record, maybe the only record, that in the past someone was in the meadow and did something while there. (As you've probably noticed, according to this definition, almost every place on earth is a site.) The ultimate goal of an archaeological excavation is to collect as much information about the past as possible, so it's lucky that ancient people weren't any tidier than we are. The debris they left behind is just what you'd find in an abandoned village today, and in order to study it, archaeological teams include all sorts of experts: architects, art conservationists, art historians, biologists, botanists, chemists, economic theorists, ethnographers, geneticists, geographers, geologists, graphic artists, historians, linguists, materials

Figure 1.1 Centuries of rebuilding on the same site can create mounds like this one in Turkey with its attached modern village.

scientists, osteologists, pathologists, photographers, physical anthropologists, physicists, sociologists, surveyors, and zoologists all study archaeological data. And all of them, regardless of their backgrounds, share a set of assumptions about the archaeological process, and about what excavations can reveal about the past.

The most basic archaeological assumption is that sites are created over time – even that broken bottle in the meadow is the result of several sequential actions. Material remains accumulate in layers, or strata (usually identified by significant changes in the finds or by visible differences in the soil). On some sites the strata are so thin they're hardly visible above the ground, but Neolithic villagers from Iran to Greece built their houses using mudbrick, and on these sites the living debris built up in thick layers that eventually created large mounds that can be seen for miles: they're referred to variously as *magoulas*, *tepes*, *tels* or *tells*, and *höyüks*, all of which simply mean hill. But whether the layers are thick or thin, archaeologists assume that they contain a chronological record of what happened on a site, with the earliest evidence at the bottom and the most recent evidence at the top. This concept of chronological deposition is so important that it's reflected in two of the four Laws of Archaeology: the Law of Stratigraphy – archaeological layers are deposited one at a time – and the Law of Superposition – the lowest layers were deposited first.

Understanding that archaeological strata are deposited over time, and that layers near the bottom are older than those near the top, allows archaeologists to trace cultural changes on a site. For example, when archaeologists write that the process of animal domestication took place in a particular place, what they mean is that they've compared the animal remains in the strata, and seen a change from wild forms in the lower (earlier) levels to

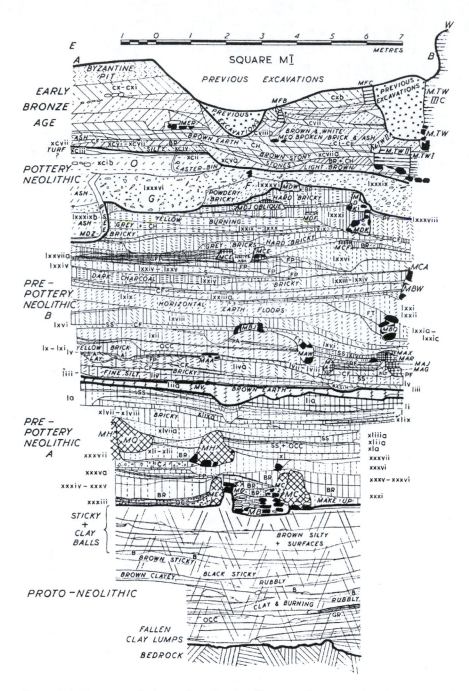

Figure 1.2 This vertical section from Jericho illustrates the way archaeologists record complex stratigraphy on a multi-period site.

domestic forms in the upper (later) levels. A report that ceramic technology was introduced from the outside means that pottery suddenly appeared in one layer and was found in all subsequent layers. And when excavators report that social elites developed on a site, they base that conclusion on a sequence of changes in the material remains from level to level that suggest the evolution of a class system.

The second assumption made by all archaeologists is that everything found on a site can be assigned to one of four broad categories of remains. The first category is artifacts, which are defined as portable objects made or modified by people. Pottery jars, stone tools and beads are examples of typical Neolithic artifacts. The second category, features, is used for non-portable artifacts like ovens and hearths. The third category is structures, and it includes everything from houses and sheds to roads and bridges. And finally, there are ecofacts – animal and plant remains that haven't been made into artifacts or used in structures. If a length of wood found on a site functioned as a digging stick it's an artifact, but if it was used as kindling it's an ecofact. Kitchen scraps and pollen grains are ecofacts; and so are human bones and teeth, although they're usually referred to as human remains.

The third assumption archaeologists make is that almost all of the artifacts, features, structures and ecofacts that ancient people left behind have disappeared. In the last hundred thousand years, most people have chosen to live in temperate climates, where the weather alternates between hot and cold, and wet and dry: the worst possible conditions for the preservation of organic material.[1] Inorganic remains have a better chance of surviving the weather, but they're often destroyed by later people on the site. New inhabitants knock down old buildings to make space for newer, and larger,

Figure 1.3 Villagers built this wall using column drums from a nearby Roman city.

ones (a process that's all too familiar in modern communities). Sometimes the old building materials are reused, but usually they're thrown away. Even if archaeological remains survive urban renewal, armies (and mobs) pull down walls, tear up roads, burn houses, loot graves, deface art and melt down metal artifacts. When you consider the amount of natural decay, plus this purposeful destruction, it seems miraculous that anything at all survives after a few hundred years, much less the 10,000 years since agriculture was first invented.

On the other hand, some natural environments encourage preservation. Organic remains survive surprisingly well when the environment is constant: consistently dry deserts, constantly wet lake bottoms and bogs, and constantly cold glaciers have all produced well-preserved Neolithic remains. The body of the famous European Iceman, Ötzi, survived for over 5,000 years because for most of that time it was frozen.[2] Examples of Neolithic sites with consistently wet environments include 7,000-year old Hemudu in China, where archaeologists found wooden architecture, red lacquerware bowls, rice grains and thousands of bones and bone artifacts; the Swiss lake villages described at the end of the chapter; and the Ozette site on the Northwest American coast (destroyed by a mudslide) where the entire contents of the houses were preserved.

Ethnographic analogy

A different type of archaeological assumption is based on analogy – the concept that like objects can be compared. Archaeologists study material remains, and since they know that people today surround themselves with things that reflect what's important to them, they assume that ancient artifacts reflect what was important to ancient people. This theory is supported by ethnographic reports. Ethnographers are cultural anthropologists who study individual cultures by living in them and observing the way people behave. All archaeologists rely on ethnography to some extent, but prehistorians don't have any other sources of information about the people they study, so they find ethnographic reports particularly useful. And since for much of the twentieth century ethnographic studies concentrated on traditional societies (many of which were pre-literate) there are plenty of sources with insights into why prehistoric people make and use various artifacts. For example, in almost every known culture – both historic and prehistoric – hemispherical bowls are used to hold liquids and soft foods like porridge. Archaeologists apply ethnographic analogy and assume that ancient hemispherical bowls were made for similar foods.

Archaeologists also apply the concept of analogy to broader issues than the probable function of an artifact or feature. Ethnographic reports reveal that there are universals of human behavior. In all known societies people work hard to make a living, love their families, worry about their health,

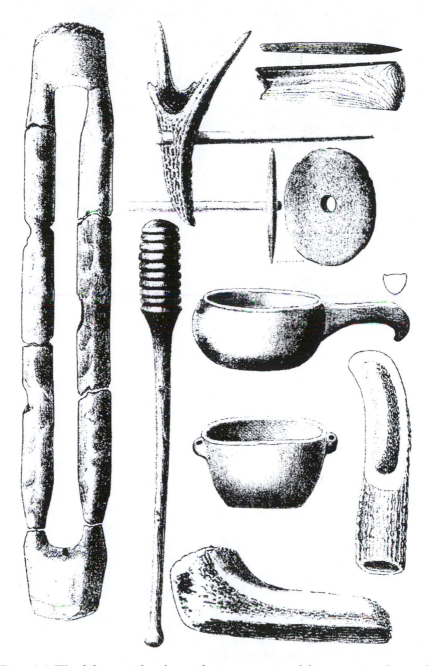

Figure 1.4 Wood, bone, and antler artifacts were preserved for over seven thousand
years in the muddy bottoms of Swiss lakes.

and mourn their dead. There are also universals of social organization: all societies have a political structure, a system of social organization, and a form of religion. Based on ethnographic analogy, archaeologists assume that prehistoric people were a lot like us, and that their shared values guided them as they interacted with their families and other group members. In other words, like us, prehistoric people lived in cultures. When anthropologists and archaeologists talk about a culture, they mean a group of people with a set of common attitudes and customs that they transmit from generation to generation. This definition is implicit in names like the Linearbandkeramik Culture – the Neolithic people in Europe who made and used Linear Band decorated pottery – and the Mississippian culture – Neolithic people who farmed along the lower Mississippi River. The last use of analogy has to do with specific attitudes and beliefs. Archaeologists know the explanations living cultures give for why they bury their dead, so through analogy archaeologists might propose that prehistoric people who buried their dead had similar reasons.

Dating

Now we turn to archaeological dating. How do archaeologists know that a site is Neolithic? The most basic answer is that they recognize the features, structures, and particularly, the artifacts typically made by Neolithic-stage people. Another common strategy is to examine the stratigraphic sequence on a site, and if there are the remains of pre-Neolithic cultures below a given layer, and the remains of post-Neolithic cultures above, it's likely that the layer in the middle is Neolithic. But unlike the cultural term "Roman," for example, "Neolithic" doesn't refer to a specific time in the past. Instead, it refers to a general stage in cultural development, and people around the world moved into this stage, and then beyond it, at different times. So while archaeologists have always been able to date a Neolithic site relatively (as earlier than or later than other sites in the region), until about fifty years ago they had no way to date prehistoric sites absolutely – in terms of years ago. Then a series of scientific breakthroughs radically changed the world of archaeological dating. The first of these was the invention of radiocarbon dating (commonly abbreviated as Carbon-14 or ^{14}C dating).

Many elements naturally occur in both stable and unstable (radioactive) forms. The radioactive elements are unbalanced and they lose particles at a known rate called a half-life (which is defined as the amount of time it takes half the total radioactivity in a given sample to disappear). Both stable carbon (^{12}C) and radioactive carbon (^{14}C) – which has two extra neutrons – are constantly absorbed by all living things. When a plant or animal dies, the amount of ^{12}C in its body stays the same but the ^{14}C begins to decay at a half-life rate of 5,730 +/– 40 years. Scientists can calculate how long ago an organism died by comparing the amounts of ^{12}C and ^{14}C left in it: the smaller the proportion of ^{14}C in the sample, the longer ago the death occurred. Organic remains that are less than 40,000 years old retain enough ^{14}C for radiocarbon analysis, but in samples older than that there's too little left for accurate measurement.

Carbon-14 dating was developed by two physicists, J.R. Arnold and W.F. Libby. They published their ideas in 1949, and in 1961 Libby was awarded the Nobel Prize in Physics for their work. When Arnold and Libby established their process, they collected about 10–20 grams of organic material and refined it into about 5 grams of pure carbon. This may not sound like much, but removing 10–20 grams of material from an object can be very destructive, which is why most early ^{14}C dating used charcoal from hearths or other burnt deposits. Then, in the 1980s, radiocarbon accelerator mass spectrometry (AMS) was invented and it became possible to measure tiny amounts of organic matter. Today labs routinely test samples as small as 5 milligrams, or the equivalent of a single charred seed or one tree ring.

Although radiocarbon dating revolutionized archaeology, and rapidly became the most common scientific dating method, it turned out to be less accurate than everyone had assumed. In the first place, ^{14}C dates are expressed in terms of one standard deviation. When a lab reports a radiocarbon date of 1510 +/− 25 bp it actually means that there's a two in three (or 67 percent) chance that the actual date falls between 1485 and 1535 years before present. Since historians already know that Ferdinand and Isabella expelled the Moors in CE 1492, carbon-dating an artifact from that time of the expulsion wouldn't make any sense: the historical data would be much more accurate than the radiocarbon dates. A second significant problem is that Libby based his calculations on the assumption that the amount of ^{14}C in the upper atmosphere has never changed, but scientists now know that sunspots and other atmospheric phenomena have caused significant fluctuations in ^{14}C. Before 1,000 BCE, for example, there was more ^{14}C in the atmosphere than there is today. This means that samples older than 1,000 BCE have more ^{14}C left in them than Libby expected, and that labs using Libby's calculation tables underestimate the time that has passed since the organism died. The dates they report are too recent. By 4,000 BCE, radiocarbon dates based on Libby's calculations are nearly 400 years too young, by 9,000 BCE they're off by about 2,000 years, and the calculations get more and more inaccurate as you go back in time. Obviously, this is a serious problem for archaeologists who are trying to pinpoint the first experiments in food production. And there's a third problem, this one concerning the accuracy of the labs. Different radiocarbon labs produce different dates for the same material. Archaeologists had suspected this for some time, and finally one scholar tested four labs by sending them identical samples from a Neolithic site. The results were sobering: none of the labs agreed about the age of the samples, and to make matters worse, the results from one lab were consistently too recent, while those from another were consistently too old.[3] Archaeologists try to compensate by sending samples to more than one lab and averaging the results, but it's an expensive and time-consuming solution to an unnecessary problem. Luckily, there's another scientific dating system – one that's amazingly accurate – that scientists can use to correct the radio-carbon dates. It's called dendrochronology.

Dendrochronology, or tree-ring dating, is based on the fact that every year trees lay down a double ring of growth – during the main growth season the ring is wide and light-colored, while during the other seasons the ring is thinner and darker – and because no two years have exactly the same weather, each year's pattern of thick and thin rings is unique. Because each pair of rings records one year of growth, if you have a cross-section of a trunk including the bark you can figure out how old the tree was when it was cut down. You simply count the number of double rings. More significantly, if you know when the tree was cut down, you can figure out when it first sprouted by counting the number of rings and subtracting the total from the year it was felled. A tree with 52 double growth rings that was cut down in 2006, for example, sprouted in 1954. When scientists realized that they could calculate the age of trees in this way, they began creating

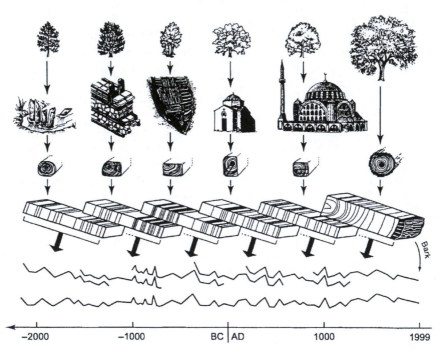

Figure 1.5 Dendrochronological sequences are created by matching patterns of annual growth rings found in increasingly ancient samples.

tree-ring sequences by putting together overlapping growth ring patterns from different samples. They started with living trees, and then moved on to older and older pieces of wood, including some from archaeological sites. Dendrochronologists haven't been able to develop long continuous sequences for any part of the world – after all, very old wood is rare – but there are discontinuous sequences (separated by periods for which they don't yet have data) going back 10,000 years.[4]

Almost as soon as radiocarbon dating was invented archaeologists began comparing dendrochronological dates with radiocarbon dates from similar contexts: it was these comparisons that revealed the fluctuations in atmospheric ^{14}C. Because a dendrochronological date is accurate to the year, any radiocarbon date of the same material can easily be recalibrated, and once that's done, the dates of other samples with the same radiocarbon reading can be changed without running additional tests. The recalibrations are plotted on a curve, which allows archaeologists to estimate the amount of correction they need to make when their radiocarbon dates fall into gaps in the dendrochronological sequences.

Other scientific developments

The scientific advances in dating are not the only new techniques adopted by archaeologists in the past few decades. Like all scientists, excavators constantly fine-tune their methods as new discoveries are made, and among other advances, satellite mapping, exploration using sonar, and a plethora of increasingly sophisticated scientific tests for artifacts have become increasingly important. Excavators now collect and analyze all sorts of finds that they used to throw away. The new information has led to an increasingly sophisticated picture of life during and after the Neolithic transition, and that picture is often surprising. Most people assume that once Neolithic villagers began growing their food and raising animals for meat and milk, their health improved. Paleopathologists have discovered that the opposite is true: Neolithic people generally weren't as healthy as their Paleolithic ancestors. Archaeologists used to believe that early experiments in agriculture involved every available species, but they now know that Neolithic villagers concentrated on a few plants and animals and ignored the rest. Perhaps the most significant new realization is that the Neolithic transition was haphazard rather than part of an inevitable linear progression of human culture from hunting/gathering to urbanism. Agriculture, ceramics, village life, and the other important Neolithic cultural innovations were invented at different times in many places and they turn up in different combinations depending on the culture being studied. Sometimes the new ideas were readily adopted, but other times they weren't. And sometimes it's difficult to decide if a culture is actually Neolithic.

11

Figure 1.6 The site of Robenhausen.

Preservation at the Swiss lake villages

During 1853 and 1854, a prolonged drought in Switzerland caused the water levels in alpine lakes to drop more than a foot below the lowest recorded levels. During the winter of 1854, the commune of Obermeilen took advantage of the low water in the Zürichsee to begin a land reclamation project, and as the workmen began to dig up the muddy ground, they uncovered a prehistoric "lake village," the first of hundreds that were subsequently discovered in alpine Europe. The sites were called lake villages because the original excavators assumed they were built on platforms stretching into the water,[5] but archaeologists now believe these communities were actually built on the ground at the water's edge. (However, on the larger lakes where seasonal flooding occurred, the houses were raised on stilts made of oak, beech, birch, and fir.[6]) But no matter where the houses were constructed, an enormous amount of building material has been preserved: remnants of wooden frames, plank floors, wattle and daub walls, and thatched roofs have all been found. In fact, so much wood survives that archaeologists have been able to use dendrochronology to construct year-by-year site histories, firmly identifying the earliest villages – on the Bodensee, Zürichsee, and in Wauwilwemoos – as more than 5,000 years old.[7] Neolithic villagers continued to live by the lakes for the next three millennia. In fact, the preserved material remains span two cultural transitions: from seasonal foraging to sedentary agriculture, and from stone tools to the use of bronze.

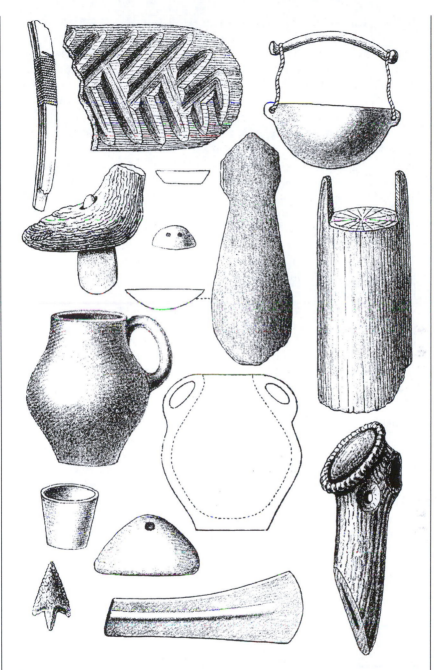

Figure 1.7 Clay jugs and cups, wooden farming implements like the yoke (upper right) and hoe (lower right), architectural remains (right center), flint points (lower left), and bone chisels (bottom center) found at Robenhausen.

The preservation of organic material from these settlements is extraordinary. Artifacts from almost every aspect of everyday life in Neolithic Europe survived. The lake dwellers relied heavily on wood. Besides using it for their houses, and dugout canoes, they made wooden bowls, spoons and ladles; chisels, hooks, and knife handles; bows and "clubs"; and loom parts. They also used animal bones, teeth, tusks and antlers to make beads, needles, pins, awls, chisels, saws, arrowheads, handles for stone axes, and at least one fish hook. They made chipped and ground stone tools, and at some sites, they made pottery.

The list of plant remains gives some idea of the wealth of material on these sites. The original report mentions hulls, husks, and stalks; and fruit seeds, pits and stones. Some seeds, nuts, fruits and legumes were preserved intact, and the list of plants includes wheat, barley, and millet; peas; apples, pears, plums, sloes, raspberries, blackberries, and strawberries; dog rose, elder, and bilberry; and caraway seeds, beech nuts, hickory nuts, and water chestnuts.[8] Botanists have refined the identifications to include einkorn, emmer, and bread wheat; six-rowed barley and broomcorn millet; peas, and perhaps fava beans, all of which the villagers may have grown.[9] Two other plant varieties found at the lake villages, flax and opium poppy, are rarely preserved on European sites, and provide particularly interesting cultural information.

Flax (*Linum usitatissimum*) is the first plant fiber known to have been used for textile-making and the oldest fragments of woven linen in Europe come from these lake sites. The cloth is highly sophisticated in technique and design, which suggests a long tradition of textile development that's otherwise invisible archaeologically. But even though the remains of woven cloth are rare, they're not as rare as examples of the tools needed to process flax from the raw plant to finished cloth. Flax-processing begins when the weaver pulls up the plants (which grow in damp and marshy areas) and puts them aside to dry and rot (this is called retting). When everything has decayed except the bast (the tough inner fibers), the flax is broken up and beaten (scutched); then combed (heckled), spun into thread, wound into skeins, and woven into cloth. The lake villages produced examples of all the tools needed for every step of this process, including spindle whorls and skeins of linen thread, and looms and loom weights.[10] Flax was also woven into baskets and mats by the lake dwellers, and its seeds were probably pressed for linseed oil.

Most of the examples of the second unusual plant found at the lake villages, opium poppy (*Papaver somniferum*), were preserved as seeds pressed into cakes, but one unripe charred capsule also survived.[11] Although people today think of poppies mainly as the source of a powerful analgesic drug, for Neolithic villagers the opium in the pods wasn't nearly as important as the seeds. Poppy seeds are a good food

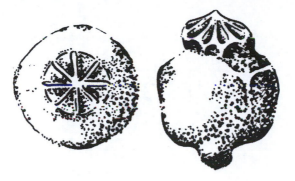

Figure 1.8 A poppy capsule from Robenhausen.

source – they're highly nutritious, containing relatively large amounts of carbohydrates and fats, as well as vitamins, proteins, calcium, and small amounts of minerals. People can eat them raw, bake them into poppy seed cakes, cook them into a porridge or cake filling, grind them into poppy flour, and add them to dough for flavor. About three-quarters of the weight of poppy seeds is in their oil, which can be burned in lamps without needing to be processed or refining.[12] And the young poppy leaves are edible as salad greens. There's no doubt that it was their nutritional value, not their opium, that made poppies so important to the Neolithic villagers in Switzerland. Still it's likely that the lake dwellers knew that the milky juice in the pods could reduce intense pain, so maybe poppies were also part of the Neolithic medical kit.

2

THE GENETICS OF DOMESTICATION

No matter where you are, sometime in the last 24 hours you probably ate a meal based on domesticated plants and animals. It's doubtful you thought about the agricultural processes that resulted in your pizza or lamb stew or sushi, because raising plants and animals for food is so fundamental that you never stop to consider it. And why should you? After all, people have always farmed and herded – in fact, many myth cycles tell us that as soon as people were created they started cultivating crops and raising animals. The stories you probably know best are the verses about Cain and Abel in Genesis 4 of the Hebrew Bible or the Surah of the Bee – Surah XVI – from the Quran; but there are examples from many cultures including ancient Mesopotamia, the Quiché Maya, the native Hawaiians, the Barotse and Dogon people of Africa, and the Hopi of the American southwest.[1]

The stories all tell us that agriculture has been our way of life almost from the moment that people were created. Science, on the other hand, reveals that growing plants and animals for food is a recent development. For hundreds of thousands of years, our human ancestors ate wild plants they gathered and wild animals they killed, a subsistence strategy anthropologists call foraging. No matter where they live, foragers are constantly on the move, harvesting the plants as they ripen and intercepting migrating herds of wild animals; and no matter how skilled they are they have to eat everything they find in order to survive. Occasionally, for some reason, foragers become semi-sedentary and begin to settle down. When this happens they continue to hunt and gather, but at the same time they take the first steps toward farming (raising plants) and herding (raising animals) – they begin nurturing some wild plants and animals and discouraging others. Over time, they learn to grow and store surplus food, and eventually they produce most of what they eat. In other words, they develop agriculture.

The transition from foraging to food production occurred with surprising speed. Fifteen thousand years ago, no one living on earth grew food. Ten thousand years ago only a few people in a few places were actively engaged in controlling plants and animals. But by 5,000 years ago, many people were involved in agriculture; and today, although a few isolated communities of foragers may remain, almost everyone on earth produces food (or buys it from farmers and herders who produce it). Although archaeologists disagree about the specific causes leading to food production, they're generally in agreement about when and where it first arose, and about the biological and cultural phenomena underlying plant and animal domestication.

Cultivation, taming and domestication

Scientists define domestication as the purposeful manipulation of plants and animals by humans in a way that causes genetic and morphological (physical) changes. In other words, domesticated plants and animals differ genetically and physically from their wild ancestors; and domesticated animals behave differently, too. During the domestication process, a symbiosis develops in which agriculturalists, their plants, and their animals become interdependent, relying on one another for survival: as people rely more and more on the plants and animals they're domesticating, they become less able to hunt and gather wild foods, and as the domesticates become more useful to people, they're less able to live in the wild. For example, many wolf cubs have been raised and even bred by people, but wolves aren't domestic animals. They're wild and can survive very well without human intervention. Modern dogs are the descendants of wolves, but their relationship with humans has changed them: they've become domesticated and they depend on people for food and shelter.

Domestication did not appear overnight. The development was comparatively rapid, but it still took 3,000 years for the first Neolithic cultures to move from foraging to full-scale agriculture.[2] So it may be useful to think of domestication as a process rather than an event. The process begins when people first interfere with plant and animal reproduction and ends with fully domesticated species. To put it another way, at one end of the process are wild plants and animals (teosinte – a wild grass, for example, or wolves) and at the other end are their domestic descendants (Silver Queen corn and

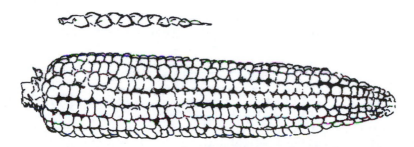

Figure 2.1 The seed heads of teosinte (above) and modern sweet corn (below).

Figure 2.2 A grey wolf and one of its descendants.

Yorkshire terriers). Plants on the way to domestication – but not yet domesticated – are technically "cultivated," and animals in the same situation have been "tamed": between the two extremes represented by teosinte and wolves at one end, and sweet corn and Yorkies at the other, there's a range of cultivated grasses and tamed canines. Fully wild and fully domestic plants and animals don't look alike, and it's easy to tell them apart, but those on the way to domestication are much harder to differentiate, and at the very beginning of the domestication process it's almost impossible to tell them apart.

The genetic and morphological changes that occur during domestication are encouraged by human decisions, because people identify characteristics they like in a plant or animal and try to reproduce them in a larger population through selective breeding (sometimes called "artificial selection" to differentiate it from "natural selection," which takes place without human intervention). Russian wolf hounds, boxers, cocker spaniels and chihuahuas don't look alike – or like wolves – because on the way to domestication people decided to encourage certain characteristics and discourage others. Cauliflower, kale, broccoli, kohlrabi and brussels sprouts are all cabbages, but they're not all alike because people took advantage of different characteristics that occurred naturally in the cabbage population, and selectively bred five different vegetables. In some cases, selective breeding results in plants or animals that are so different from their closest relatives that scientists identify them as new species.

Taxonomy

A species is a group of organisms that can interbreed and produce fertile offspring. The term comes from a classification system, or taxonomy, invented in the eighteenth century by the Swedish botanist Carolus Linnaeus. He developed a series of categories based on the external appearance of plants and animals, and placed all living things into them, creating a logical framework still used today. The categories descend from the broadest (any organism that can move, digest and breathe is a member of the Kingdom *Animalia*) to the most specific. To simplify scientific discussion, Linnaeus established binomial nomenclature, or double names, that identify plants and animals by the last two categories in his taxonomy – Genus (a group of similar species) and Species. Linnaeus actually described each species with a twelve-word Latin sentence, which became its official name, and then abbreviated that to a two-word common scientific designation. For example, the official name for spiderwort is *Tradescantia ephemerum phalangoides tripetalum non repens virginianum gramineum* which can be translated as "The annual, upright Tradescantia from Virginia which has a grasslike habit, three petals, and stamens with hairs like spider legs." The common designation is *Tradescantia virginiana* or "Tradescantia of Virginia."[3] Later taxonomers added one more category – Subspecies – to identify small populations within species that become isolated and genetically distinct from the larger group, which means that some plants and animals have three-part common names.

Genus, species, and subspecies names not only differentiate similar plants and animal, they also demonstrate how various plants and animals relate to one another. Figure 2.3 illustrates this. Domestic sheep, domestic goats, gazelles, and ibexes are all mammals and they're also members of the same Family (*Bovidae*). But then they part company taxonomically. Sheep, goats, and ibexes belong to the Subfamily *Caprinae*, while gazelles are *Antilopinae*; at the next level – Genus – goats and ibexes are grouped together in *Capra*, while sheep are placed in *Ovis*. Ibexes and goats are differentiated at the species level: the ibex is *Capra ibex*, and the goat is *Capra hircus*. The taxonomy makes clear that ibexes and goats are more alike than either is like sheep, and that ibexes are more like goats and sheep than they are like gazelles.

Kingdom: *Animalia*
move, digest, and breathe

Subkingdom: *Metazoa*
many-celled

Phylum: *Chordata*
spinal chord

Subphylum: *Vertebrata*
internal segmented skeleton
with vertebral column

Class: *Mammalia*
mammary glands, warm blood,
specialized teeth, hair

Order: *Animalia*
move, digest, and breathe

Family: *Bovidae*
horns not antlers

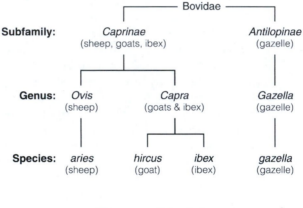

Sheep = *Ovis aries*
Goats = *Capra hircus*
Ibex = *Capra ibex*
Gazelle = *Gazella gazella*

Figure 2.3 Taxonomies are organized from the broadest categories to the most specific. Sheep, goats, gazelles, and ibexes are all members of the Family *Bovidae*, but each is a separate species.

Genetics

The first agriculturalists certainly had a practical understanding of selective breeding: they could see that if they bred their smallest cows with their smallest bulls, the offspring tended to be small. But they had no idea how or why it worked. In fact, until the twentieth century no one really understood the mechanics underlying selective breeding. There wasn't even a name for the study of genes until 1909, when an English scientist, William Bateson, coined the term genetics. Today the science of genetics is well established and an explosion of research in cell biology – which continues unabated – has made it possible for scientists to understand and even manipulate the basic mechanisms of life. And even non-specialists understand that parents contribute genetic material (or traits) to their offspring.

Although it may seem unlikely, we have a mid-nineteenth-century Augustinian monk and abbot of the monastery of St Thomas at Brno in Moravia, Gregor Mendel, to thank for modern genetic engineering. During his studies in Vienna he became so interested in the way traits appeared in garden plants that he decided to study garden peas. Peas are typical flowering plants. They reproduce sexually, producing pollen (the fertilizing or male element) which joins with ovules (the plant part that contains the embryo sac and the female germ cell) to create the seeds. Most peas are self-pollinating: the pollen and ovules from the same plant come together to create the next generation, so the offspring have only one parent and they're all identical to it. In order to produce different varieties of peas, gardeners take pollen from one type of pea and place it in the ovules of another type of pea, a process called cross-breeding. Mendel decided to cross-breed different varieties of peas, hoping he could learn how to predict the appearance of the hybrids that resulted. Along the way he discovered the basic laws in inheritance.

Mendel chose to breed two strains of garden peas: one with tall stems, and one with stems that were short. When he bred a pair of short plants all the offspring had short stems. Similarly, a pair of tall plants produced offspring that were all tall. When he cross-bred the two strains (pairing a tall plant and a short plant) the resulting hybrids were also tall, so Mendel decided that the trait for tall stems had somehow cancelled out the trait for short stems, and he designated tallness as a dominant trait and shortness as a recessive trait. Then he cross-bred two first-generation hybrids. When he saw that three out of every four offspring had tall stems, and one had a short stem, he realized that recessive traits weren't permanently lost, but could reappear in later generations. Based on his experiments, Mendel developed a general theory about the inheritance of dominant and recessive traits. He decided that each parent provided a set of traits, and that one of those sets cancelled out the other. He didn't know how the traits were passed from parent to offspring, or why recessive traits disappeared in the first generation and reappeared in a quarter of the second generation offspring, but he had demonstrated that it happened. He presented his conclusions in a series of articles, the first of which, "Versuche über Pflanzenhybriden" or "Experiments in plant hybridization" is the best known. Unfortunately, they appeared in a local journal, *Verhandlungen des Naturforschenden Vereines in Brünn*, and were essentially ignored until the early twentieth century.

Mendel's first article appeared in 1865, and it took almost exactly a hundred years before anyone figured out why Mendel's pea experiments turned

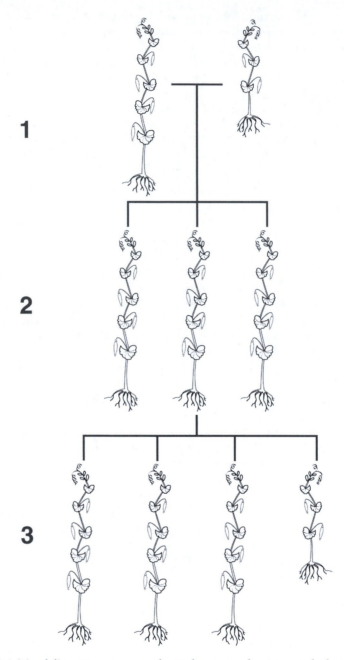

Figure 2.4 Mendel's experiments with garden peas demonstrated that recessive traits disappear in the first generation of offspring, but reappear in later generations.

out the way they did. Geneticists now know that traits like tall stems and short stems in peas are determined by genes, which are found in the molecules of two acids, deoxyribonucleic acid (DNA) and ribonucleic acid (RNA) in plant and animal cells. The connection between DNA and the transmission of traits was first suggested in the 1940s;[4] and a few years later, when James Watson and Francis Crick proposed a model for the structure and function of DNA, their work revolutionized biology and medical science, earning them the 1962 Nobel Prize for Medicine.[5]

It turns out that the mechanisms of inheritance are rather simple. Cells reproduce in two ways: through cell division and through sexual reproduction. Cell division is asexual and takes place continually as your body heals itself or replaces old cells with new ones. During cell division, the DNA in the nucleus (the nuclear DNA) becomes tightly coiled into structures called chromosomes, which occur in pairs. Each new cell receives the pairs of chromosomes and all the original genetic information is transferred from the old cells to the new ones. In sexual reproduction, on the other hand, an organism produces either egg cells or sperm cells, each of which carries half of every chromosome pair. When the egg and sperm cells join, the chromosomes match up to form the original number of pairs and create a composite set of genetic information, with half of the nuclear DNA coming from each parent. The new cells also contain some DNA inherited from only one parent. Plant and animals cells contain structures called mitochondria in which the DNA (mtDNA) comes from the mother. Plant cells contain a third kind of DNA (chloroplast DNA or ctDNA) also inherited only through the maternal line. Because mtDNA and ctDNA pass directly from a mother to her offspring without genetic mixing, they're relatively unchanged from generation to generation, which makes them very useful in the study of genetic diversity.

If mistakes occur in the transmission of the genetic information, the new cells may be abnormal in some way, and abnormalities may also occur if the DNA changes spontaneously or mutates. Abnormalities aren't necessarily a bad thing: like all traits, they can be unfavorable, favorable, or neutral. What do geneticists mean when they call a trait favorable (or unfavorable or neutral)? The distinction has to do with its effect on reproduction. A favorable trait improves a plant or animal's ability to survive into adulthood and pass on its genes, an unfavorable trait lessens that ability, and a neutral trait doesn't affect reproduction one way or the other. Not many unfavorable traits become part of a population's shared genetic material – or gene pool – because they're seldom passed on to offspring. On the other hand, there's a good possibility that when a new favorable trait appears it will move into the gene pool. When this happens repeatedly over a long period of time, the gene pool may change so much that the population becomes a separate species. This slow alteration of the gene pool is what the nineteenth-century naturalist, Charles Darwin, meant when he talked about evolution.

Natural selection

Like Linnaeus, Darwin was fascinated by the sheer number of different plants and animals found in nature; and like his contemporary, Mendel, he wanted to understand how this diversity came about. After his 1831 voyage to the Galápagos Islands, where he discovered a surprising variety of beak shapes in the finch population, the prevailing explanation for biological diversity no longer satisfied him. When Darwin was growing up, most

Figure 2.5 These finches are among those Darwin studied.

English Protestants believed that the earth was created in 4004 BCE (a date based on the number of generations listed in Genesis). But a new science, geology, had challenged that belief, and Darwin (like most scientists) became convinced that the earth was actually millions of years old. In light of this newly revealed antiquity, fixity of species – the notion that life hadn't changed at all since creation as described in the Bible – seemed less and less tenable, and although he never doubted that God created life, Darwin began looking for a scientific explanation for the vast number of different plants and animals alive on the earth. He developed a new theory that explained biological variability as the result of natural changes taking place over time. But he couldn't figure out how it worked.

Several scholars had already tried to explain biological variability, and some – among them Darwin's grandfather, Erasmus Darwin – believed that natural change was a factor. The most influential of these theorists was a Frenchman, Jean-Baptiste Pierre Antoine de Monet Chevalier de Lamarck. Lamarck, who gave the science of biology its name and who was internationally known as the finest biological thinker of his time, believed that the environment caused animals to change, and he developed a hypothesis, the Theory of Acquired Characteristics, to explain the mechanisms.

According to Lamarck, if natural conditions forced animals to adjust the way they used various muscles, their bodies would change physically in response, and the physical changes would then be passed on to their offspring. His most famous explanation concerned the long necks of giraffes. Lamarck believed that the earliest giraffes had short necks, and that as individual giraffes kept stretching to reach leaves above their heads, their necks grew slightly longer. (Anyone who's spent time in a gym trying to build muscles is familiar with this concept.) Although he thought the giraffes acquired their longer necks through exercise rather than genetic inheritance, Lamarck also believed that they could pass the acquired characteristic on to their offspring. This process, he said, continued generation after generation until giraffes reached their modern profile. The modern view, of course, is that only traits encoded in the genes can be passed on from parents to offspring, and that exercise – or the lack of it – doesn't alter DNA.

Lamarck convinced many naturalists, but others were skeptical, and after his experiences in the Galápagos, Darwin became one of the skeptics. Instead of adopting Lamarck's explanation for biological diversity, he formulated his own, which he explained as "descent with modification based on the principle of natural selection" (sometimes referred to as Darwinian evolution). Darwin borrowed the word "selection" from animal breeders; but although the results may be similar, natural selection is profoundly different from selective breeding. When people engage in selective breeding, they decide which traits are favorable and work actively to encourage them. Traits that are defined as favorable by the breeder may or may not be biologically favorable to the plant or animal being manipulated: thoroughbred horses are routinely bred with hips too narrow to allow the foal's head to pass unassisted during birth; maize (the term botanists use for what Americans call corn) can't disperse its seeds without human help; and the ratio of male to female trees in date palm plantations has been reduced to the point that pollination has to be carried out by hand.[6] In the absence of human intervention, these traits would definitely be unfavorable. During natural selection, on the other hand, no one decides which traits are favorable and which aren't. Instead, over millennia, the environment in which the plants and animals live – or nature – determines the favorability of traits.

Although he didn't explain it exactly like this, Darwin's argument had five main points. First, he believed that all species are capable of producing offspring faster than their food supplies increase. (He adopted this from the works of Thomas Malthus.[7]) Second, because food is limited, individual members of a species have to compete for it: individuals with traits that make them better able to compete have an advantage, and are more likely to survive. (This is the so-called "survival of the fittest.") Third, the environment determines which traits are favorable, or, to put it another way, individuals with favorable traits are better adapted to their environment. (Darwin noted that what's favorable at one time or place may be a liability elsewhere.) Fourth, although he didn't know how or why this happened, he believed that all traits are inherited and passed from generation to generation. Because individuals with favorable traits are more likely to survive than those with unfavorable traits, they're more likely to reproduce, and to have offspring with those traits. Fifth, natural selection encourages changes in the gene pool, but it doesn't cause them. Over long periods of time, favorable traits become dominant in the gene pool, while less favorable traits disappear: natural selection is an extremely slow process, and populations, not individuals, evolve. For Darwin's contemporaries, two of these points were particularly troubling. Whereas the mechanisms of natural selection seemed possible, the idea that it wasn't directly guided by God's plan offended many people who relied on traditional religion-based explanations of natural diversity. The scientific community found the statement that populations (not individuals) evolve equally disturbing, because the majority of them ascribed to Lamarck's Theory of Acquired Characteristics, which was based on individual evolution.

For twenty years, Darwin sat at home refining his ideas. But in 1858 he was shocked to learn that a younger naturalist, Alfred Russel Wallace, was about to present his own version of natural selection to the English scientific community. Darwin hurriedly submitted a paper to the Linnean Society of London, and a year later he published one of the pivotal scientific works of the modern period, *On the Origin of Species by Means of Natural Selection, or, The Preservation of Favored Races in the Struggle for Life*. (Darwin used the term "race" in its biological sense; that is, as a population within a species that differs from other populations in some aspect of appearance.)

Darwinian evolution is quite simple, and (probably because of that) from the moment it was presented to the public, scientists have been testing its validity,[8] and while the basic mechanism, natural selection, has been fully established, other aspects have not. For example, Darwin assumed that all evolutionary change was gradual and constant, but this is no longer accepted: biologists now believe that evolution occurs at variable rates, sometimes with great rapidity, and at other times very slowly. But despite some fine-tuning, Darwin's organizing principle of natural selection, and his assumption that the environment (however it may be defined by the various schools of evolutionary theory) determines which traits are adaptable, continue to be the accepted scientific explanation of biological diversity.

How does this relate to a discussion of the Neolithic? At the beginning of the Neolithic transition the wild ancestors of domesticated plants and animals had evolved to be well adapted to their environments – if they hadn't, they would have become extinct. But when people began intervening in plant and animal reproduction, their presence changed the natural environment. Some of the traits that had always helped wild plants and animals survive became maladaptive and at the same time, a few traits that were harmful to the wild species made it easier for cultivated plants and tamed animals to survive. Without the mixture of the natural changes that occurred in potential domesticates and the human intervention that encouraged further changes, successful domestication could not have taken place.

Natural selection and the peppered moth

When most people think of evolution, they imagine slow incremental changes in a population of plants or animals. But as I mentioned above, evolutionary changes can also appear suddenly. This is what happened at the beginning of the domestication process, when interactions with people radically altered the gene pools of early domesticates. Rapid evolutionary changes can also occur without human help, which is illustrated by the most famous example of natural selection at work – the changing coloration of the peppered moth (*Biston betularia*). The story of this population of light-colored moths that turned dark and then light again in response to environmental change is an elegant (and irrefutable) example of Darwinian evolution at work. What happened to the peppered moth reminds us how easily populations can adapt to new conditions in times of environmental stress.

The peppered moth, easily recognizable by its distinctive off-white wings "peppered" with black specks, is common in England, where its preferred daytime environment is light-grey lichen-covered trees. The species, which includes a variety of color gradations from dark to light, has always been popular with insect collectors because it's easy to

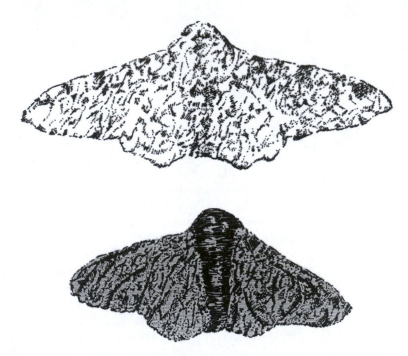

Figure 2.6 Peppered moths vary in color from light grey to almost black.

preserve and because the specimens generally maintain their color after death. Before 1850, most of the specimens netted by English collectors were a speckled light grey – roughly the color of the lichens. But then the collectors noticed a change: increasingly, the moths they captured had dark wings, and many of them were almost totally black. British entomologists were fascinated by this rapid change in the peppered moth population, especially when they realized that it was almost entirely restricted to polluted industrial areas. They began to realize that what they were seeing was the process of evolution through natural selection.

Because the light grey moths resembled the lichens on the trees, they were relatively safe from their main daytime predators, birds. But the darker moths were easy to see, and this disadvantage limited the percentage of genes for dark coloration in the peppered moth gene pool. When, in the mid-nineteenth century, industrial pollution in England began turning the lichen on the tree trunks black, the darker moths were suddenly protected while the light-colored moths became vulnerable, and as more and more dark moths survived, the gene pool shifted toward darker coloration. Similar examples of "industrial melanism"

Figure 2.7 On a dark tree trunk, the light coloration is maladaptive.

were identified in Europe, Japan, the United States, and Canada, and in every case, the mechanism for evolution seemed to be the same.

For about a century, dark peppered moths continued to dominate the populations. Then, in the 1950s, scientists noticed that the gene pool was rapidly shifting back toward the lighter coloration. As a result of anti-pollution legislation, the air was cleaner, the lichen on the tree trunks was becoming lighter, and so were the moths. In fact, this second shift in the gene pool was so radical that many entomologists believe the genes for dark coloration may disappear completely, and that soon, the dark peppered moths will be extinct.

The story of peppered moth evolution is so simple that many evolutionary biologists and entomologists have wondered if it could possibly be true, and several of them have tested it. Although the results of their experiments have been reported in the popular press as "debunking" Darwinian evolution, what they actually revealed both supports the main points of Darwinian evolution and emphasizes its complexity. The coloration of the peppered moth population definitely shifted in response to environment factors, but almost every aspect of the process was more multifaceted than anyone thought.[9] For example, during the day peppered moths rest on a number of locations besides tree trunks, and their survival is less dependent on their coloring than was originally assumed. It also turns out that the changes in the peppered moth gene pool didn't parallel the changes in pollution levels as closely as had been reported (migration, as well as bird predation, also had an effect on the ratio of dark to light forms). In short, far from illustrating the elegant simplicity of natural selection, the story of the peppered moth highlights its elegant complexity, and reminds us that even simple evolutionary changes aren't easy to trace. And this is important to remember as we examine the genetic mechanisms underlying domestication.

3

ARCHAEOLOGICAL EVIDENCE FOR DOMESTICATION

Although most of the world's population has been fully agricultural for millennia, only a handful of cultures actually invented farming and herding. They shared their knowledge with their non-agricultural neighbors, most of whom eventually became food producers (although a few adopted cultivation or taming but never took the final step into agriculture, and one or two learned about it and rejected it, continuing to forage into the modern colonial era). Today, almost everyone on earth relies on food production to survive.

The earliest archaeological evidence for agriculture comes from sites in southwest Asia and the Levant. It dates to more than 12,000 years ago, at the beginning of the current geological period, the Holocene, when a rise in world temperatures caused the glaciers covering much of the northern hemisphere to retreat. There's evidence that people had begun experimenting with cultivation and taming thousands of years before the onset of the Holocene, but their earliest efforts didn't leave tangible remains, and by the time that the physical changes in plants and animals caused by cultivation and taming became visible in the archaeological record, the process was well on its way.

Areas of primary and secondary domestication

Scientists looking for evidence of early agriculture concentrate on areas where the experiments could have succeeded. It may seem obvious, but you can't invent domestication without plants and animals that can be domesticated, and in general you need several of these potential domesticates in order to become fully agricultural. There are a few notable exceptions to this rule. Until maize arrived thousands of years later, squash seems to have been the lone domesticated crop at Guilá Naquitz in Mexico's Valley of Oaxaca;[1] and excavators at the site of Kuk in highland New Guinea recently suggested that agriculture there was originally based on a single crop, taro (but this interpretation isn't accepted by all scholars).[2] In any case, most prehistorians interested in early agriculture focus on regions with clusters of suitable

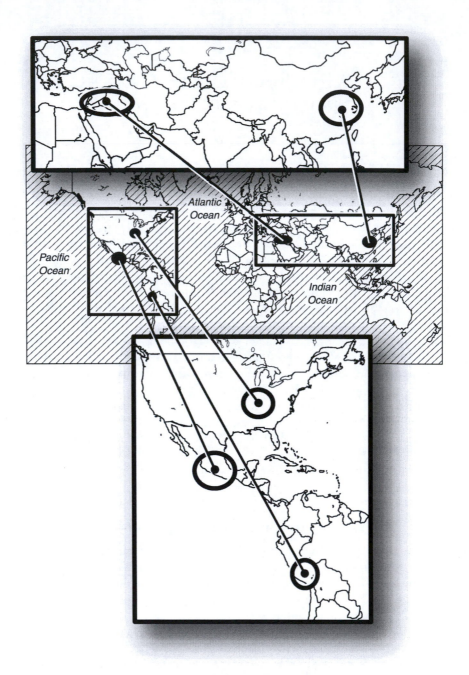

Figure 3.1 The five areas of primary domestication: China, southwest Asia, Mexico, South America, and the eastern United States.

plants and animals: it turns out there are only a handful of these scattered around the globe. Usually referred to as areas of primary domestication, they were first identified in the 1930s by a Soviet biologist and plant geneticist, Nikolai Vavilov, who based his research on the ideas of a nineteenth-century Swiss botanist, Alphonse de Candolle.

Candolle had collated botanical, geographical, philological and archaeological evidence as he tried to locate the earliest areas of domestication.[3] He knew that in evolutionary terms domestication is a recent event, and he thought it likely that many of the wild ancestors of modern domesticates were not only still alive, but still living in the wild ranges they inhabited at the beginning of the Holocene. Vavilov adopted these ideas, tested them, and eventually located many of the Holocene habitats of the wild ancestors. He took note of any regions where several habitats overlapped because he assumed that the first successful domestications must have taken place where several domesticable species were available. This assumption turned out to be true: in southwest Asia, for example, the natural ranges of wild sheep, goats, wheat, barley, lentils, peas, and flax (among others) all coincide.

Vavilov's research led him to identify seven regions as areas of primary domestication: China, India and southeast Asia, southwest Asia, the Mediterranean, the Sudanic-Abyssinian area, central America and the Andes, and the South American tropics.[4] Genetic research over the past half century has reduced the number to five: China (the Yangtze and Yellow River basins), southwest Asia, Mexico, South America (the Andes mountains and the Amazon basin), and the eastern United States (the Mississippi basin). It's also possible that agriculture was invented in India, Sub-Saharan Africa, and, as mentioned above, New Guinea, but more research is needed before scientists can be sure.

The domesticated plants and animals in areas of primary domestication are called founder populations, because they founded – or were the foundation of – agriculture in those regions. Founder populations include rice, foxtail millet, soybean, other tubers and fruits, pig, and poultry in China; wheat, barley, pea, lentil, sheep, goat, pig, and cattle in southwest Asia; maize, bean, squash, manioc, other fruits and tubers, turkey, and dog in Mexico; maize, quinoa, bean, squash, manioc, potato, llama, alpaca, and guinea pig in South America; and in the Mississippi basin, where there were no domesticable animals, the founder crops are squash, gourd, goosefoot, marsh elder, and sunflower. Identifying these founder populations has been a (relatively) straightforward process, but locating their wild ancestors hasn't been easy. After all, dozens of wild grasses grow in southwest Asia. How can an archaeobotanist (a scientist who specializes in plant remains found in archaeological contexts) determine which one is the actual ancestor of domestic wheat? The most accurate method is genetic analysis, especially studies of DNA, because the more closely the genetic structure of a domesticate resembles that of a possible progenitor, the more likely it is that the wild species is an ancestor. Using this technique, botanists have identified the wild ancestors of many crops including most of the world's important cereals. (Because farming maintains their genetic stability, cereals are very conservative genetically, and for this reason matching them with their ancestors is relatively uncomplicated.[5])

Once the wild progenitors are identified, scientists look for their early Holocene habitats, because this information would help archaeologists decide where to look for sites with evidence of early domestication. Archaeobotanists have been fairly successful at locating the habitats of the ancestors of cereals: the grass that gave rise to einkorn wheat has been traced to the Karacadağ mountains in eastern Turkey,[6] and recently the Balsas River basin in southern Mexico was identified as the habitat of the teosinte ancestral to modern maize. Archaeozoologists, on the other hand, haven't been as successful. Unlike most crops, domestic animal species often have several equally likely potential ancestors. Some of these are now extinct and many are no longer living in their ancient habitats, so even if they can be firmly identified they're not much help in locating sites with evidence of early experiments in animal domestication. Another problem is that wild and domestic animals have interbred for millennia, with the result that domestic animals are much less genetically stable than most crops, and this makes genetic analysis difficult. So does the fact that after centuries of intensive selective breeding, the gene pools of modern animal species have been so radically changed that even if their wild progenitors could be identified, it might be impossible to make useful genetic correlations.[7]

Change

Archaeologists are interested in finding out about the wild ancestors of domestic plants and animals, but because their focus is human behavior, not botany and zoology, they're much more interested in why people chose to domesticate some wild plants and animals and not others. They also want to know how the Neolithic transition changed the way people lived – in fact, all archaeologists, regardless of the periods they study, focus on cultural change. Speculation about how cultures change has a long history, beginning with the Greeks, and over the centuries many theories have been advanced. Today, there's general agreement that cultural change occurs when people make decisions (some are conscious and some are not) that set the change in motion. This idea refutes earlier theories that concentrated on outside factors and assumed that people changed only when new conditions forced them to.

When new ideas or customs arise inside a culture the process is called independent invention – the development of agriculture in areas of primary domestication is an example of this kind of change. When change is introduced from the outside, the process is called diffusion – agriculture was introduced to most of the world's populations through diffusion. There are several kinds of diffusion, some accidental and others purposeful, among them the movement of peoples (new people enter a region bringing new ideas) and the movement of ideas and technology (traders and travelers carry ideas and technology with them as they move from place to place). In the case of the spread of agriculture, both patterns are seen: in some places agriculturalists migrated into adjacent areas and lived with or replaced the local non-agricultural populations; while in other places they shared the concept and practices of agriculture – and their already-domesticated plants and animals – with people living nearby. Diffusion can also result from conquest, and when that happens the cultural changes may be imposed. Most of the time, however, people seem to have willingly adopted the new way of life, and once they did, they sometimes began inventing new ideas and technologies themselves: when the diffusion of agriculture led people to domesticate local plants and animals, creating what archaeologists call areas of secondary domestication. Because primary and secondary domestication reflect different kinds of cultural change, scientists studying the origins of agriculture are interested in both.

Agriculture may have been independently invented in only a few places, but once it was established, it diffused with surprising speed, at first locally, and then across the globe. In only a few thousand years, southwest Asian domesticates had moved west through Europe to Spain, the British Isles, and Scandinavia; east across central Asia to Pakistan; and south to Egypt and North Africa. Similar patterns can be seen in China, where agriculture spread from the Yellow, Huai, and Yangze river basins east to Korea and Japan, south to southeast Asia, and west to India; in Africa, where the movement was generally from the north to south; and in the Americas, where maize cultivation diffused from Mexico into both North and South America.

Material remains

When agriculture arrives on a site as the result of diffusion, there are often dramatic changes in the archaeological record. Suddenly domesticated plants and animals (along with the equipment needed to deal with them) appear, and so do new technologies like pottery and ground stone tools. If the diffusion involved the movement of people along with their ideas, excavators may find new burial customs, new forms of architecture, or new social patterns. The situation is quite different, however, on sites where independent invention took place. There, archaeologists find continual changes as early experiments turn into full-blown technologies or customs.

Before discussing the specific artifacts, ecofacts, structures, and features that point to the presence of agriculture on a site, we need to take a quick look at human remains. Human skeletons provide information on all aspects of Neolithic life. The bones and teeth of early agriculturalists are distinctive in several ways: they show the physical effects of eating a diet high in cereals; of living in densely populated year-round settlements; and of growing and processing crops. Human skeletons also provide glimpses of the social, political, economic and religious systems that developed in the Neolithic, but there are limits to the amount of useful cultural information they can convey. Relatively few Neolithic burials have been found, and even on sites where they're fairly numerous they don't represent the entire population. In the first place, not everyone died at home (it's unlikely that traders and herders were returned to their villages for burial, for example) and those who did die at home weren't always buried there. Secondly, in most Neolithic cultures it appears that only the members of the social elite were buried. And no matter who was interred, bodies that were treated with great care are likely to be preserved, while those that were treated casually, or thrown away with the rest of the community's garbage, have long since disappeared. So even if it were possible to locate and excavate every single burial on a site, the information gained would be incomplete.

Similar limitations affect other categories of remains. Since domesticates don't look like their wild ancestors, distinguishing between fully wild species and fully domesticated species can be relatively simple: it isn't that hard to separate teosinte seeds from kernels of sweet corn or wolf skulls from the skulls of Yorkshire terriers. But the dramatic physical changes brought about by domestication took a while to develop, and in the earliest stages of food production plants and animals look wild, which means that these early experiments are essentially invisible. Even potentially useful finds like the cache of wild grains recently discovered at a site near Jericho[8] don't prove that the domestication process was underway. All they imply is that (perhaps) experiments with cultivation were taking place. To add to the confusion, Neolithic people didn't switch to food production overnight. As they experimented with agriculture they also continued hunting and gathering, and excavators of early agricultural sites usually find a mixture of wild and cultivated/tamed species. Often, they can't be sure which are which. The ideal site, with remains of clearly identified wild species in its earliest levels, remains of clearly identified domesticated species in its upper levels, and remains of clearly intermediate forms in between, is just that – an ideal.[9]

Even in the best preservation contexts, organic remains dating to the Neolithic are rare. Occasionally caches of grains are found like the one near Jericho and the almost pure deposits of emmer, einkorn, pea, grass pea, and bitter vetch found at Nea Nikomedeia in Macedonian Greece, but usually excavators rely on indirect evidence that agriculture is underway. Rather than studying actual plant remains, for example, archaeobotanists look at impressions of stalks and seeds left on the site. Neolithic streets weren't paved, and most people swept their garbage out the door and into the street where it was trodden into the mud. People dropped seeds on their mud or

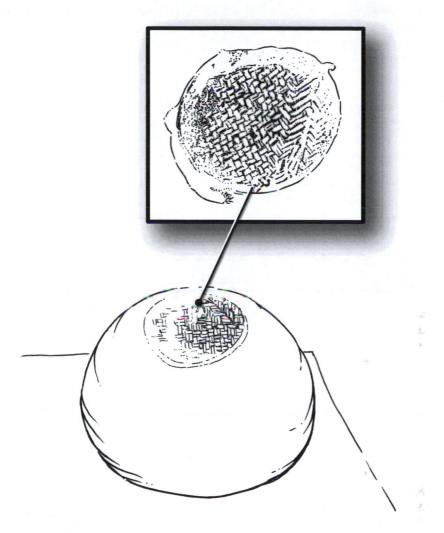

Figure 3.2 Mat impressions like this one can help botanists identify the plants on a site.

plaster house floors, they discarded stalks and stems as they wove mats, and they mixed plant material with clay to make mudbricks and pottery. If the impressions are clear enough, archaeobotanists can identify the species, and sometimes they can distinguish between wild plants and their cultivated des-cendants. Similar information comes from a different type of imprint, the woven patterns on the bottoms of pots that were dried on woven reed mats or textiles. Phytoliths (silica structures that line the stalks and stems of some grasses and give them stability) are another important source because they're left behind when reed baskets and floor mats decay. Pollen found in the soil is also helpful, if only in reconstructing the general environment at the time the site was occupied; and animal dung, which was used in construction, and as a common fuel, contains plant remains which can sometimes be identified.

Archaeozoologists also study dung because wild sheep and goats had very different diets from their tamed cousins.[10] They look at hoof prints left in streets and floors, and examine handles, beads, buttons, needles, and pins made from bones, teeth, tusks, and horns as they try to identify which species were present on the site. Occasionally a domesticable animal is found buried beside a human, and is assumed to be a tamed pet; and on a very few sites, paintings and sculpture depicting hunting scenes have been found.

Archaeologists also study the percentages of various plants and animals

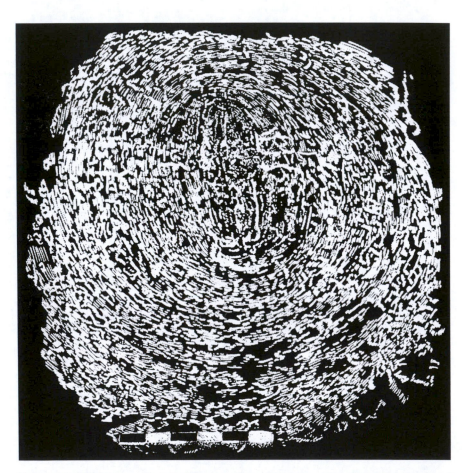

Figure 3.3 All that remains of a floor mat from Jericho are the phytoliths that lined the woven stems.

on a site: if the numbers suddenly change when domesticable plants or animals appear (especially if the new species aren't native to the region), even if the new remains look wild excavators assume that domestication is underway.

But perhaps the strongest indirect evidence pointing to domestication is the presence of artifacts, features, and structures relating to processing food. For example, when excavators find specially-constructed threshing floors where an entire harvest of seeds can be separated from their stalks and husks, they assume that food production based on growing grain is underway. Tools like grinders and mortars and pestles used for grinding grain can point to food production, especially if they're found in permanent settlements. Ovens (especially bread ovens), and grain storage bins are also strong indications of farming; and sheds, stables, and pens point to herding.

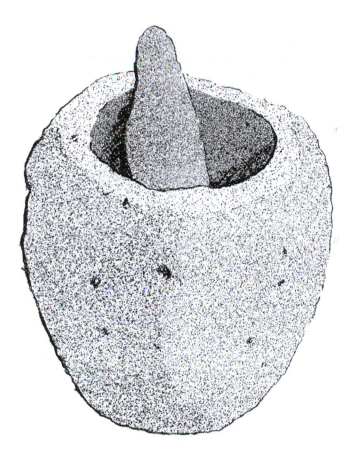

Figure 3.4 The presence of mortars and pestles on a site suggests that food-processing was an important activity.

Animal demographics

As I mentioned before, because their goal is to reconstruct prehistoric cultures, archaeologists want to know why villagers were attracted to particular plants or animals. It's easier to make bread with wheat than with rye, because wheat rises when leavened. But wheat was being cultivated long before bread-making was invented. Why? Did it make better porridge? Was flatbread made with wheat more appetizing? And what about animals? Were they hunted for food or for sacrifice? Were they raised as a source of meat? Or for milk and cheese? Or for their hide, hair, or wool? How important in general were they to the culture? Unfortunately, most archaeological evidence isn't much help with questions like these. After all, an archaeologist excavating a Masai camp wouldn't even realize that the Masai have domestic cattle – much less that the cattle are the main source of protein – because there are no cattle bones in Masai camps: the Masai drink the blood and milk of their cattle, but they don't butcher them.[11]

Just because it's hard to figure out why certain plants and animals were attractive to prehistoric people doesn't mean that archaeologists stop trying. Archaeozoologists have had more success at it than archaeobotanists. Bones and teeth, while often fragmentary, survive in large numbers on most sites,

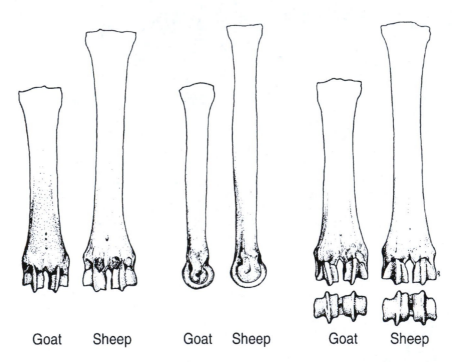

Goat   Sheep   Goat   Sheep   Goat   Sheep

Figure 3.5 Unless certain bones like these metacarpals are preserved, archaeozoologists cannot differentiate between sheep and goat skeletons.

which means that calculating the demographics of the animals may be possible. For demographic studies to be really useful, however, they have to provide nuanced information, and this is only possible if archaeozoologists are able to identify all the species on a site (domesticable or not), record their sexes and ages at death, speculate where they are in the domestication process, and calculate percentages based on all these factors. This isn't an easy proposition. In the first place, it's often impossible to identify all the species present on a site: some remains are too fragmentary, while others in good condition are non-diagnostic (they don't provide information that's helpful). The most troublesome identification problem involves sheep and goats. Faunal remains of these two earliest domesticates are largely indistinguishable. It's so hard to tell them apart that in many site reports they're lumped together as caprovines or ovicaprines or ovicaprids – all somewhat awkward amalgamations of their two genera: *Capra* (goats) and *Ovis* (sheep). Obviously, demographic studies that don't distinguish sheep bones from goat bones are almost useless, because archaeologists need to know if one or both species are present, if either one is new to the site, and if both are there, which is more numerous.[12] Until recently, the only sheep and goat remains that could be easily differentiated were a few small bones in the hoof (the distal metapodials) and toes (the phalanges), the horn cores, and the juvenile teeth. But now one leg bone (the distal tibia), the ankle (the astragulus), and the heel (the calcaneum), along with the shoulder blades (the scapula) and – in immature specimens – some elements of the jaw have been added to the list. Of these diagnostic remains, the horn cores and leg bones are the most likely to survive well enough to be studied.

After archaeozoologists have identified the species on a site, they turn to the questions of age and sex. It turns out that animal bones and teeth are relatively easy to age: a fairly precise measure is possible because all mammals have two sets of teeth – their milk teeth and their permanent teeth – which erupt on a predictable schedule. Teeth have two parts: a crown that's exposed above the gum, and a root that lies below. The crown is made up of an outer layer of enamel and an inner layer of a hard substance called dentine, both of which surround a pulp chamber containing blood vessels. The root and all or part of the crown are covered by yet another hard material called cementum, which protects the enamel and reduces the possibility of chipping. In many animals, the tooth enamel wears down over time, providing a general measure of age, and because the cementum constantly renews itself, if archaeozoologists section teeth and count the cementum lines on them, they can calculate the age of the tooth and by extension, the animal it came from.

The easiest way to determine sex is to look for sexual dimorphism, the physical differences between males and females seen in many species including humans. The most obvious dimorphism is in size – males are usually larger and have heavier bones than females – so the percentage of male animals to female animals on the site can be estimated by sorting the bones into groups based on their size. Dimorphism also shows up in horns and tusks: boars, for example, have tusks, but sows don't; and rams have horns, while ewes lack them. Sometimes sexual dimorphism in a species is particularly striking (it was so extreme in the aurochs, the wild ancestors of modern cattle, that taxonomers originally identified the two sexes as separate species) but more often it's subtle, and since individual members of a species vary considerably, demographics based on dimorphism are always tentative.

Two applications of demographic information that might provide information on human behavior (as opposed to animal morphology) were proposed in 1947 by a Russian archaeologist, A.W. Arcikjowski. If the applications are valid, they provide new ways for archaeologists to address some difficult questions: whether the animals on a site were wild or tamed, why they were tamed (for meat, milk, and/or wool), and where the tamed animals lie in the domestication process (usually, animals are tamed first for meat and later for milk or wool).

The first application addresses wild and tamed animals. Arcikjowski had a good knowledge of ethnology, and based on that he suggested that the demographics of animals killed by hunters would be different from those of animals raised and slaughtered by agriculturalists. Because hunters target healthy adult animals of either sex, but will settle for anything they can catch, and because they leave undesirable body parts behind when they return home, Arcikjowski thought that the faunal remains of hunted animals found on sites would be incomplete, would come equally from males and females, and would include some bones from very old animals. In contrast, on sites where animals were raised, he assumed there would be complete skeletons of many adolescent and young adult male animals, a few skeletons of old male animals, and many skeletons of old female animals. He knew that modern herders need very few males to impregnate their female animals, and that while males provide more hair or wool and/or meat than females, they're aggressive and territorial, and difficult to control. He also knew that herders routinely slaughter more males than females: Kurdish pastoralists, for example, keep only one male for every ten to thirty females, while Turkish villagers report a one-to-fifty/sixty ratio.[13] Based on statistics like these, Arcikjowski assumed that most of the faunal remains on sites where animals were raised would come from young or castrated males.[14] (Castrates mature later than other animals, their bones are lighter and thinner than those of intact males, and if performed early enough, castration also affects the growth of horns,[15] so their remains are relatively easy to recognize.)

Arcikjowski's second theory addressed the different demographics found in flocks raised for meat, those raised for milk, and those raised for wool. Once again, he based his theories on ethnographic studies. In milk herds, he suggested, male animals would be slaughtered before they were weaned so

Figure 3.6 Some archaeologists believe that animal demographics can help them distinguish the ways the animals were used.

that their mothers would continue to provide milk for human consumption. In meat herds, on the other hand, male animals wouldn't be culled until they'd reached their maximum body mass just before they became sexually mature. In herds kept for wool, males not needed for breeding would be castrated (castrated males produce the best – and the heaviest – fleece) and all adults would be killed when their wool production decreased.[16] In all the herds, unless they were weak or very old, females would be the least likely to be slaughtered.[17]

Applying animal demographics to archaeological sites is so common-sensical that as soon as the concept was proposed it won converts. Because the studies didn't rely on difficult-to-see morphological changes, they pro-mised to revolutionize the identification of tamed and early-stage domesti-cated animals, and they rapidly became an important interpretative tool. In one of the best-known applications, for example, animal demographics were used at Zawi Chemi Shanidar in northeastern Iraq to support the claim that sheep were domesticated there at a very early date. But while many archaeo-zoologists began relying on demographic studies, others questioned their validity as research tools, citing the problems of poor bone preservation and species identification, and pointing out that they would have to process thousands of bones in order to obtain useful statistics. As one specialist wrote ". . . 10 identified bones will tell us which species were exploited; 100 identified bones can tell us roughly in what proportions man exploited them; 1000 identified bones will be just enough to provide us with intra-specific information such as the proportion of different age groups and sexes culled. In a sample of 10,000 identified bones there should be enough

43

mandibles to plot a continuous age distribution of the herbivores."[18] Ethnographers also weighed in, reporting that decisions about which animals to kill often rest on social customs rather than economic need. They pointed out that animals are most often killed on feast days, at weddings and funerals, and to honor special guests, and that the age of the animals when slaughtered has more to do with the time of year than with anything else. Ethnographers also cited studies of hunter-gatherers who hunt selectively, deliberately choosing to target young males and preserve female animals and their young even if this results in less animal protein for the group or who avoid an entire species for ritual reasons. Faced with this diversity of customs, how, they asked, can a simple count of animal bones reveal much of anything useful?

Evidence for domestication at Abu Hureyra

In 1963, despite the fact that the project would eventually flood dozens of modern villages and ancient sites, the government of the Syrian Arab Republic decided to construct a dam on the upper Euphrates river. Under the patronage of UNESCO, the Syrians undertook a ten-year program of archaeological salvage in the area to be flooded, culminating in a series of rescue operations, among them the excavation of an extraordinary prehistoric site, Abu Hureyra. The excavation and publication of this site are a testament to the amount of detailed information about early domestication that can be discovered through archaeological research.

Abu Hureyra was a prominent feature in the pre-dam landscape because it sat on a low terrace above the Euphrates flood plain, and because it covered almost 30 acres: it was larger than any contemporary site in southwest Asia. It had been continually occupied for a long time, and the project directors (Andrew Moore, Gordon Hillman, and Anthony Legge) hoped that the deep occupation deposits filled with well-preserved material would provide new information about the transition from foraging to farming in northern Syria. The finds from Abu Hureyra did prove to be very important to the study of early agricultural communities, but not exactly in the way they had expected. While their two seasons of excavation and quarter-century of analyzing the finds from Abu Hureyra did provide new information about the Neolithic transition, the more significant contribution was a new set of archaeological standards for research into the origins of domestication.

The most important aspect of salvage archaeology is that there's not much time to do anything, so excavators limit their work: sometimes they focus on creating a chronological sequence, sometimes they concentrate on one period and ignore the rest, and sometimes they

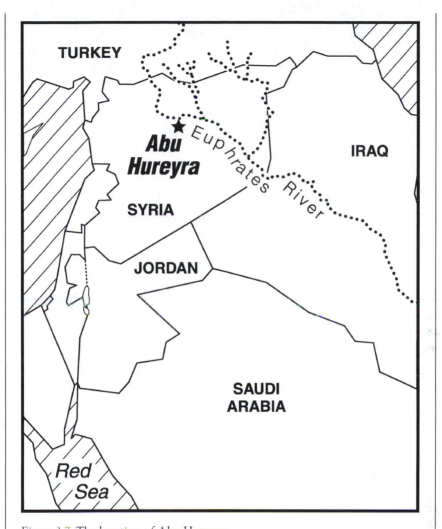

Figure 3.7 The location of Abu Hureyra.

excavate only one area of the site. At Abu Hureyra, the excavation combined two of these strategies. In the first season a vertical history was established using a series of deep trenches. Then, having discovered that there were two main periods of occupation at Abu Hureyra, the team spent the second season expanding their trenches horizontally, in order to learn more about the people who lived there. What they discovered was that the original inhabitants of the site were sedentary hunter-gatherers who followed an annual cycle of foraging. The area near the site was especially rich in foodstuffs, and the people appear to have been healthy. They collected over 250 different species of wild plants – a well-balanced mix of wild rye and wild wheat, feather-grass, club-rush, knot-grass, wild millets, and a few others (all of which were found on the site); plus nuts, tubers, and leafy greens that weren't preserved.[19] They hunted a small number of animal species, the most common of which were gazelle, onager, deer, cattle, sheep, hare, and fox. But then, about 15,000 years ago, the climate changed and many of the plants on which they based their diet became less common in the region. The villagers at Abu Hureyra responded by beginning to cultivate rye, and then (probably) by domesticating it.[20] This is the earliest transition to farming found anywhere in the world.

After a short period during which occupation on the site was very reduced, a new village emerged. This Neolithic community lasted for 2,500 years, and grew in population from about 3,000 to nearly 6,000 inhabitants.[21] The farmers continued to gather wild wheat, barley, and rye; but at the same time they grew domesticated wheat (einkorn, emmer, and bread wheat), domesticated two- and six-rowed barley, lentils, large vetches, and flax,[22] and toward the end of the occupation period they added chickpea and field bean to their crops. They hunted wild animals, and also herded domestic sheep and goats. The wheat, lentils, and goats may have been domesticated elsewhere and imported, but the other crops and the sheep were probably domesticated locally.[23]

When the results of the excavation were published in 2000 it became clear that despite having spent only a few months in excavation, the Abu Hureyra team had gathered more information about the transition to agriculture than had been found by many decades-long projects.[24] They did it by collecting thousands of organic samples and then subjecting them to an extraordinarily broad program of analysis. From the very beginning, all the excavated soil was dry-sieved, which allowed the team to recover thousands of seeds, small bones, and small artifacts of the kind that are usually thrown away. Large soil samples were water-floated – the first time this method had been used systematically on a large site. (In water floatation, the excavated dirt is mixed with water and forced through successively smaller meshes. It's the only method archaeologists have for retrieving very small ecofacts and artifacts). The excavation team saved all the charcoal for radiocarbon dating and species analysis, they took soil samples for later pollen and insect analysis, and they collected mudbricks to study the plant remains in them. In the end, they collected several metric tons of flints, 4,000 artifacts, the remains of 200 people, 2 metric tons of animal remains, and 500 liters of plant material from floatation.[25]

Over the 25 years that followed, the Abu Hureyra team built up a complex picture of life in the village. They returned to the area after it had been flooded to survey nearby sites, and to study the local ecology. Trying to figure out how the artifacts were used, they studied tools described in ethnographic reports of hunter-gatherers and traditional farmers. The paleopathologists coaxed an astounding amount of information about cultural practices from the human skeletal material; and as they searched for evidence of animal domestication, the archaeozoologists applied every measure they could find to the extremely fragmentary animal remains, including demographic analysis. The archaeobotanical team set new standards in botanical research: to differentiate wild and domestic cereals they used every scientific method available to them, including bran histology, pyrolysis mass spectrometry, infrared spectrometry, gas chromatography mass spectrometry, scanning electron microscopes, and Fourier transform infrared spectrometry. Many samples were too fragmentary to identify in the usual ways, so they developed a new system of identification based on internal anatomy. As the range of wild and domestic plants at Abu Hureyra became clear, the botanical team searched for ethnographic parallels, and they also began a series of practical experiments: they harvested, processed, cooked, and ate most of the foods the prehistoric people had gathered and grown.[26]

An entire generation of young scholars were trained by working on the material from Abu Hureyra, and their research continues as new techniques for analyzing finds are developed. Although the directors have moved on to other projects, they think about how much more they could have learned if they'd had the time. They write "We continue to be astonished at the richness of the evidence we were able to recover. It is thus with a poignant sense of loss that we reflect on the now inaccessible information . . . covered by the waters of the new lake in the Euphrates Valley."[27]

Note: The primary data from the excavation has been placed in an electronic archive (http://www.ret.edu./abuhureyra) that is available to anyone with internet access.

4

PLANT DOMESTICATION

The chances are good that at some time in your life you've grown a plant. When you prepared the soil (whether in a garden or a flower pot), planted the seeds or young plants, and cared for them as they grew, you were mirroring practices that developed when foragers living in the areas of primary domestication took their first steps toward farming. The plant species they targeted for domestication were well-known – they'd been gathering them for food for millennia – but they were only a few of the thousands of plants their ancestors had eaten. These few species were preadapted to human intervention: that is, they had natural characteristics that encouraged the domestication process, and many were prone to routine mutations that made them even more attractive to early farmers.[1] The importance of this preadaptation becomes clear when we consider the mechanisms of plant reproduction.

Because most of the first crops reproduce sexually, our discussion begins when pollen and ovules join. Many plants are cross-pollinators: their pollen is carried from one plant to the next either by the wind, or by insects and animals attracted to the fruit and flowers, but the earliest crops were all self-pollinators, a factor that was essential to their successful domestication. Once plants have been fertilized, they begin to grow seeds. Each seed contains food – mainly starch, protein, and oil – which builds up until the seed is ripe, at which point most of them fall off the parent plant and embed themselves in the soil where they rest until they germinate (that is, change into seedlings). Germination occurs when the seeds begin absorbing water, which sets in motion a biochemical reaction that causes the embryos to elongate and form baby plants. If all goes well, the young plants establish themselves and a new generation is on its way. But sometimes heavy rains wash the germinating seeds away, or a sudden freeze or drought kills the embryos before they're established, or predators eat the seeds and the germinating plants. If all the seeds on a plant ripen and fall to the ground and germinate at the same time, they're even more likely to be destroyed. And even if they survive and germinate, the new plants compete with one another (and sometimes, with their parents) for moisture, sunlight, and nutrients in the soil, and some of them die.

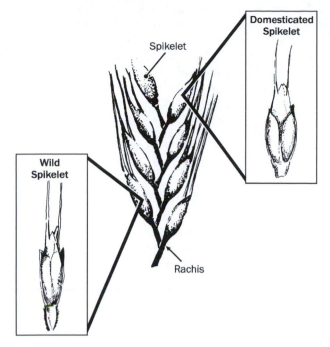

Figure 4.1 An ear of grain is composed of spikelets, attached to short stems called rachises. Wild and domestic spikelets are shaped differently.

In response to these factors, seed-bearing species evolved a set of adaptive strategies, one of which is delayed germination. In many species, seeds germinate only under special circumstances. Some seeds need a certain amount of light before they begin to grow, others need to come close to freezing during the winter, and a few species developed a more elaborate strategy in which some of the seeds from each plant lie dormant for months, or even years, before they sprout. The most common adaptive strategy is shattering, a term botanists use to describe seeds that fall off the stalk or out of the pod at the slightest touch. Shattering occurs when the rachis – the stem that attaches the seeds or spikelets to the stalk, and through which nutrients pass – becomes extremely brittle and breaks, allowing the mature seeds to fall to the ground.

In the wild, shattering is adaptive (it's a favorable trait) because it developed together with a second strategy called sequential ripening, which ensures that the seeds on a stalk or in a pod don't become ripe all at once. Instead, over time, as each cluster of seeds ripens, its rachises become brittle and shatter, and the seeds fall to the ground. Shattering is especially important for plants with heavy seeds, because they tend to drop their seeds straight down, but less important in species with small, light-weight seeds because they've developed other mechanisms that disperse the seeds away from the parent plant. There are pods that burst and eject seeds in all directions, wings that catch the wind and carry seeds far away, and spines that attach themselves to passing animal fur. An exceptionally effective dispersal mechanism is the evolution of a seed coat so resistant that seeds can pass unharmed through the digestive tracts of animals that eat them – birds, in particular, disperse these seeds over a wide area.

Cereals and legumes

Cereals (the name comes from the Roman goddess of agriculture, Ceres) are flowering grasses that sprout, flower, seed, and die every year, which is why gardeners refer to them as annuals. Grown for their seeds or kernels, cereals are excellent sources of energy: although they lack some amino acids, as well as calcium, vitamin A, and vitamin C, they provide starch and oil, and in some cases, considerable amounts of protein. Once ripe, the kernels are relatively easy to store and they retain their nutrients for a long time. Even the stalks of cereals are useful as animal food, as bedding in stables and barns, and as a building material. A major drawback with cereals is that they depend on the soil for nitrogen, and without artificial fertilization they eventually exhaust the fields they're growing in, but despite this, two cereals (wheat and barley) were the very first plants to be domesticated; and a third (rye) may have been cultivated, or even domesticated, at about the same time. Today, cereal crops including wheat, rice, maize, sorghum, millet, and oats provide most of the calories in the human diet.[2]

Like cereals, legumes are annuals. Some legumes are grown for animal fodder, but many other legumes are cultivated for their seeds, which ripen in pods. The seeds are rich in B-vitamins and iron; contain on average two times the protein but less starch than cereals; and can be eaten, sometimes pods and all, while they're still green. (Snow peas and green beans are familiar examples.) Legumes are characterized by a long period of sequential ripening, during which a single plant may have ripe pods, green pods, and flowers, all at the same time, which means that a stand of legumes can be harvested again and again over several weeks. Like cereals, legumes can be dried and stored for later use (the pods open easily when dry), and again like cereals, legumes provide food for both people and animals. Unlike cereals, however, legume plants add nitrogen to the soil, so when they're grown in the same fields as cereals they can replace much of the nitrogen the cereals have depleted.

Growing cereals and legumes together is good for the fields, and eating them together is good for the farmers. In order to build and maintain body tissue, people need protein – or more specifically, the amino acids in protein. Some amino acids are synthesized in the adult human body, but eight essential ones can't be, and have to come from food. Although all eight are

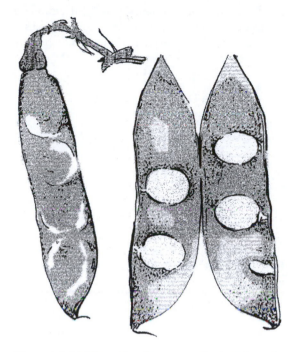

Figure 4.2 Unlike grains, legume seeds ripen in pods.

present in animal protein, plant proteins are usually missing one or two. When cereals and legumes are eaten together they provide all eight of the essential amino acids,[3] a fact that the ancestors of early agriculturalists they undoubtedly understood – at least on a practical level – and their descendants took advantage of that knowledge. In Asia, rice, wheat, and barley were grown along with soybeans; in India rice was paired with hyacinth bean, black gram, and green gram; in the African savannah, pearl millet and sorghum were domesticated along with cow pea and Bambara groundnut; and in the New World, maize and Phaseolus beans in Mesoamerica, and maize and groundnuts in South America were the bases for agriculture.[4]

Cereals and legumes are technically dry fruits (they have a hard dry layer around their seeds). Early agriculturalists also experimented with growing succulent fruits like apples, olives, grapes, and melons, but most of these were brought into domestication much later than cereals and legumes, and in most cultures they've always been supplementary foods rather than staples. Many of them are propagated vegetatively – asexually through offshoots, cuttings, tubers, bulbs, and corms – rather than sexually through seeds, so they're more complicated to grow than cereals and legumes, and this may account for their typically late addition to agricultural assemblages. It should be noted, however, that recent research in Israel suggests that figs may have been domesticated at a site near Jericho in the Jordan Valley at about the same time as the first experiments with cereals and legumes,[5] and some archaeologists believe that in New Guinea tubers may have been domesticated long before other crops were imported.

Southwest Asian founder crops

The earliest evidence archaeologists have found for plant domestication comes from southwest Asia, where the founder crop assemblage includes three cereals (two wheats – emmer and einkorn – plus barley) and four legumes (lentil, pea, chickpea, and bitter vetch). Early farmers in southwestern Asia also grew flax, probably both for its oil and its fiber; and as I just mentioned, may have grown figs. The complex lineages of the eight traditionally recognized founder crops (that is, all but the figs) have been traced genetically: some wild progenitors were widely spread, while one – wild chickpea – grew only in southeastern Turkey. We're going to look more closely at three of the founder crops: wheat, barley, and lentils.[6]

Wheat (Triticum)

Wheat, an annual, self-pollinating, flowering grass with considerably more protein than any other cereal, is the most significant cereal crop in the world. Among its most useful characteristics is its ability to rise if leavened with yeast. Since its domestication in southwest Asia, wheat has become an important staple in all major cuisines: it's grown world-wide, food made with it accounts for 20 percent of the total calories consumed by the world's populations, and a failure of the world wheat crop due to a disease or infestation would be an unmitigated disaster for us all. The three most important wheat species brought into domestication, einkorn wheat (*Triticum turgidum*), emmer wheat (*T. monococcum*), and bread wheat (*T. aestivuna*), have been widely studied and archaeobotanists understand more about their transition from wild grasses to domesticated cereals than about any other domestic crops. It's now known, for example, that the most commonly grown modern wheat – bread wheat – is a hybrid of emmer and a wild goat grass, *Aegilops squarrosa*. Unlike many early crops, the other two early wheats, emmer and einkorn, also continue to be grown: a variety of emmer called durum wheat is used in making pasta, and einkorn is grown as an heirloom crop.

The wild progenitors of domesticated wheat grow in open areas on upland hillsides and slopes. They do well in bitterly cold winters; and need cool weather during their germination period, moderate to warm temperatures during their growing cycle, and warm dry weather as they ripen. In this environment, the ancestral grasses of einkorn and emmer evolved four adaptive germination strategies: shattering, sequential ripening (a stand of wild wheat ripens over a two-week period), delayed germination (spikelets of

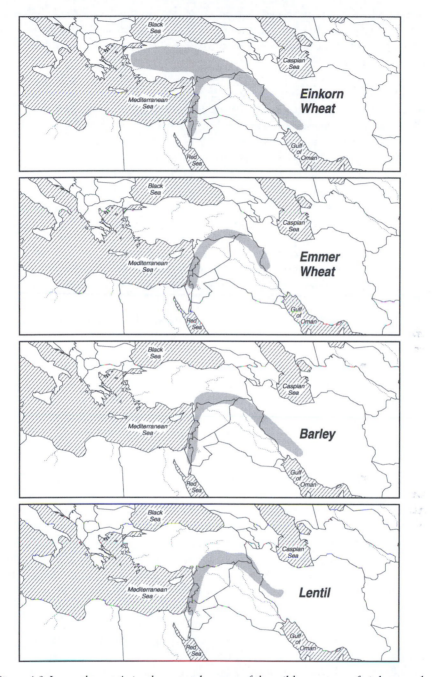

Figure 4.3 In southwest Asia, the natural ranges of the wild ancestors of einkorn and emmer wheat, barley, and lentil overlap.

emmer wheat contain two seeds, one of which frequently does not germinate for a year), and the development of a tough husk around each kernel, which protected the small seeds from frost and dehydration during the cold winter months.

There's plenty of evidence that besides wheat seeds, foragers routinely collected the seeds of other annual grasses in the area. Some of these, like wild rye, would seem to be a lot more attractive as a domesticate than wild wheat. Rye is exceptionally easy to harvest because it grows in very dense stands, the seeds can be freed from the husks in a mortar and pestle (this isn't true of the wild wheats, which have tough husks), and the grains are less floury than wheat grains, so they're less gritty when roasted. Rye seeds are also easier to crush, easier to cook into mush, and easier to grind into flour, and the low glycemic index of rye-based foods makes them more sustaining than wheats, so that people who eat them feel full for longer periods of time.[7] Why, then, did wheat (not rye) become the world's single most important crop? The answer is complex, as answers involving natural selection and human behavior often are; and even though the process of wheat domestication has been extensively studied, archaeobotanists and archaeologists don't agree on all the details. Everyone does agree, however, that experiments in wheat domestication began because of a recurring natural mutation of a single wheat gene.

In all stands of wild wheat there are likely to be a few stalks with non-shattering spikelets: a single gene controls the brittleness of the rachis, and a common mutation of this gene produces plants whose spikelets are tightly bound to the stalk. Non-shattering inhibits – or prevents – seed dispersal and it's distinctly disadvantageous because few, if any, of the seeds from plants with tough rachises fall to the ground and germinate. So, although the non-shattering mutation reappears periodically, it doesn't move into the gene pool. When people began collecting wild wheat, they changed the environment and the reproduction odds because they concentrated on the tough-rachis mutants.

Experiments have shown that when shattering wheat is harvested – whether by hand stripping, flint-bladed sickles, beaters and baskets, beaters and boats, steel sickles, scythes, mechanical strippers, mechanical blowers, binders, or power mower/swathers followed by pickup combines and grain combines – the results are the same: about half of the potential yield is lost.[8] But because tough-rachis spikelets are bound to the stalk, fewer of their ripe kernels fall to the ground during harvesting, and a greater percentage of them end up in the harvesting baskets. At the same time, during the harvest some tough-rachis kernels that would otherwise dehydrate on the stalk are knocked off and fall to the ground where they germinate. Over time, as people returned to the same wild stands to harvest grain and continued to select the stalks with tough-rachises, the percentage of plants with tough rachises in the wild wheat population became significant and the gene pool began to shift. As people moved from foraging to cultivating, it's likely that more and more of the seeds saved from the last harvest were tough-rachis mutants, and eventually, the non-shattering type (which couldn't survive without human intervention) became the dominant strain in the population under human control.

Because the issue of shattering is essential to any discussion of wheat cultivation and domestication, identifying the presence of non-shattering strains on a site is important. The main diagnostic test used by archaeobotanists to identify grains that are in the process of domestication or that have been domesticated is to examine the scars left when the kernels separated from the rachis: brittle rachis kernels detach easily and their scars are clean, but those from tough-rachis heads have to be torn off the stalk, and the scars that are left are rough. If a significant percentage of the wheat remains on a site have rough scars (that is, they come from non-shattering plants) archaeologists assume that the domestication process has started.[9]

Barley (Hordeum vulgare)

Barley, another annual, self-pollinating, flowering grass, is almost always found as a companion crop with wheat. The wild progenitors of wheat and barley grow on many of the same upland slopes: barley tolerates poorer soil and can survive in hotter and drier conditions, but doesn't do as well in very cold winters. Like wild wheat, wild barley shatters but has a recurring mutation for non-shattering, so the mechanisms of domestication in wheat and barley are largely the same. The presence of significant amounts of non-shattering barley on a site is a marker for the domestication process.

The non-shattering mutation alone would have made barley attractive to early cultivators, but barley has other mutations that encouraged its domestication. The first has to do with the seed heads. In wild barley, the seed heads carry two rows of seeds arranged in spikelet groups of three on alternating sides of the rachis. Only the middle seed in each triplet is fertile. The seed heads of domestic barley, on the other hand, have six rows of seeds, all of which are fertile. Two mutations govern these changes, and it's very likely that when the mutant plants appeared people concentrated on harvesting them: the archaeological record certainly reveals that over time domestic barley became six-rowed. A second important mutation produces naked barley kernels (a naked kernel is one without the tough hull). Hulled grains take a lot of time to process because you have to pound or grind them to free the kernels, whereas naked kernel grains are much easier to thresh: in fact, they're often referred to as "free-threshing" because the seeds are so easy to process. Archaeologists assume that people actively selected free-threshing mutant barley, causing the gene pool to change. Barley continues to be grown today in both its hulled and naked forms. There are also free-threshing varieties of wheat. However, domestic einkorn and emmer wheats are hulled and modern cross-breeding experiments indicate that the first bread wheat probably was too. In fact, archaeobotanists believe that (unlike free-threshing barley) un-hulled wheats appeared only after the hulled varieties were domesticated.

In the West people rarely eat barley and its main uses are in beer-making – malt is a powder made from hulled barley grains that have germinated for about a week[10] – and as an animal feed. In times of famine, people grind barley to make bread, but its flour produces a heavy, coarse, and unappetizing product, and as soon as possible bakers revert to wheat flour. In east Asia, on the other hand, barley is an important food crop. In both China and Korea barley is eaten mixed with rice, and in Tibet it's mixed with yak butter and salted tea to make the staple food, *tsampa*. Koreans drink hot tea made from roasted barley grains and water (*bori-cha*) while the Japanese prefer the mixture cold (*mugi-cha*): in both cases it serves as a mild laxative.

Lentil (Lens culinaris)

Lentil, one of the earliest of the domesticated grain legumes, has a high protein content – about 25 percent. It's a self-pollinating annual that grows

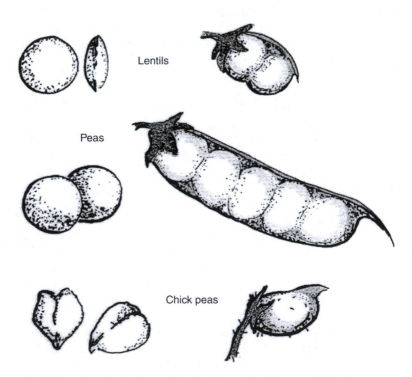

Lentils

Peas

Chick peas

Figure 4.4 Three southwest Asian founder crops: lentil, pea, and chickpea.

on the same upland slopes as wild wheat and wild barley, and it's often found with them on archaeological sites. Today, lentil colonizes the borders of cereal fields, a habit that was probably common in antiquity, too. In wild lentil, the ripe seed pods burst and expel the seeds, but in domestic lentil this characteristic has been lost, which makes it easy to harvest. Once again, the change was caused by a common mutation on a single gene. Another common mutation replaced the thick, coarse seed coat of the wild lentil (which insulated the seeds and served to delay germination over several years) with a thinner coat that encouraged the annual germination needed in crops.

As they moved toward domestication, the other members of the south-west Asian founder assemblage – pea, chickpea, bitter vetch, and flax – also developed non-splitting pods, and the seed coats in pea and chickpea became thinner. And, as all eight founder crops became more and more dependent on human intervention for their survival, they lost the strategies of sequential ripening and dormancy (which the new farmers didn't like) and developed larger, heavier, seeds (which the farmers preferred), probably as a result of additional natural mutations.

Self-pollination

We need to return briefly to the subject of self-pollination, a characteristic shared by all the southwest Asian founder crops. Unlike non-shattering seeds and thin seed cases, self-pollination didn't appear because of human selection. Instead, it was a pre-existing condition that facilitated successful domestication. Self-pollinating plants, you remember, deposit their pollen on their own ovules: botanists say that they breed "true" because there's no genetic mixing (there's only one parent, after all) and each generation pre-serves all the genetic characteristics of its parents. The importance of self-pollination to the domestication process is enormous, because once a change has occurred in a self-pollinator's gene pool, it's firmly established

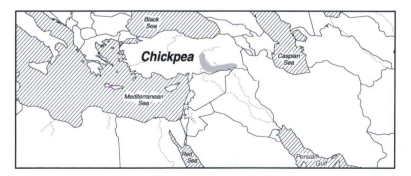

Figure 4.5 The wild range of chickpea is very small.

and there's no danger it will be removed by cross-breeding. This means that once people began encouraging the new mutant forms, the mutations were carried forward into all subsequent generations. Self-pollinating plants are also relatively easy to transplant to new areas because their reproduction is entirely self-contained. In fact, self-pollination is the main reason that it took only a few decades, or perhaps a few hundred years, for the gene pools of the founder crops to be permanently changed by human intervention.[11]

Other founder crops

Botanists know much less about the genesis of crop assemblages in the other areas of primary domestication. This is due partly to a frustrating lack of evidence (both archaeological and botanical) and partly to the characteristics of the crops themselves. For example, the wild progenitors of domesticated sorghum have been identified: they're found mainly in the African savannah belt south of the Sahara, where sorghum was probably first domesticated. Unfortunately, no archaeological evidence supporting this probable domestication has been discovered, and in fact, the earliest remains of domesticated sorghum are found on the Indian subcontinent. The situation with rice domestication is just the opposite: there's clear archaeological evidence for China as the locus of rice domestication, but the wild progenitor of this grain hasn't been found. Rice cross-pollinates, and its history of constant hybridization between wild and cultivated forms has created a genetic tangle that hasn't yet been unraveled – and may never be.

It's clear that the simple task of harvesting wild grains didn't automatically lead to domestication. It was only when people began selecting seeds with certain characteristics that the process was set in motion. Planting the seeds in fields near villages – that is, isolating the crops outside the natural ranges of the wild progenitors – sped the process along, and soon the cultivated plants were quite distinct from their wild progenitors. Their gene pools had changed, and they were on their way to becoming crops.

The domestication of maize (corn)

In many ways, the fact that maize (*Zea mays mays*) was ever domesticated is surprising. Its ancestor, teosinte (*Zea mays parviglumis*), is an unlikely progenitor – it took seventy years and the invention of genetic research to establish the relationship. An annual wild grass native to southern and western Mexico, teosinte is a thick-stemmed, branching grass that shatters, seed by tiny seed, as it ripens. Technically, each seed is a fruit, and the fruitcases are so hard that the seeds pass unaltered through digestive systems. It's hard to imagine how teosinte could have evolved into a naked-grained, single-stalked crop with many large seeds

---

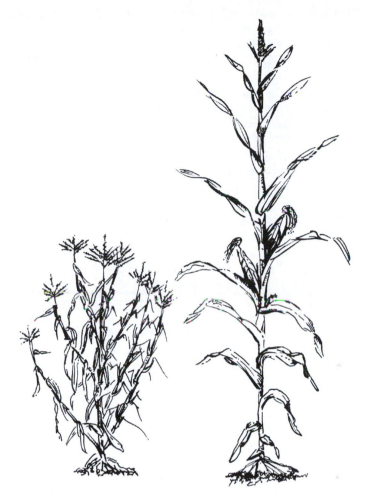

Figure 4.6 Teosinte is a branching annual grass with tiny seeds that disperse easily, while its descendant, maize, is a single-stalked crop with many large seeds permanently attached to cobs covered with husks that cannot open by themselves.

permanently attached to cobs, cobs permanently attached to their shanks, and husks that need human help to open. But that's what happened.

How did it occur to people to domesticate teosinte? Ancient people chewed maize stems for sugar,[12] so perhaps they used teosinte in the same way. Unlike the southwest Asian cereals, teosinte certainly couldn't have been a major source of food because its fruitcase-protected seeds are indigestible.[13] Still, botanists know that teosinte

was harvested because when foragers encountered a spontaneous mutation on one gene that freed the seeds from the fruitcases, they began
actively selecting the mutant plants. The mutant teosinte couldn't
propagate by itself, so it required human intervention to move the trait
for naked seeds into the teosinte gene pool. Geneticists believe that
only a few other mutations were necessary for teosinte to become
primitive maize, among them loss of shattering, the development of
upright architecture with female cobs on the primary branches, and
increased kernel nutrition. By about 9,000 years ago – according to the
molecular data – farmers in the Balsas River basin of southern Mexico
had taken advantage of these mutations to create a small population of
mutant teosinte (as few as twenty plants would have been enough)
which then gave rise to maize.

The new maize farmers had to contend with problems unknown to
the Neolithic people of southwest Asia. Unlike wheat, barley and the
other Old World cereals which are self-pollinating, teosinte and maize
are both wind-pollinated and they're very susceptible to unwanted
cross-pollination. Some teosinte-maize hybrids are so different from
either parent that until genetic analysis they were classified as different
species,[14] so the early maize growers had to be vigilant in maintaining
their mutant stocks. Another difference was the continued presence of
sequential ripening. One of the first genetic changes in Old World
cereals was the loss of sequential ripening, which meant that the crops
could be sown in large fields and harvested all at once.

Maize, on the other hand, maintained the long sequential maturation
of its ancestor, so it had to be harvested again and again, plant by
plant.[15] Eventually a system developed in which the farmers took
advantage of this characteristic by planting maize, beans, and squash
seeds together in little mounds of earth. As the maize grew up, the bean
twined around it and the squash formed a groundcover that discour-
aged weeds,[16] and when they were ripe, more than one crop could be
harvested during each sweep of the fields.

Maize was so superior to the other New World grains that it was
rapidly adopted by cultures to the north and south. Its only drawback
is that it's unusually low in niacin (it also lacks the amino acids lysine
and methionine) and so people who depend heavily on maize can suffer
protein hunger and also niacin deficiency or pellagra. But cooking
maize in lime water or pounding it with wood ash increase the niacin,
and eating maize with beans adds both niacin and protein.

The oldest archaeological evidence for maize is from southern Central
and northern South America, where pollen, phytoliths and starch
grains that date to between 7,700 and 6,000 years ago have been found.
Maize pollen from a site on the tropical Gulf of Mexico has been dated
to 7,100 years ago,[17] and in Mexico, actual cobs dating to 6,200 years

ago have been excavated at Guilá Naquitz, a small camp site in the Valley of Oaxaca not too far from the Balsas River basin.[18] By 3,000 years ago maize had reached northern Mexico and the southwestern United States,[19] and at about the same time, maize with kernels the size of modern varieties was used to make impressed decorations on pottery in Equador.[20] By 2,100 years ago maize had reached the eastern part of the United States, although it didn't become an important crop there until a thousand years later. And all the time, the genetic manipulation continued. For the first two millennia, farmers seem to have concentrated on increasing the size of the cobs and improving the quality of the kernels, and by 4,400 years ago most of the genetic components of modern maize were present in Mexico, but farmers have continued to experiment with new varieties, probably because maize is constantly crossing-breeding with wild teosinte.

Today, maize – the New World's most important contribution to the human diet – is second only to wheat in the numbers of acres planted each year.[21] The story of its domestication is a reminder that prehistoric people were just as intelligent, creative and capable of genetic engineering as people today.

5

ANIMAL DOMESTICATION

In many ways, animal domestication and plant domestication are similar. The early agriculturalists knew a lot about potential animal domesticates because their ancestors had eaten them for centuries. Like plants, some of the animal species turned out to be easier to domesticate than others, and natural genetic changes played an important role in the decisions about which of them to tame. And in concept, there's not a lot of difference breeding cows to give more milk and breeding grain to produce larger kernels. But in one important way, raising animals isn't at all like growing crops because, unlike plants, animals have personalities. Farmers certainly interact with their plants – after all, they take care of them as they grow – but the plants are passive. There's no social relationship between vegetable growers and their tomatoes. Animals, on the other hand, are active social creatures, which means that successful animal husbandry (the term used to describe raising and breeding animals) involves changes in both behavior and morphology. Some of the behavioral and physical changes that appeared in tamed and early domesticates weren't intentionally caused by their keepers, while others were clearly the result of deliberate selective breeding. But the behavioral characteristics that were essential – those that made some animals easy to pen, easy to breed, easy to herd, and easy to protect – were inherent in the species themselves. In other words, like the earliest crops, the first domesticated animals were preadapted – in this case to interactions with humans.

There are three preadaptive traits that allow animals to be easily domesticated, all of them present in the first three animals to live closely with humans – dogs, sheep and goats. The first characteristic is gregariousness. Species that are sociable and live in groups are predisposed to domestication because they congregate (they tend to stay close to one another in large groups) and because no matter how widely they roam during the day, they always return to the herd at night. Since they tend to stay close to one another in the wild, they don't mind being bunched up in captivity, which means that they're comfortable when crowded together in a pen, and crowded conditions don't affect their ability to reproduce, bear multiple offspring, or mature rapidly into adults. With a very few exceptions (most notably, the cat) all domestic animals are gregarious, but not all gregarious animals can be domesticated. Unless they have the second essential behavioral trait – acceptance of hierarchical social systems – even gregarious animals will resist human control. Dominance hierarchy social systems are important because animals with them are predisposed to follow leaders, and will readily accept humans as the dominant animals in their group. Again, almost all domestic animals (except the cat) fall into this category. The third essential trait is an absence of aggression or territorialism. Territorial species defend their home ranges, while non-territorial species can live comfortably almost anywhere, and find it easy to share their habitats with other animals.[1] In general, they're placid and slow to panic, and when threatened they tend to move into tight defensive groups and face their attackers rather than running away. Only a few domestic animals (like the horse and the cat) are territorial.

Morphological changes caused by domestication

Domestic animals share many behavioral characteristics with their wild progenitors, but they don't look much like them. All animal species on the way

Figure 5.1 Neotony is easy to see when you compare the faces of the grey wolf and the Yorkshire terrier.

to domestication went through a series of similar physical changes, many of which seem to be linked to a single factor – neotony, or the retention of foetal or juvenile characteristics in the adult animal. Both the bodies and the behavior of early domesticates were affected by neotony, and scientists still don't understand exactly why. Some zoologists have suggested that neotony was triggered by genes controlling the timing of maturation, which resulted in a change in the growth rate or an early onset of sexual maturity. But no matter what the cause, shortly after the domestication process began, tamed animals stopped maturing before they reached their adult proportions. They began to look younger (and cuter) than their wild cousins, with bigger eyes, larger heads in relation to their bodies, and softer fur. And they began to behave differently, too. In the wild, juvenile animals are easier to tame than their parents: they're curious and willing to play, they're less likely to run away from new experiences, and they're not afraid to explore new locations. Because domestic animals never matured, they retained these behavioral characteristics, as well as the ability to keep learning, something that wild animals lose in adulthood. The old adage to the contrary, you *can* teach an old dog (but not an old wolf) new tricks.

A mid-twentieth-century experiment in selective breeding offers some interesting clues to the origins of neotony. A Russian geneticist, D.K. Belyaev, spent twenty years trying to breed red foxes with dog-like temperaments. Like wolves, foxes can be tamed, but they've never been domesticated, and in captivity they display one of three distinct attitudes towards people: 60 percent are afraid, 30 percent are aggressive, and 10 percent are curious. When Belyaev bred only the curious foxes the results were surprising. They developed elevated serotonin levels (serotonin lessens some kinds of aggression and fear): rather than acting aggressive or running away – normal fox behavior even in tamed animals – they wagged their tails when people approached, licked their keeper's hands, and whined for attention. They also changed morphologically: their ears dropped, their tails curled, and their fur became patterned – some with border collie-like white markings on their muzzles and underbellies.[2] Without meaning to, Belyaev had produced foxes with neotony. Something similar probably happened in the early stages of domestication: neotony appeared spontaneously, and when it did, Neolithic breeders encouraged it.

Other changes appeared in animals on the way to domestication, some of them quite striking. One of the earliest and most recognizable is a considerable reduction in size. At some point Neolithic farmers must have decided to breed smaller-sized animals because they're easier to control and more likely to survive in marginal conditions, but the reduction in size I'm talking about appears at the very beginning of the domestication process, long before selective breeding could have made a difference. It's so common that the appearance of noticeably smaller faunal remains on a Neolithic site is automatically interpreted as an indication of early-stage domestication. As in the case of neotony, zoologists don't know what triggered size reduction, but some believe that it was simply a matter of natural selection: the smaller size, they theorize, was adaptive in the new, crowded living conditions. Other zoologists believe that it was caused by stress-related hormonal imbalances, or by a general decline in health in tamed and early-stage domesticates since they probably suffered increased levels of disease and parasitic infections. Another possibility is malnutrition. Tamed adults may well have been malnourished because they were forced to adjust to a new diet and a new schedule of feeding, and because an animal's appetite and growth rate are set in the last stages of gestation, the offspring of these malnourished parents would be small at birth, would eat less than normal juveniles, and would never catch up with their peers. Or maybe the babies were normal, but when people began to milk their animals, they forced the young animals to be weaned at an earlier age than their wild cousins, and this affected their growth.[3]

The reduction in size is general, but it's especially pronounced in the skull. The jaws and muzzles of domesticated animals are shorter than those of their wild cousins, and their teeth are smaller. Archaeozoologists think that the shorter jaw developed first, because the earliest specimens are filled with badly crowded big teeth. But within a few generations the teeth have shrunk to fit the smaller jaw, and once they have, they become a permanent characteristic: Great Danes have larger bodies than their wolf ancestors but their teeth are much smaller.[4] Another result of the smaller skull was a reduced cranial capacity and a smaller brain – in relation to their body size, domestic animals have much smaller brains than their wild ancestors. Although you might not think so, the development of a smaller brain in domestic animals was adaptive. Brains consume an enormous amount of energy. Animals don't evolve larger brains than necessary, and while wild animals need large brains (they have to be able to react quickly to a variety of situations, so the energy needed to keep their brains going is well spent), domestic animals lead regular and regulated lives, and large brains aren't essential to their survival: their energy is better spent elsewhere. Like the smaller teeth, once the smaller brains develop they became a permanent feature. Even when domestic animals revert to the wild (that is, become feral), and have to face difficult challenges to their survival, their brain size doesn't increase. Studies of dingos, feral in Australia for thousands of years, and of the Soay sheep, feral on the island of St Kilda in the Hebrides since the Neolithic period, have proved this to be true.[5]

Another skeletal change that may indicate domestication is found in the horns. Horns are composed of a dead sheath covering a living bone core. The sheath rarely survives, but the horn cores often do, and they're differently shaped in domestic and wild animals: the horns of domestic caprovines are essentially triangular or almond-shaped in section, while those of their wild cousins are four-sided. In general, domestic sheep and goats also have smaller and shorter horns than wild sheep and goats (but because some domestic sheep have larger horns than their progenitors, horn size isn't always a useful distinguishing feature).

When sheep and goats were domesticated, their coats changed, too. Wild caprovines have stiff hairy outer coats – the hairs are called kemps – and shorter, finer, undercoats which grow in the winter and are shed each spring. The outer hair on domestic goats is similar to kemps, and goats still shed their undercoats spontaneously (cashmere and mohair are woven from the undercoats grown by goats), but domestic sheep have lost their kemps and their undercoat has become a woolly fleece that grows year round. Because it's no longer shed spontaneously it has to be sheared, which is an improvement (at least for their human keepers) because all the wool can be harvested at the same time. Although more research is needed before they can be sure, many archaeozoologists believe that genetic mutations in sheep initiated both the loss of self-shedding and the disappearance of the kemps. Because hair and wool don't survive in the archaeological record except under extraordinary circumstances, archaeologists don't know when domestic-type coats first appeared, but Neolithic sculptures of woolly sheep indicate that the change occurred early in the domestication process.

Another morphological change associated with domestication is the retention of body fat. Healthy domestic animals have a layer of fat under the skin, and more fat marbled throughout their muscles. (Modern beef cattle and pigs illustrate this trait.) The fatter bodies may be a side-effect of breeding for calm temperaments: recent experiments have shown that in pig and cattle breeds, leaner strains are more excitable than fatter breeds.[6] Although all domestic animals are fatter than their wild cousins, some domesticates, like camels and fat-tailed sheep, evolved special accumulations of fat to help

Figure 5.2 Wild sheep and goats have shaggy outer coats and woolly undercoats that shed annually.

Figure 5.3 Fat-tailed sheep store excess fat in their tails. This one has almost depleted its supply.

them survive long periods with little food and water. Once again, archaeozoologists don't know what caused this adaptation or when it first occurred, but depictions in art suggest it appeared in the early stages of domestication.

There's one more morphological characteristic that points to domestication: the skeletons of tamed and domestic animals show the effects of disease and have skeletal malformations that aren't seen in the wild. Although some of the problems, such as stress fractures in draft animals, don't appear until animals have been domesticated for millennia, as soon as sheep and goats came under human control they began to suffer chronic arthritis and gum disease.[7]

Archaeozoologists estimate that it took less than two hundred years (or about 30 generations) for neotony and the other physical changes to appear.[8] And as Neolithic breeders took more active control of their animals, subjecting them to new diets and crowded quarters and selecting for personality traits like placidity, the morphological and behavioral changes in the animals accelerated. It wasn't long before the tamed animals were so different from their wild cousins that they had become new – domestic – species.

The earliest domestic animals

We now turn to some specific animal species. Once again we're going to focus on southwest Asia, because that's where the earliest experiments in animal husbandry took place. Four mammal species were important there: sheep and goats, pigs, and cattle. But before I discuss them, we need to take a quick look at an southwest Asian animal that wasn't domesticated.

Figure 5.4 Syrian gazelles were an important food source for early farmers in south-west Asia, but were never domesticated.

Archaeologists know that gazelles were the favorite prey of pre-Neolithic people in southwest Asia because they've found more gazelle bones on pre-Neolithic sites than those of any other animal, and because there's evidence that herds of gazelles were driven into corrals and slaughtered by the hundreds. Gazelle meat was so popular that the animals were hunted in large numbers long after people had domesticated other sources of animal protein but early farmers never tried to domesticate them. Why? The answer is simple: they weren't able to because gazelles lacked the characteristics necessary for successful domestication. Although they travel in groups, gazelles can't be herded because when threatened, they run away. They're fiercely territorial and sometimes nasty-tempered, and they don't breed easily in captivity. They're also intensely nervous, and when they're penned up they panic – some die of shock and others batter themselves to death against fences trying to escape (which may be why the strategy of using corrals for killing them was developed). Neolithic farmers had no choice: the only possible domesticates in southwest Asia were sheep, goats, pigs, and cattle.

Sheep (Ovis aries) *and goats* (Capra hircus)

The Asiatic mouflon (*Ovis orientalis*) is probably the ancestor of all domestic sheep, and the bezoar goat (*Capra aegagrus*) is the main, if not the sole, ancestor of domestic goats. In antiquity these wild animals inhabited foothills and mountains from Turkey and the Levant to southern Iran, and this is the region in which archaeologists have found the earliest evidence for animal husbandry. In the wild, their habitats don't overlap – sheep live in the foothills, and goats live high up in the mountains – but because neither species is territorial, they're willing to be herded together and to share their ranges. Sheep and goats have complementary eating habits: sheep are grazers that prefer grass, while goats are browsing ruminants that concentrate on thorny shrubs (although they'll readily accept a wide range of food). Ruminants have multiple stomachs, allowing them to digest woody cellulose. They browse for a time, stop and regurgitate the partially digested material, ruminate or chew it – zoologists say they chew their cud – and then swallow it into another stomach.

For both sheep and goats, the main survival problem in the wild is finding enough food, not running away from predators, so when they're frightened they bunch up, and if a sheepdog or herdsman comes close, they'll turn and walk away. They congregate naturally, so they're easy to pen; they actually

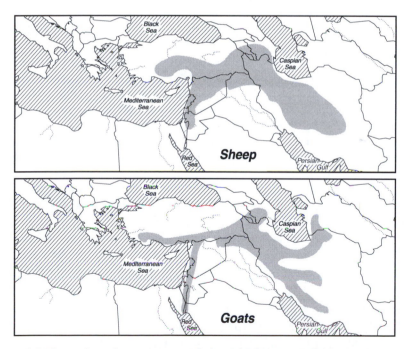

Figure 5.5 The earliest domestication of sheep and goats took place in southwest Asia and the Levant, where their natural ranges overlapped.

69

thrive in crowded conditions, and because their social systems are based on a dominant leader, they readily accept a herdsman in that role. Sheep and goats are also amazingly useful. They provide meat, milk, yoghurt, and cheese for food; fibers, horns, hides, sinews, and bone for artifacts and clothing; tallow for lubrication and lighting; and dung for building material, fuel, and fertilizer. It's hardly surprising that they continue to be the basis for pastoralist economies around the world.

Although most Neolithic faunal assemblages include remains of both species, they seem to have been domesticated independently of one another: the earliest known remains of domesticated goats come from Ganj Dareh in western Iran, and the site of Zawi Chemi Shanidar in northeastern Iraq may be the site of the earliest known domesticated sheep. Early domestic sheep are also found in Syria at Bouqras, where the evidence suggests that domestication had just begun, and at Argissa-Magoula in Greece where they seem to have been imported after domestication (sheep weren't native to Greece).[9]

Pigs (Sus scrofa domestica)

Domestic pigs are descended from the wild boar (*Sus scrofa*), which is still relatively common in Europe, Asia, and North Africa. The genetic relationship between wild and domestic pigs is confusing – in many places wild and feral populations have interbred with domestic pigs, creating about twenty-five sub-species – but there's some evidence that pigs were independently domesticated in southwest Asia and in China, and maybe in a few other places, too.[10] Pigs are browsers. They live in river valleys and marshes, and move around very little, spending their time eating and sleeping, and because they naturally eat for long periods and then sleep for long periods they easily adjust to the rhythms of farm life. Unlike sheep and goats, pigs don't live in herds. A sow and her piglets form a group, huddling together in nests, and staying together even when they're foraging. Boars, on the other hand, are solitary and can be very aggressive (since antiquity boar hunts have been noted for their danger), but they're not territorial: they only fight each other over sows or food. Pigs aren't as useful as sheep and goats, but because they can eat the same foods as people, they can be trained to clean up garbage, and of course they can provide animal protein (and pigskin). But even though they bear litters and grow quickly, pigs don't seem to have been a particularly popular source of meat in Neolithic southwest Asia. Maybe, because pigs don't do well in dry, hot climates, they were simply harder to raise than sheep and goats.

Cattle (Bos taurus)

Cattle were the last of the four important early domesticates to be brought under human control. Except for the domestic breeds of southeast Asia,

Figure 5.6 The aurochs is the extinct ancestor of most breeds of modern cattle: male aurochsen stood 6 ft tall at the shoulder.

modern cattle are descended from the extinct wild ox, or aurochs (*Bos primigenius*), a grazing and browsing ruminant that stood about 6 feet tall at the shoulder. Aurochsen survived in Europe until the modern period: the last one was killed in Poland in 1627. Until very recently it was assumed that *Bos taurus* was domesticated once, in southwest Asia, and then exported (along with sheep and goats) to Europe and Africa. However, new archaeological and genetic research supports the theory of a second, independent domestication in the eastern Sahara,[11] and a third domestication – of Indian humped cattle or zebu (*Bos indicus*) – probably occurred at Mehrgarh in northwestern Pakistan.[12]

Cattle are ruminants, and they need to be able to graze at night. Confining them in pens without food affects their growth, which may account for the rapid decrease in size in cattle as soon as they're tamed, without which it's unlikely that aurochsen could ever have been successfully domesticated, because cattle more nervous than caprovines and much harder to control. Even modern breeds of cattle are more difficult to milk than the caprovines: the cow has to know her milker, her calf must be present, and the milker may have to stimulate the genital area before the milk flows. Given this difficulty, some archaeozoologists believe that aurochsen were originally tamed for sacrifice and barter, not for their meat and milk.[13] But no matter the reason for their domestication, cattle rapidly became the most versatile of all farm animals, providing everything herders get from sheep and goats; plus butter, cream, and traction; and all of it in a bigger package.

Other domesticates

One other important large mammal domesticated in the Old World is the horse (*Equus caballus*). The wild progenitor of modern horses is known: it was a wild Mongolian steppe horse (*Equus ferus przewalskii* or Przewalski's horse) which still survives in zoos. Horses were domesticated long after cattle, and there's quite a lot of disagreement about whether it happened more than once. But zoologists all agree about why it took so long for people to domesticate these aggressive, nervous, territorial grazers – they are clearly not predisposed to human control.

In the New World, large-animal domestication was limited to the llama (*Lama glama*) and the alpaca *(Vicugna pacos)*. While both animals provide meat, the llama is primarily a pack animal and the alpaca is raised for its hair. MtDNA studies have identified their wild ancestors – the llama is descended from the guanaco (*Lama guanicoe*), and the alpaca from the vicuña (*Vicugna vicugna*) – but unlike most animals under domestication, llama and alpaca morphology didn't change when humans began controlling them, so archaeologists don't know exactly when selective breeding began. Some zoologists doubt that llamas have ever been truly domesticated.[14] Although llama owners mark their animals, and consider them to be property, during most of the year groups of llamas are left alone – that is, not herded – and they spend their days on the mountain slopes in mixed groups with vicuñas (which are wild). Sometimes they cross-breed. Since llama owners do castrate or kill most of the young male animals, in a sense they control the gene pool, but because llamas reproduce without human control, their owners don't engage in direct selective breeding.

Figure 5.7 Llama behavior suggests that they have been tamed, but never fully domesticated.

Dogs and cats

Over ten years ago I made the acquaintance of a English cocker spaniel puppy. The first thing he did when we met was show me his favorite toy, a stuffed animal of indeterminate species. Of course, I praised him extravagantly. He's gone now, but almost until the day he died, when he saw me he came running, tail wagging, stuffed animal in his jaws. At about the same time, I adopted a grey-tabby kitten. These days she's a very dignified lady cat, and every now and then (but only when she feels like it) she brings me an animal, too – a dead mouse. Dogs and cats are uniquely connected with people. They live in our houses, sleep on our beds, and curl up next to us when we read or watch television. We think of them as family members: we worry about their appetites, nurse them when they're sick, and grieve when they die. They're our two most intimate animal companions, but they're not at all alike.

Dogs (*Canis familiaris*)

The grey wolf (*Canis lupus*), the ancestor of all modern dogs, was the first animal people domesticated. Wolves are the perfect potential domesticate: in the wild they live in packs (they're gregarious), and they have a strongly developed dominance hierarchy system. Once a wolf accepts a dominant animal – including a human – as its leader, it's fiercely loyal; and because wolves are intelligent, they can be trained to help their human owners. Wolf society is a lot like human society in

Figure 5.8 Dogs and cats interact with humans in very different ways.

that it's based on relationships between individuals that are constantly expressed through facial expressions and body language. Dogs have retained this behavioral pattern, which you can see in action during what people interpret as affectionate interactions between dogs and their owners. The pattern also explains why a puppy with an owner who smiles a lot smiles back, even though this expression is never seen in the wild.[15] As you would expect, in many ways dogs are immature wolves. They exhibit both physical and behavioral neotony: their heads and teeth are smaller and their brains are roughly like the brains of 4-month-old wolves.[16] Dogs are curious and friendly, which are typical juvenile wolf behaviors; they bark, and so do immature wolves when they want attention; and dogs' vocalization pattern resembles the calls of young wolves.[17]

Unlike most domestic animals, dogs were independently domesticated in several regions, including southwest Asia, northern and eastern Europe, Russia, Japan, and North and South America, and although many scientists have worked on the issue, we don't know where or when the first experiments took place. The authors of a recent analysis of mtDNA from 162 wolves and 140 dogs that confirmed the ancestry of the grey wolf suggested that dogs were fully domesticated more than 100,000 years ago,[18] but this seems unlikely. People kept tamed wolves for thousands of years before domesticating them, and the earliest archaeological record evidence for domesticated dogs – two sets of remains – date to only about 15,000 years ago: one is the skeleton of a clearly domesticated animal from an Upper Paleolithic site in Germany; the other, a puppy buried with an elderly woman, was found in Israel, but the skeleton is so fragmentary and the animal was so young that scientists can't tell if it's a dog, a wolf, or a jackal.[19]

Of all domesticates, dogs have been the most radically changed morphologically by their relationship with humans. They've been selectively bred to perform a wide range of tasks for their owners, and the result has been as varied as the dachshund, the St Bernard, and the teacup chihuahua. We may imagine that we know what dogs think, but we really have no idea how they feel about us. Our feelings about them, however, are clear: our long partnership with dogs has been extremely satisfying.

Cats (*Felix domestica* or *F. catus*)

Cats are descended from two subspecies – the African wild cat (*Felix sylvestris lybica*) and the European wild cat (*Felix sylvestris sylvestris*). The two are somewhat different morphologically, probably as a result of their environments: *Felix s. sylvestris*, a short stocky animal, with thick fur, small ears and a short tail, evolved in northern Europe; while *Felix s. lybicus* evolved in much warmer surroundings, and is long and thin with tall ears and a long tail. There's been relatively little selective breeding of cats based on morphology (it hasn't been necessary because all cats perform the same task: they hunt vermin), which means that domestic cats closely resemble their ancestors and that there's not much variation among modern cat breeds.

Unlike wolves, wild cats exhibit none of the characteristics we expect in potential domesticates. They're solitary, territorial, aggressive, and (mainly) nocturnal hunters. Domestic cats act in much the same way, which is one reason some zoologists think they're still partly wild.[20] This inability to agree on whether or not cats are "fully domesticated" may explain why studies of animal domestication spend a lot of time on dogs, but say very little – sometimes nothing at all – about cats. Because they're territorial, cats mark their home ranges using scent: when they sharpen their claws, for example, they're laying down scent from glands on the underside of their front paws. There are also scent glands at the base of the tail and on the sides of the face and the edges of the mouth, so when a cat rubs against you and twines its tail around your leg, it's marking you with its scent and identifying you as part of its territory. (This is the reason that some zoologists believe it's the territory, and not the social relationship with human owners, that's important to cats.) But whether they're only tamed or fully domesticated, cats thrive equally well as pampered pets or as half-tamed animals in barns and urban areas, and even the most highly bred feline could probably survive in the wild if it had to.

Because the morphology of wild and domestic cats is so similar, it's impossible to pinpoint the earliest examples of cat domestication, or even to figure out why people began living with them. Cat remains have been found on several prehistoric sites in Cyprus, and since they aren't native to the island, they must have been intentionally imported. But archaeozoologists can't tell if they were tamed or domesticated, and there's some suggestion that the cats, along with dogs and foxes (all three were brought to Cyprus at the same time) were largely feral, and were hunted and eaten rather than tamed.[21] At one site, however, a young cat seems to have been placed in a small pit next to a human burial,[22] which suggests it had some value beyond a hot meal.

Cats don't work for people on demand, nor do they supply food or raw materials. Their fur is sometimes was used for clothing (I once noticed a large tiger cat hanging from a hook in a Turkish fur market), but cats have never been systematically raised for fur because neither the color nor texture can be easily controlled through selective breeding. Instead, cats pursue their normal behavior – hunting small animals – and in return receive food, shelter and (whether they want it or not) affection from their owners.

6

ARCHITECTURE

When people invented farming, instead of moving seasonally like their ancestors they began to live in one location all year (a pattern anthropologists call sedentism). Settling down and living in year-round communities was an enormous change: almost every aspect of daily life had to be reinvented, from the way people cooked to how they related to their neighbors. The most basic change was in the concept of "home." Mobile foragers, by definition, are always on the move. They may establish seasonal camps, but after they've harvested the ripe plants, or after the animal herds have migrated past, they pack up and head for another location. Because they think of themselves as living in the whole area, they rarely define one camp or location as "home." Sedentary people, on the other hand, live in established communities with permanent houses. Generation after generation live in the same place, and for them, their villages are "home."

Because they assume that only sedentary cultures live in permanent villages, when archaeologists are trying to figure out if a site is Neolithic or not, they usually check for evidence of year-round occupation. But some sites are confusing. A few foraging cultures in Europe and Asia built permanent

Figure 6.1 The presence of human commensals like house mice indicates that a site was occupied year-round.

settlements, some quite elaborate, and lived in them for at least part of every year. The Serbian site of Lepenski Vir is a good example. It was a planned community of trapezoidal structures (all with the same internal organization) that were carefully lined up side by side beside a river. This level of village organization is characteristic of the Neolithic, and archaeologists can't agree if the people at Lepenski Vir were pre-Neolithic or not. They also can't agree about what the buildings were used for, and whether or not they were in use year-round, all of which makes it difficult to know how to categorize this site.[1]

Another traditional measure of year-round occupation – ecofacts that include plant species that ripen in all seasons – has also been open to question since the discovery of the extraordinarily well-preserved ecofacts from the Upper Paleolithic site Ohalo II, on the Sea of Galilee. Archaeologists have found the remains of plants that ripen in all four seasons, which certainly indicate that Ohalo II was occupied year-round. If it was, it's the earliest evidence for sedentism in the world, predating the Neolithic transition by at least 10,000 years. A third characteristic used to identify sedentism is animal remains that reflect slaughtering on the site throughout the year.[2] But the most telling indication of permanent occupation is the presence of so-called human commensals, including rats, house mice, and sparrows. These species are attracted by the stored grain in agricultural communities, and their remains are almost certain proof that a site was occupied year-round.

Whether seasonal or permanent, all communities include two types of buildings: domestic buildings where people live, and public buildings where they go for other reasons. Sometimes the structures are dispersed – that is, free-standing – and at other times they're agglomerate – connected to one another with party walls. Because the artifacts associated with households are distinctive, and because patterns of daily life haven't changed much in the last 10,000 years (i.e. most people live where they cook, eat, and sleep) domestic architecture is fairly easy to recognize from archaeological evidence. Buildings without the remains of daily life are assumed to have been non-domestic, but their actual functions are often impossible to ascertain.

Circular and rectangular buildings

Although it's quite varied structurally, Neolithic architecture around the world went through similar stages of development. From China to the Americas, the earliest village dwellings were circular semi-subterranean pit-houses with lightly built superstructures. Because the ground provided insulation, pit-houses were warmer than the surface shelters used by hunter-gatherers, but they were dark and damp and almost impossible to enlarge, and in most regions they were quickly replaced by free-standing houses. Still, earth-sheltered buildings never completely disappeared. At Neolithic sites like 'Ain Ghazal in Jordan, houses continued to be partially dug into

Figure 6.2 Mesa Verde is a site with agglomerate architecture.

Figure 6.3 Free-standing circular houses were an early development.

hillsides. At others, like the Chinese site Banpo Ts'un where archaeologists found semi-subterranean circular houses, semi-subterranean rectangular houses, and free-standing circular houses in use at the same time, pit-houses and free-standing houses stood side-by-side. And since the Neolithic period, communities here and there have continued to live fully or partially underground. Among the most famous examples are the underground villages in Cappadocia (Turkey) and in the Chinese loess belt, but semi-subterranean houses built into caves are found from Asia to western Europe and the American southwest; the sod huts constructed by pioneers in the North American Great Plains were semi-subterranean; and so are many finished basements in modern housing developments.[3]

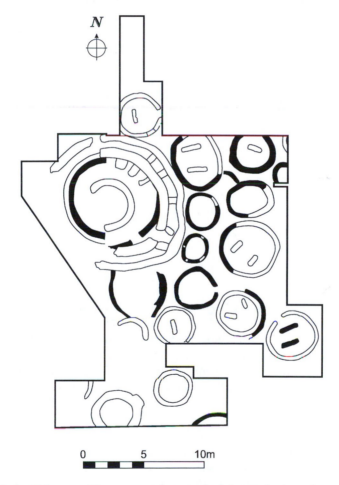

Figure 6.4 At Kalavassos-Tenta some houses had internal piers that may have supported second stories. (On this plan, mudbrick walls are shown in black and stone walls are shown in white.)[4]

Like the pit-houses, the first free-standing Neolithic houses were circular in plan. But as Neolithic life became increasingly complex, and the need for multi-room structures and well-organized communities grew, circular structures were gradually replaced by a Neolithic innovation: rectilinear architecture. Circular buildings are easier to build – square corners and right-angle joins require considerable precision – but they're much less practical. Rectilinear modules are simple to divide or enlarge, can be easily standardized, and can be stacked to produce two or more stories, which is probably why most Neolithic cultures invented the new plan. Like pit-houses, however, circular structures never completely disappeared. In southeastern Turkey and Iraq they continued to be common,[5] and in other regions, builders combined the two shapes. In the Halaf culture in northeastern Syria, for example, builders added flat-roofed rectangular entrances to their circular domed houses, resulting in a "key-hole" plan. A similar floor plan developed in the Shulaveri-Somutepe-Group culture in the Republic of Georgia, whose villages included both flat-roofed and domed circular houses: builders enlarged the domed houses by adding semi-domes, and expanded the flat-roofed houses by joining a square addition to a half-circular main structure.[6]

Circular-plan buildings are found today in tribal compounds in several parts of Africa, and in villages in northern Syria and Apulia (Italy). Circular granaries are found from Africa to Iberia; in the North American grain belt cylindrical grain silos are a common sight; the cylindrical oast towers of England (now often converted into expensive country homes) originally contained kilns built for drying hops or malt; and cylindrical pigeon towers are still in use from the Nile valley to China.

Foundations

Every building project begins with the ground on which the structure will stand. Pit-houses don't need foundations, and the earliest builders of free-standing structures didn't bother with them, either. But as construction techniques advanced, foundations became necessary, both to provide a solid footing and to protect the walls from rising damp. Neolithic foundations were typically a few courses high. Where wood was plentiful, foundations were sometimes made of logs, and as we know from the extraordinary preservation at the Chinese site of Hemudu and the Swiss lake villages, pile foundations were used in some marshy areas. The most common material, however, was fieldstone, occasionally augmented by household debris and old mortars and other grinding stones.[7] Often, these sturdy foundations are the only surviving evidence we have for Neolithic buildings.

Because the sides of the pit hold up the superstructure, pit-houses don't need framing, but once free-standing structures became common the builders had to frame the walls to keep them from falling down. The most common

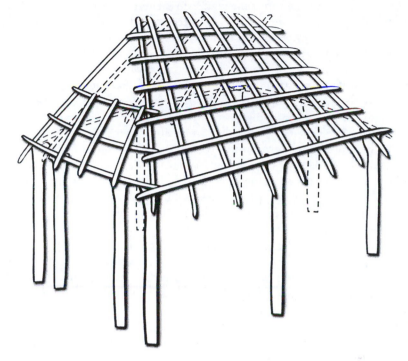

Figure 6.5 Post and lintel construction is the most common type of framing.

framing, both in prehistory and in the modern world, uses post and lintel construction in which upright posts support the horizontal elements. The wall supports (studs), floor and ceiling supports (joists) and roof supports (rafters) can be attached to the frame in various ways: by tying, by using pegs or mortise and tenon joints (a mortise is a slot and a tenon is a projection that fits into it), or by that modern invention, nails. Based on the presence of postholes, post and rafter sockets, the impressions of framing members on plastered walls, and in rare cases the timbers themselves, archeologists believe post and lintel construction first appeared in the Neolithic.

Walls

While most people probably assume that a wall is a solid structure, that's not always the case. Walls can be broken by openings, made up of rows of columns, or indicated by nothing more than corner posts; but solid or not, they always serve the same purpose – they establish two spatial zones – outside and inside, or here and not here. Walls delineate private and public spaces, separate domestic activity areas from one another, and (in religious structures) protect sacred space from the pollution of the everyday world.

Most walls are finished in some way. The earliest pit-house builders probably smoothed or tamped the earth walls to make them less friable, but bare
earth walls aren't very appealing or practical, and before long a number of
wall treatments appeared. Some, like the mud and straw plaster found on
some sites, were minimal but others were more elaborate, and much more
time-consuming to apply: the inhabitants of Tell Ramad in Syria used a fine
plaster that had been stained red. At some sites interior stone walls were
built against the sides of the pit, at others (like 'Ain Mallaha in Syria and
Ramat Harif in the Negev) the walls were lined with stone slabs, and at
Hallan Çemi in southeastern Turkey the pit walls were reinforced with small
stones cemented together using a white plaster-like substance.[8] Like so many
Neolithic innovations, all of these treatments are still in use today.

When people began building free-standing structures, they also began
experimenting with different materials to use for the walls. The earliest walls
may have been pisé or rammed earth, which is made by tamping a mixture
of sand, loam, clay, and other ingredients into forms. Because it cracks and
is easily eroded by water and wind, pisé needs a protective outer coating.
It's heavy and bulky, and was most successfully used for large earth platforms and defensive walls: the architecture at Agia Sofia in Greece, Hallan
Çemi in Turkey, and Hougang in Henan Province, China are good examples.
(China is particularly known for its substantial pisé city walls, with examples
ranging from the Neolithic to the modern period.) In the Americas, remarkable rammed-earth features have been found at Late Archaic sites such as
Poverty Point and Watson Brake in Louisiana, and at various Hopewell and
Mississippian centers. The largest prehistoric structure in the United States
was Monk's Mound, a rammed-earth monument at the Mississippian site
of Cahokia (Ohio).

While a few Neolithic builders, like those at Khirokitia in Cyprus, may
have used pisé for the upper walls of houses (with lower courses of mudbrick or stone) this application is rare. In Europe, the upper stories were
probably made of wattle and daub,[9] another wall construction technique that
was invented in the Neolithic. Wattles are poles or stakes around which twigs
and branches are woven and daub is a plaster made of clay and straw that
covers the wattles. Walls made of wattle and daub are light and flexible; and
although making them requires skill, and the daub has to be renewed annually, they're easy to build. Like pisé, wattle and daub was widespread in the
Neolithic – it's been found at the Neolithic village at Karanovo in Bulgaria,
at early Neolithic sites in Greece like Nea Nikomedeia, across Europe at the
many Linearbandkeramik settlements with their timber longhouses, and in
China at sites such as Banpo Ts'un. Wattle and daub is also typical of the
Late Archaic culture in the American Southwest – one of the best examples
is the Hohokam village of Snaketown in Arizona. And although it's not
often found today, until about 150 years ago wattle and daub was commonly
used for new construction in northern Europe and the British Isles.

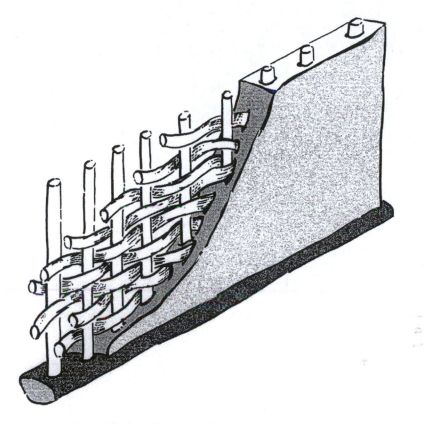

Figure 6.6 Wattle and daub walls are made by weaving twigs and branches around
vertical stakes and then plastering both sides with mud.

Mudbrick is a third wall material that first appears in the Neolithic.
Known as adobe in the Americas, mudbricks are exactly what their name
suggests – bricks made of mud, dried in the sun and laid in courses around
timber framing.[10] Like pisé and wattle and daub, mudbricks shrink and crack
as they dry, but early brick-makers learned to add straw and chaff (and
sometimes, dried dung) to reduce the shrinkage. In the beginning, mudbricks were probably formed by hand one at a time, but soon builders began
pouring the mud and straw mixture into rectangular molds, the process
that's used today, and in doing so, they established the first mass-production
system. The earliest mudbricks are from southwest Asia, where (at Jericho)
they were made by hand and shaped "... rather like flattened cigars" with
rows of indentations on the upper surface "to provide keying for the mud-
mortar in which they were set"[11] (see Figure 7.7). Later mudbricks on the site
are plano-convex with a flat bottom surface and a humped or convex upper
surface, a shape that must have complicated the construction process.

Figure 6.7 In some regions, modern houses are still built using mudbricks made on the site.

In many respects, mudbrick is a perfect construction material, especially in steppe and desert environments. Except for the framing, no wood is needed; because mudbrick walls are solid there's little insect or rodent infestation; and mudbrick houses provide excellent sound and temperature insulation. (During the year I lived in one in Cyprus I rarely heard any street noise, and no matter the outside temperature, the rooms stayed between 60 and 70 degrees F.) Mudbrick architecture is inexpensive, and almost anyone can build a mudbrick house: all kinds of dirt can be used for the bricks; straw, chaff, and dung (natural byproducts of farming and herding) are readily available; the bricks are easy to form; and the walls are easy to construct. Like pisé and wattle and daub, mudbrick has to be plastered annually to protect it from wind and water, but mud plaster is cheap and easily made, and the lower courses of bricks can be protected by stone slabs. In fact, mudbrick houses have only one serious disadvantage – the walls are heavy and inflexible and when destabilized they collapse inward, crushing everything beneath them. In the earthquake-prone regions of western and central Asia, where mudbrick is still the main building material in rural areas, falling walls kill hundreds of people every year.

Neolithic people in temperate zones usually didn't build with mudbricks. Instead they used stone and wood. In Europe the timber longhouses of the Linearbandkeramik and North European Plain cultures have been thoroughly investigated at sites like Brześć Kujawski in Poland, and in North America the Iroquoin longhouses in the eastern United States and the log houses built by Pacific Northwest coastal tribes are also well known. But because wood decays rapidly in damp climates, although archaeologists know that both logs and planks were used for walls, they don't know much more than that about the details of wooden construction. Little is known about stone construction, either. Stones don't decay, of course, but they're likely to be pulled out and reused by later cultures. Archaeologists do know that while some stone walls were solid, in many regions the builders used a more efficient option (casemate walls) where the exterior surfaces were slabs or boulders and the interior was rubble fill.

Roofs

To roof their buildings, Neolithic people invented four basic methods, all of which are still used today. The simplest method is to sink a tall central post into the floor, stretch rafters diagonally from the walls to the top of the pole, and then cover the conical frame with bundles of straw or reeds (the ancestors of modern thatch). Conical thatched roofs are easy to build, can be used on both circular and rectangular structures, and if thick enough, shed water effectively. But they provide nesting places for insects and vermin, they decay rapidly and have to be continually replaced, and they're very flammable: over the last half-century many of the thatched farmhouses houses in Europe, the British Isles, and (especially) Japan have been re-roofed in tile, safety having won out over aesthetics and tradition.

The second method is to build a flat roof supported by post and lintel construction. In small houses, posts can be attached to the walls and the rafters will span the entire room, but larger houses need more complex treatments. Some Neolithic builders placed one end of the rafters on the walls and attached the other to a centrally located post and lintel support, others set up a number of posts across the room and stretched the rafters between pairs of them. Once the flat roof was framed, the rafters (or joists placed on the rafters) were covered with a layer of wattle or reeds or matting, and then sealed by a thick layer of mud. Flat roofs were solid, waterproof

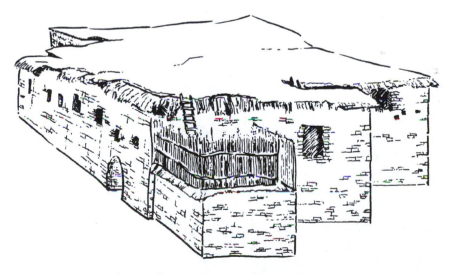

Figure 6.8 In many places, villages architecture has not changed since the Neolithic.

surfaces on which people could work or sleep. They were fire-resistant, and could be kept in good repair with an annual layer of mud plaster. They've never gone out of style in arid regions, and are found today from Arizona to Xian.

The third kind of roof is pitched. Pitched roofs are normally used on rectangular buildings because they consist of a central ridge pole supported by posts, and rafters that stretch from that ridge to the walls. Archaeologists usually reconstruct Neolithic pitched roofs as gabled (the most common roof profile in the world), with two sides sloping down from the ridge pole and unroofed triangular faces on the ends. A variation found mostly in Asia is the hipped roof, which slopes down on all four sides. In areas without much timber, pitched roofs were probably thatched, and where wood was plentiful, split logs or wattle and daub might have been used. Pitched roofs shed water, and snow and ice, and are typically found in temperate wooded settings.

The fourth Neolithic roofing technique is a corbeled vault. Corbeled vaults are made by laying each course of masonry so that it extends slightly inside the course below. They're rarely found intact, and some archaeologists believe that full corbeling wasn't used in the Neolithic, but that walls were corbeled to a certain height and then covered with flat roofs. Corbeling creates a flow of air that provides natural cooling, which may be why the circular houses in northern Syria mentioned above are beehive-shaped. But they're difficult to build, and they've never been as popular as the other options.

Figure 6.9 Hipped thatched roofs are still found in Asia.

Figure 6.10 Corbeled arches were used to create beehive-shaped structures.

Floors

Floor treatments in the Neolithic ranged from tamped earth to stone slab paving. Like the pit-house walls, the earliest floors were made of mud that was beaten smooth and colored with layers of pigmented clay, or that was covered with a mixture of mud and straw. As plaster technology developed in southwest Asia, true lime plaster floors became common, and decorative variations began to appear, including a kind of terrazzo in which crushed stone, stone chips, or pebbles are added to the plaster surface and polished smooth. One of the most elaborate examples was found at the north Syrian site of Çayönü, where a red terrazzo floor was inset with two pairs of parallel white terrazzo lines. Plastered floors were common in hot, dry climates, but in damper regions stone slab paving and planks were used. Like so many Neolithic inventions, all of these floor types are used today.

Except for the invention of the true arch, and the addition of new building materials like concrete and metal, construction hasn't changed much since the Neolithic period. The function of the buildings hasn't changed much either, because once invented, the sedentary village became the dominant built environment in the world.

Monumental architecture

Scholars use the term monumental architecture for structures that are unusually large. Although architectural historians usually connect monumental buildings with the rise of urban states, the earliest examples appear in the Neolithic. Archaeologists can't always figure out why a Neolithic culture built monuments, but since architecture is by definition functional, the buildings must have served a purpose. Some of them seem to be temples or shrines; others, like the burial platforms of

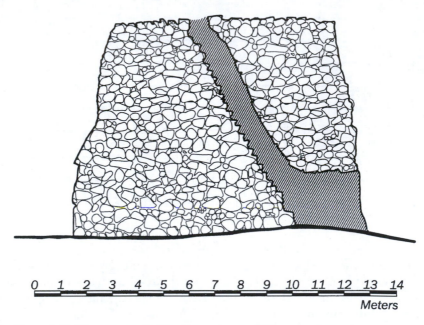

0 1 2 3 4 5 6 7 8 9 10 11 12 13 14

Meters

Figure 6.11 The tower at Jericho has an internal 22-step staircase.

the Liangzhu culture in China, clearly functioned as burial installations; and still others, like the megalithic structures in western Europe, may have been both graves and shrines.

Jericho

One of the most famous examples of Neolithic monumental architecture was found at the site of Jericho, a community near a perennial spring on the west bank of the Jordan River. Often described as the oldest walled city in the world, Jericho has been excavated over and over again since the mid-nineteenth century. The most significant project was the 1952–1956 expedition led by British archaeologist Dame Kathleen Kenyon, which opened up the Neolithic levels and uncovered a huge fieldstone wall and articulating tower. The wall, which slopes slightly inward toward the top, was originally about 6 ft wide at the base and about 12 ft tall. Below the outer face was a 26 ft wide, 6.5 ft deep ditch. The tower is on the inner face of the wall. When it was built, it was 27 ft high and 30 ft in diameter at the base, and was solid except for an interior staircase of twenty steps that led to the roof. The wall and tower complex lasted about 700 years, but eventually an accumulation of debris buried it and it disappeared.

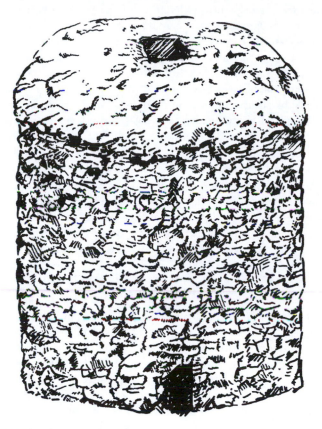

Figure 6.12 The almost 30-ft tall tower has survived in excellent condition.

When Kenyon announced that she'd found the wall, archaeologists were astonished that it dated to the Neolithic (reactions included phrases like "without modern tools!"). Then a more substantive issue arose: without a coercive system of forced labor how could the wall and tower have been built? Assuming that only a serious threat to the entire population could explain it, and undoubtedly influenced by the biblical Book of Joshua, scholars decided that it was defensive, but subsequent exploration hasn't supported that theory. The wall doesn't seem to stretch all the way around the site, and the tower is on the inside, which doesn't make sense if it's part of a fortification. No one has found clear evidence for warfare at Jericho, or anywhere else in the Neolithic Levant, and there are no similar towers or walls in the region. If the wall at Jericho was defensive, who, one wonders, was the enemy it was intended to defend against?

Furthermore, there's no evidence at all that the construction was driven by fear. One excavator calculates that as few as 200 laborers could have built it in a week, a considerable undertaking for a community of at most 1,000 people, but not an impossible task requiring coercion.[12] So why did the Jericho community build the tower and the wall? Some archaeologists have argued that the city was a regional collection and distribution center and that the wall was to keep animals (and other goods) safely inside instead of marauders outside. Another, more recent suggestion is that, like a much smaller wall at the site of Beidha in Jordan, the Jericho wall was a defense against sudden rainstorms. All the settlements in the region, including modern cities, are threatened by sudden flash floods, and at Jericho, water, silt, and debris pour down the slopes behind the site. The ditch outside the wall seems to have been filled up with water-borne sediments shortly after it was completed, which supports the theory of flood control,[13] but this explanation doesn't explain the tower, and so the discussion continues.

Stonehenge

A second famous Neolithic monument, Stonehenge, was constructed over a period of about 1,500 years. This megalithic stone circle on Salisbury Plain in southern England began its existence as a ditch about 330 ft in diameter surrounding a 6 ft high bank and a wooden palisade.[14] A circle of upright posts was added in the center, then replaced by a horse-shoe arrangement of five pairs of upright sandstone pillars with lintels that came from a quarry about 20 miles away. The pillars, which weighed about 40 tons and were 24 ft high at their tallest, were surrounded by a circle more than 100 ft in diameter constructed of 20 ft sandstone uprights (each weighing more than 50 tons) that supported a single curved lintel. Later additions to Stonehenge included rings of bluestone uprights, a stone that may have been an altar,[15] and an avenue banked on either side extending to the Heel Stone (a pointed piece of grey sandstone).[16]

Figure 6.13 Stonehenge's function as an astronomical calculator was probably tied to the local religion.

Stonehenge has a long history of use as a sanctuary (modern Druids worship there on Midsummer's Eve), but because when the last stage of the monument was constructed the sun rose directly over the Heel Stone on the morning of the summer solstice, for the last half-century scholars have wondered if it might not have had a practical purpose, too. In 1965, English astronomer Gerald Hawkins proposed that the main function of Stonehenge, whatever ceremonies might have taken place there, was astronomical; and that Neolithic observers used it as a giant calculating machine, perhaps to record stellar and lunar alignments and to predict eclipses. Recently the renowned British astronomer, David Hughes, revisited the issue and agreed that Stonehenge had an astronomical function. After all, he wrote, "[t]he task of understanding the journeying of Sun, Moon, Mercury, Venus, Mars, Jupiter and Saturn kept the enquiring mind gainfully occupied from the dawn of antiquity to the time of Kepler."[17] Hughes then proposed another use for the monument – to calculate and compensate for the difference between the length of the tropical and lunar years.[18] Today, most archaeologists believe that Stonehenge was probably used for astronomical observations, but they still aren't sure what exactly was being observed, who did it, or why.

7

POTTERY

Most of the craft technologies used by Neolithic villagers were refinements of earlier traditions. The shapes of the finished products – baskets, stone tools, bone needles – were sometimes different, but the process was generally the same: raw material was braided or chipped or carved into useful items. But perhaps the most important Neolithic craft technology, pottery-making, was an entirely new concept because it involves turning raw materials into something else entirely. Pottery, after all, doesn't occur in nature. Unfired clay isn't pottery, and when a potter picks up a lump of earth and forms it into a jar, the result still isn't pottery. But when the potter fires the clay jar, it's transformed into a new – artificial – material, and this makes the invention of ceramic technology one of the most interesting developments in human history.

When pottery appears in the archaeological record the technology is already fully developed, so archaeologists don't know where or when people first realized that fired clay could be useful. The basic principle of firing

Attributes of a Clay Vessel

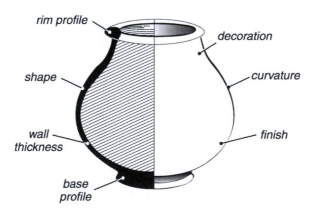

Figure 7.1 The attributes of a pot make it distinctive.

(that clay gets hard when it's heated) was certainly known for tens of thousands of years: our Paleolithic ancestors lined their fire-pits with clay and could hardly have failed to notice what happened to that lining. But since the firing was incidental to the fire makers' purpose (in other words, they didn't care about making the clay hard), it didn't result in a new technology except at one site – Dolní Věstonice in the Czech Republic. About 30,000 years ago, Paleolithic hunter-gatherers living there made and fired thousands of small clay figurines. But they don't seem to have taught anyone else to fire clay, and almost twenty thousand years passed before people in the western world reinvented the practice of firing clay figurines, this time at a number of sites in southwest Asia.

Firing clay figurines isn't quite the same as pottery-making, because the word pottery refers to specifically fired clay containers. A few non-farming cultures did make pottery: semi-sedentary nomads in North Africa and hunter-gatherers in the central Nile Valley fired pots; pottery appears in forager contexts in the Amazon basin, in Colombia, and in the American Southeast; and in Japan, the Jōmon culture (which may or may not be pre-Neolithic) made the first Asian pottery. Eventually, pottery was invented in dozens of places all over the world, most often by early agriculturalists. The earliest known Neolithic wares appeared about 8,000 years ago at scattered sites in southwest Asia, and because archaeologists have identified the precursors of ceramic technology in this region, it makes sense to concentrate our discussion there.

For archaeologists, pottery is the largest, and most important, type of artifact. Fired clay objects break relatively easily, as anyone who's dropped a coffee cup knows, but the broken pieces themselves (called sherds) are essentially indestructible: they aren't affected by changes in temperature and humidity; they don't rust, rot, dissolve, or crumble after they're discarded; and they're almost never reused by later cultures. Sherds are so ubiquitous on ceramic-period sites that many cultures (including the earliest Neolithic groups in Europe, the Linearbandkeramik, Cardial, Starčevo, and Rubanée cultures[1]) are named after their distinctive ceramic wares.

Pottery carries all sorts of cultural information: sherds can be used to trace long-lost trade routes, to establish cultural links between sites, and to reveal the presence of social stratification. The decorative patterns on ceramic vessels, which are often the only surviving examples of a culture's artistic sensibilities, have been interpreted by some archaeologists as carrying coded messages.[2] Sherds also provide information about ancient diets: the very presence of cooking ware implies certain dietary characteristics, and food residues left on sherds can be analyzed and identified: the earliest evidence for winemaking comes from a sherd.[3]

Clay

Pottery-making is a manufacturing process, and like all manufacturers, potters developed a specialized vocabulary to describe their work. Modern potters refer to the material of a fired vessel as the fabric of the pot. Clay, the stuff gardeners hate because it packs down into layers that shed water and discourage root growth, is the main component of all fabrics. The particles in clay are plate-shaped (that is, thin and flat), and slide over one another because moisture collects in a thin layer on their surfaces: this is what makes clay malleable when mixed with water. Clay often includes iron oxides, alkalines, and alkaline earths, and the mixture of these minerals makes some clay beds better than others.

Neolithic craftsmen sometimes traveled for days to collect raw clay. They brought it home in lumps, removed the large pebbles and other impurities, and ground it into a sort of meal that could be mixed with water. Then, to make the clay less sticky and easier to work, they added tempering agents like sand, volcanic and wood ash, small stones, potsherds, broken shells, straw, chaff, bark, and feathers. Temper reduces shrinking and cracking both as a pot dries (because it helps the moisture evaporate evenly) and during firing (because organic temper burns away, leaving the vessel walls filled with small air spaces). The advantages of tempering clay greatly outweigh the drawbacks, but there are some. If a potter adds too much temper the walls may be weakened and when the vessel is first used it will break. Temper can also cause unattractive holes on a pot's surface – not only does organic temper burn away leaving holes, but large pieces of inorganic temper can dimple the surface like a bad rash, or catch on the potter's finishing tools and fall out.

Making a pot

After mixing in the temper, potters added water, and kneaded (or wedged) the clay to the right consistency. Like modern ceramicists, Neolithic craftsmen probably formed the wedged clay into a ball and allowed it to rest for a while, then wedged it again to make it easier to work with and to get rid of air bubbles that could cause breakage during firing. And finally, after days of preparation, the potters were ready to begin making pots.

The basic methods of pottery-making haven't changed much since they were invented. There are only three, all still in use today. Potters can build their vessels (shape them by hand), throw them (use a potter's wheel), or mold them (press soft clay/pour liquid clay into a mold). The earliest pottery was all hand-made. When the potter's wheel was invented, however, most people adopted it because it greatly increased productivity. Molding, a much later technology, increased productivity even more.

The easiest way to build a pot is to pick up a lump of clay and pinch and

Figure 7.2 Clay has to be wedged to force out trapped air bubbles.

Figure 7.3 The simplest pots are pinched.

stretch it into the desired shape. It's hard to control the wall thickness of these pinch-pots, so they tend to be very small. When making larger vessels, potters sometimes pat or roll out slabs of clay and join them together (a technique called slab building), but the easiest way is to use coils – that is, to roll the clay into long ropes and coil them the way children make

Figure 7.4 Most hand-made pottery is coiled.

birds' nests out of modeling clay. Coiling is a slow process which allows potters to make incremental adjustments to wall thickness and shape as the vessel grows, so it's often used for large (and even enormous) shapes. Not all coiling techniques are the same, of course. In some cultures potters use coils that are oval in cross-section while in others they prefer cylindrical coils; some potters overlap the coils and press them together, others stack the coils carefully and add a thin coat of clay on the outer and inner surfaces to hold them in place, and some do nothing more than lightly smooth the walls of the pot.

After a coiled vessel is fully built, the outside surface has to be smoothed to get rid of fingerprints, coil bulges, and other marks. Although some potters use complicated methods, the simplest way is to wipe the outer surface with a wet cloth or hand, and run a finger around the top of the rim to even it up. Then the pot is allowed to dry slowly and naturally until it's stiff but malleable (a stage potters call leather-hard). At this point, potters add handles, trim the rim and base, and apply the final treatments to the walls. The most common finishing technique is dipping the vessel in slip (a suspension of fine clay particles in water) to fill in any tiny irregularities in the fabric and to prepare the pot for decoration. Many pots are self-slipped with a solution of the clay they're made out of but sometimes slips are used to change the color of the surface.

Most Neolithic pottery was decorated. In many regions, including south-west Asia, the earliest decorative finish was burnishing – rubbing the surface of the pot with a smooth pebble, a flat bone, a piece of wood, or a handful of cloth – which aligns the clay particles and makes the surface hard and shiny. Normally, potters burnished the entire pot, a practical as well as decorative practice because burnishing slows the evaporation of liquid through a vessel's

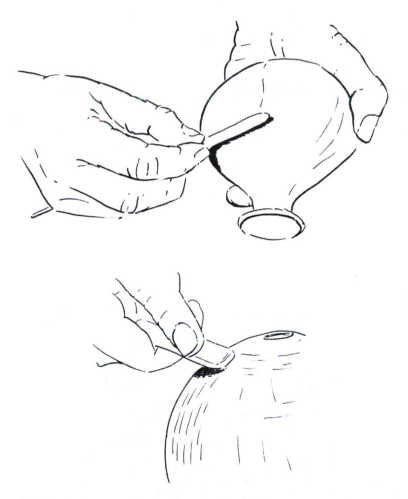

Figure 7.5 Burnishing creates a hard, shiny surface and slows evaporation.

walls. But some potters pattern-burnished their vessels, creating lustrous net designs and other geometric shapes on a matt background. In some cultures, however, burnishing is absent, or is secondary to another type of decoration, and the earliest potters incised or combed the surfaces of their vessels using tools ranging from fingernails to reeds to carefully carved stamp-seals. For example, the rims of Ertebølle pottery, the first ware made in Scandinavia, are decorated with fingernail impressions; in the Nile Valley, decorations combine comb, cord, and stick impressions; the Jōmon wares of Japan are famous for their elaborate incised, cord-marked, and impressed surfaces; and Chinese potters cord-marked, comb impressed, incised, and press-and-picked patterns on their pots.

As ceramic traditions matured, some cultures maintained their initial decorative methods, simply creating more complex patterns. Other cultures adopted new techniques, especially painting. Most early painted patterns were geometric and fairly simple, but some were quite complex and a few, like the vessels made by Yangshao culture potters living in China's Yellow River valley, depicted animals and plants. Potters also experimented with applied decoration: in the central Balkans, Barbotine Ware was decorated with irregular ridges and stripes created by patting and rubbing a rough coat of wet clay onto the dry pot's surface. Further south, potters attached anthropomorphic and zoomorphic handles and applied elaborate relief spirals to their pots. And in a few regions like the Levant, potters employed a series of different decorative techniques: pattern-burnishing one type of vessel; burnishing and incising another; washing a third with red slip; and combing, impressing, applying plastic decoration, and painting still other vessels.

Figure 7.6 Some early pottery is painted.

Firing

Firing is the final stage of pottery-making, and it's at this point that potters part company with other craftsmen and become the first alchemists. Firing is an almost magical process, during which one material (the clay) changes into another (the fabric of the pot), and while the potter effects this amazing transformation, it's the only part of pottery-making which can't be controlled. Even modern potters using sophisticated firing technologies don't know exactly what they're going to find when they open the kiln (pottery oven) doors. In the first place, humidity has an impact on firing. If it's too damp, the pots won't dry completely and may crack or even explode in the kiln; a sudden rainstorm can douse the kiln fire, leaving the vessels partly fired and thoroughly ruined; and even without rain, fires made with damp fuel may not be hot enough. Even if the weather cooperates, there's enough dry fuel, the kiln has been carefully loaded, and the firing goes as planned, pots sometimes mysteriously slump and break during firing.

And then there's the issue of color. Most raw clay is brown. The additives in it control the color of the fired pot: relatively pure clays usually fire white, clays with lots of iron particles fire red or brown, and those filled with organic matter fire black. But even when they're made from the same clay and placed in the same kiln, pots don't always end up the same color. The kind of fuel used can make a difference, and so can the location in the kiln. Pots fired in an oxygen-rich corner of the kiln, for example, usually end up with bright clear colors, while those fired in areas with less oxygen are greyer; and when oxygen is cut off to part of a vessel (because of the way it's stacked in the kiln, for example) the colors on the surface can vary widely. Color is important aesthetically, but there are also practical reasons a potter wants to end up with one color and not another: light-colored fabrics reflect heat, for example, so they make bad cooking pots but excellent storage jars; darker fabrics retain heat, so the best cooking ware is dark brown. A potter can lose an entire kiln-load if the final color is wrong. It's remarkable that Neolithic potters were able to produce consistent color results, but they were so successful that archaeologists routinely use color to distinguish different wares.

Precursors to ceramic technology

Given all this complexity, how was pottery ever invented? It certainly didn't happen overnight. In fact, many elements of ceramic technology were perfected centuries before they were brought together. As I've explained, long before the Neolithic period, people knew that heating clay made it hard, and they applied this knowledge to another technology – manufacturing mudbricks. Southwest Asian brick-makers also understood the principle of tempering clay: more than two millennia before pottery appeared they began

Figure 7.7 The fingernail impressions on the earliest mudbricks at Jericho may have provided "teeth" for the mortar.

adding straw and chaff to the clay to reduce shrinking and cracking as the bricks dried. In the beginning, the bricks weren't fired (the heat of the sun was used to harden the bricks) but soon the brick-makers began to experiment with firing in ovens or pits, a concept they borrowed from another manufacturing process – making lime plaster. Many southwest Asian cultures used lime plaster on their floors and walls, and successful plaster-making involves burning gypsum or limestone/chalk in an oven at more than 800 degrees C, so it can't have been much of a challenge to build brick kilns. By 1,500 years into the southwest Asian Neolithic, people knew that baking clay transformed it into a durable substance, they knew where to find clay that was malleable, they knew that adding temper helped keep clay from shrinking and cracking as it dried, and they knew how to build ovens that would produce extremely hot temperatures which could be maintained over several hours or days. And then they made a final very important discovery: they figured out how to make good storage containers.

The domestication of plants created an urgent need for dry storage. Storing food wasn't a new idea (foragers cached perishables in pits, sometimes stone-lined, that they dug into the ground) but the new annual harvests produced large grain surpluses that had to be dealt with or they'd spoil. This meant that the grain had to be kept dry for months (until it was eaten or used for the next year's planting) and because village life attracted vermin, grain storage also had to be as insect- and rodent-proof as possible. At first, southwest Asian farmers dug pits in the floors of their houses, sometimes lining them with clay to increase their water-tightness. Then they began experimenting with plaster linings, which were harder and more durable than clay, and much more resistant to predators. But the pits were relatively small, and it was hard to empty them without lying on the floor, so some farmers decided to waterproof baskets by lining them with plaster.

These "white ware" vessels were as effective as the plaster-lined pits, and had the distinct advantage of being on the floor instead of under it. As the technique was perfected, white ware containers got bigger and bigger until, eventually, some could no longer be moved.[4]

At this point, all the technical knowledge necessary for pottery-making was in place. What was it that encouraged people to put it all together? One possibility is that the invention of pottery was influenced by invention of bread. In many ways, pottery-making and bread-making are parallel. In each case raw material is gathered, sifted, ground, mixed with water, kneaded, allowed to age, formed into shapes, and baked. The controlled application of heat completely transforms bread dough by making an inedible material edible.[5] Perhaps the same villagers were the cooks and the potters.

Why did people like pottery?

Once ceramic technology was perfected, it spread rapidly around the world. A few groups, like the inhabitants of Khirokitia in Cyprus, seem to have tried pottery, decided they didn't like it, and stopped using it. (At Khirokitia pieces of broken pottery were found in the lowest occupation levels, but the subsequent culture was aceramic.[6]) But most people embraced the new technology enthusiastically. No other Neolithic innovation was adopted so quickly: within a thousand years of its appearance at a few sites in southwest Asia, the entire region – from the Mediterranean coast of Turkey to modern Iraq and Iran and the Levant – was making pottery. The same pattern of rapid adoption is found in Europe. In only about 700 years, Linearbandkeramik ceramic technology spread from the Hungarian Plain through Slovakia, the Czech lands, Austria, Germany, and Poland, to Belgium, Holland, and eastern France. In most places, as pottery replaced most of the traditional containers, large storage baskets, wooden and stone bowls and white ware storage jars disappeared.

Clearly, pottery was extremely attractive to early agriculturalists. Since most cultures only adopt new technologies when they have problems they can't solve any other way, pottery must have addressed a peculiarly Neolithic situation, one that was probably linked to food production. The experiments with white ware show that farmers needed better ways to store dry surpluses, but white ware containers didn't work for milk, yoghurt, butter, and cheese. Pottery, on the other hand, could be used for the full range of storage needs. But this can't be the only factor driving the rapid adoption of pottery – after all, plants and animals were domesticated centuries before the invention of ceramic technology.

Once again, there may be a connection with cooking. Preparing food in pottery vessels greatly increases the range of nutrients available to people, which may be the reason that a few foraging cultures invented pottery before they moved into food production. Another possibility is that the increasingly complex social system required luxury goods and ceramics were the perfect status item. Or maybe it was the decoration that was most important. There's a considerable spectrum of opinion about the meaning of Neolithic pottery decoration, ranging from the assumption that it was mainly – or wholly – aesthetic to suggestions that the decoration conveyed religious power, reinforced religious beliefs, or identified the owner or village where the pot was made;[7] or addressed gender-roles;[8] or subverted the social order;[9] or was a formal system of writing. Most of these ideas are probably true to some extent in one culture or another.

In any case, shortly after it first appeared, pottery had become indispensable. People routinely ate and drank out of clay bowls and cups, and they stored their surplus foods in clay jars. Leaders used special vessels in rituals and festivals, and wealthy people collected them. Traders used ceramic containers for transporting trade goods, which often led to a separate trade in the containers themselves. People were buried in large pots, and ceramic dishes, often filled with food for the next world, were buried with them. Today, when you ask people why anyone would want to make the change from stone and wooden containers to ceramic ones, they're astounded by the question. It seems so obvious. Pottery is far superior to everything else, and they can't imagine a world without it.

Jōmon pottery

It seems logical that people became sedentary farmers before they invented or adopted ceramic technology, and this is certainly the typical pattern in Europe, Asia, and the Americas. After all, pottery is heavy and breakable, and makes no sense in a mobile foraging lifestyle. What, then, are we to make of the Jōmon tradition in Japan? Long before agriculture or permanent villages appear in the Japanese archipelago, these hunter-gatherers, who built pit-houses that they occupied seasonally, were making pottery.

When the American archaeologist Edward Morse first identified Jōmon culture at the Ōmori shell mound on the Kanto Plain, his description of the pottery as "cord-marked" was translated into Japanese as Jōmon (jō means cord and mon means pattern).[10] Jōmon pottery is often cited as the oldest ceramics in the world, which it certainly isn't – the Dolní Věstonice figurines are twice as old – but Jōmon craftsmen probably created the first useable vessels. Because Japan's temperate climate and acid volcanic soil cause organic matter to decay very rapidly, it's difficult to assign absolute dates to Jōmon sites. But most Jōmon pottery was fired at very low temperatures, and recent AMS testing of bits of organic temper that survived in the walls of pots dates the oldest Jōmon ceramics to about 16,500 years ago. If this

Figure 7.8 Jōmon pottery shapes and decoration are unlike those found in any other ware.

date is accurate, the Jōmon people were the only known pottery-makers in the world for over eight millennia.

Jōmon pottery is not only the earliest in the world, it also represents the longest unbroken ceramic tradition in the world (it continues for almost 10,000 years). Technically it's so primitive that archaeologists think it may be a rare surviving example of very early ceramic experimentation. The oldest Jōmon vessels are small, deep bowls with pointed or rounded bases that were coiled without using a tournette.[11] The clay is so heavily tempered with plant materials, sand, and grit that it hardly holds together, and the vessels, which were baked in open pits – probably one at a time – were seldom completely fired. As a result, they broke easily and many pots have cracks that were closed by drilling holes on either side and lacing a cord through them (a repair technique found in most ceramic cultures). The porous fabric kept the contents cool through evaporation, but allowed as much as 10 percent of the liquid to disappear overnight.[12] But, since the technology didn't change until the very end of the period, Jōmon potters don't seem to have been particularly interested in making better pots.

While the technology was primitive, the decoration was not. The earliest vessels are plain, but almost immediately potters began decorating their work. First they applied linear-relief and nail-impressed designs;[13] then they began twisting heavy string or twine and pressing it into the clay, or wrapping it around a stick and rolling that across the pot's surface to create the cord-impressions that give the ware its name. Later they added incised and applied images of people, animals, and fantastic figures, the most elaborate of which were concentrated near the rim, probably a practical development since the pots were placed directly into the fire.[14]

Jōmon potters created a wide variety of shapes including pedestal bowls and goblets, bowls and jars with handles, what look like drums, incense burners or lamps with handles which would have been hung, narrow-necked jugs, footed serving dishes and pots, and pots mimicking shells and other natural forms.[15] Some of the elaborate angular shapes seem more suited to metal than clay, and the entire assemblage seems strangely unfunctional, particularly in the Middle Jōmon, when the tradition reached its height in terms of cultural richness and maturity.[16] Middle Jōmon potters chose artistic impact over usefulness, and didn't seem to care if the decoration made the vessels unuseable. The handles were so heavy that they broke off, and the bases were too narrow to keep the pots upright. The rims have so much

Figure 7.9 The decoration on the rim of this Middle Jōmon bowl makes it almost impossible to use.

decoration that there's no way to pour over them, and the decoration on the bodies is asymmetrical and unbalanced the vessels so much that they fell over.[17]

Because Jōmon pots are like no other ceramics in the world, there are no ethnographic analogies to explain them. It may be that pottery was initially invented for cooking but soon became a ritual ware made by ceramic specialists and connected with mortuary practices.[18] Or perhaps it became the primary means of communicating Jōmon social connections. It certainly became an important trade item. But none of these explanations is fully satisfactory. Despite decades of attempts to explain it, Jōmon pottery is still a mystery.

8

DIET AND DISEASE

Like most people, you may have always assumed that hunter-gatherers were usually hungry, tired, and sick; and that things were much better once people began producing their food and living in permanent villages. In fact, the opposite is true: hunter-gatherers were extremely healthy and Neolithic farmers were not. Paleopathologists, who study ancient diet and disease, tell us that foragers had excellent teeth, they were rarely malnourished, they were taller than most people are today, and they didn't suffer from endemic or epidemic diseases. (Endemic diseases are constantly present in the population – tuberculosis, for example, has been endemic for millennia. Epidemic diseases, on the other hand, move rapidly through a population and then disappear.) All of this changed radically when people settled down and began farming. Food production involved constant backbreaking labor, the new diet wasn't particularly healthy, and the crowded living conditions encouraged an explosion of disease. Pregnancy, childbirth, and the care of small infants may have been less stressful; it must have been easier to care for sick people; and outright starvation was less likely; but far from improving the human condition, sedentism created a set of serious new health risks, most of which continue to threaten us today.

Once again, the question is how do we know? The almost universal evidence that health declined in the Neolithic comes from studies of human skeletal remains.[1] And despite the fact that in most regions Neolithic burials are rare (four thousand years of Neolithic culture in Iran and Iraq produced a total of fewer than 350 skeletons[2]), enough human remains have survived in reasonably good condition to provide information about sex, the average age at death, and the population's general diet and health.

Age and sex

Paleopathologists and forensic pathologists use the same measurements for the estimating the age and sex and general health of the skeletons they study even though, unlike modern skeletons, Neolithic skeletons are rarely complete – often only teeth (the hardest substance in the body), the long

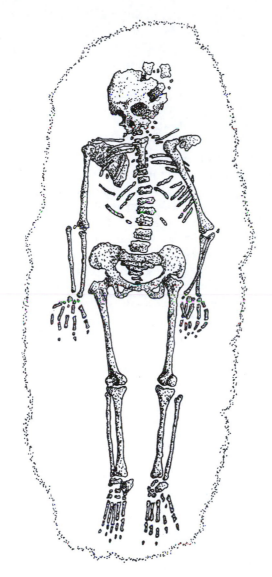

Figure 8.1 Ancient skeletons are an important source of information about health and cultural practices.

bones of the arms and legs, and the skull survive. Luckily, these elements provide most of the evidence needed to age and sex skeletons. All people mature physically at about the same rate. The floating cranial plates that let an infant's head compress in the birth canal fuse at about the same rate, and so do the long bones (which are in three pieces when we're born). We all lose our baby teeth at the same rate, our adult teeth wear down and we develop osteoarthritis and thinning bones as we age. It's difficult to determine the sex of small children, but after puberty sexual dimorphism develops: men's long bones tend to be more robust (longer and heavier) and so do their skulls; while female skeletons, besides being lighter-boned and shorter, have pelvises that are both wider and differently shaped than those of men.

Stress

Teeth, bones, and skulls can reveal more than age and sex. Studying them can also help paleopathologists gauge the general health of a population. Life in the Neolithic wasn't entirely bad, but it was extremely stressful and extremely unhealthy, and the results are clearly apparent in the human remains found on Neolithic sites.

For early agriculturalists, stress (which started in utero[3]) was constant. Episodic stress can momentarily affect the growth of teeth and bones, but the results of constant stress are much more serious: children fail to thrive and adults die young, and in cultures that don't have enough to eat it can cause malnutrition because people under stress burn up nutrients trying to combat it. There are a number of reasons for stress. It can be caused by the environment, by cultural factors like intense crowding, or by a person's general physical condition. Farming much more labor-intensive than foraging, and the new agriculturalists suffered from load-bearing injuries and severe

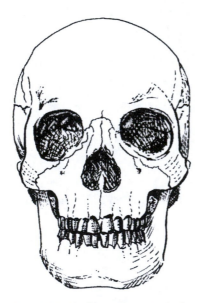

Figure 8.2 Skulls, and particularly teeth, provide evidence of nutritional and biomechanical stress.

osteoarthritis. They needed more nutrition than foragers, but ate many fewer species of plants and much less meat (and took in fewer complex amino acids), so while agriculture helped guard against famine, hunger was a universal problem and the farmers were generally run-down and susceptible to disease. It's likely that constant stress was the reason most Neolithic people were shorter than their ancestors, and didn't live as long:[4] Neolithic populations from Europe to Sri Lanka lost an average of two inches in height,[5] and in Japan, there was a two-to-five-year drop in the average age at death for men and a three-year drop for women.[6]

Nutritional stress

There are two main categories of stress – nutritional and biomechanical. Nutritional stress occurs when people don't have enough to eat, or when they don't eat foods that supply all their nutritional needs. Paleopathologists can easily identify nutritional stress because almost all forms of it leave specific markers on the human skeleton. When children suffer short periods of acute malnutrition, the linear growth of their long bones is disrupted, and dark lines (called Harris Lines) form across the bones: in many parts of the world, Harris Lines first appear in the Neolithic. The skeletons of early agriculturalists also exhibit the marks of common nutritional deficiencies like scurvy (vitamin C deficiency) which causes bleeding on the bone surface, and rickets (vitamin D deficiency) which stops growing bone from hardening. But the most common problem seems to have been anemia (which can be caused by iron deficiency or weanling diarrhea, by genetic conditions like thalassemia, by diseases like malaria, and by parasites). When people are severely anemic the skull vault and eye sockets become rough, thick and spongy,[7] a condition seen in 60 percent of the eye sockets and 50 percent of

Figure 8.3 Hypoplasia can often be seen in tooth enamel.

the skull vaults at Alepotrypa Cave in Greece and in 42 percent of the skulls at Zawi Chemi Shanidar in Iran.[8]

Because bones constantly reabsorb and deposit minerals, in adult skeletons Harris Lines may not show up even though the people were malnourished as children. But tooth enamel doesn't change once it's formed, so it provides a permanent record of childhood health. Nutritional stress or disease can cause hypoplasias (visible lines and pits of thinner enamel on the tooth surface) and microdefects (abnormal bands that lie perpendicular to the enamel) on teeth. And children who are malnourished when very young often have smaller than normal baby teeth.

Even if there were occasional food shortages as people began to adjust to farming, why, despite an abundance of food, were people often hungry and malnourished? The answer lies in the foods themselves – people whose diets are based on pounded grains, porridge, and unleavened bread are almost certain to suffer serious nutritional deficiencies – and in the way they were processed and stored. When farmers harvest food and store it for later use its nutritional value decreases. Cereals aren't particularly rich in nutrients in the first place (domesticated wheat, for example, has less protein than any of the wild varieties) so simply eating grain that's been stored for a long time can cause malnutrition. Another problem with cereals is that the digestion of carbohydrates begins in the mouth (protein digestion begins in the stomach) but the nutrients are actually absorbed into the body in the small intestine. Cereals contain salts called phytates that bind nutrients and stop them from being absorbed: the phytates in wheat and barley bind iron and zinc, and they interfere with gastrointestinal absorption of proteins and calcium. Eating cabbage family plants increases the vitamins B and C that can be absorbed, and legumes provide some protein and iron. But even with these additions, Neolithic diets never reached the quality provided by hunting and gathering wild foods.

Biomechanical stress

Biomechanical stress is the result of subjecting the body to difficult or repetitive movements – lifting bales of hay produces biomechanical stress, and so does digging in heavy clay soils. In general, bones under biomechanical stress become larger and heavier. The number of capillaries on their fibrous covering increases, stimulating growth where the muscles attach to the bones, and the resulting scars are so distinctive that paleopathologists can often identify the particular movement that caused them (although, since felling trees and tilling the soil leave similar scars, scientists can't always be sure what specific work was being done[9]). It's no surprise, given the repetitive nature of farmwork, that evidence of biomechanical stress shows up on many Neolithic skeletons. Repeated movements also cause osteoarthritis (degenerative joint disease) which develops when joints become pitted and eroded,

Figure 8.4 Biomechanical stress is caused by repetitive movements like grinding grain.

forming calluses that rub together without fluid lubrication and making it painful to move. Arthritis is still the most common pathological condition affecting human bones and joints: most modern people show signs of it while they're in their 30s, and almost no one over the age of 60 is free of it.

Severe biomechanical stress can cause broken bones and dislocated joints, and both show up in Neolithic skeletons. Sometimes bodies were buried with dislocated and displaced joints, but more often the fractures had healed, some after they were intentionally set but others without human intervention (unless the skin's punctured and the site becomes infected, even unset bones begin to reknit within two weeks[10]). Not all broken bones were caused by hard work, of course, but it's difficult for paleopathologists to tell the difference between breaks caused by accidents and those caused by work-related stress.[11] Breaks caused by violence, on the other hand, are distinctive, and so are those caused by medical procedures like amputations. (Neolithic doctors performed surprisingly complicated operations: at a site in the Zagros mountains, for example, there's evidence of trepanation, a procedure in which holes are cut in the skull to relieve pressure on the brain.[12])

One of the most thorough studies of biomechanical stress on Neolithic skeletons was conducted on human remains from Abu Hureyra, an early Neolithic site in Syria (described in Chapter 3). Life at Abu Hureyra was strenuous. Besides seasonal activities like hunting, planting, and harvesting, people built and continually repaired houses which involved digging pits and postholes, cutting wood for posts and framing, and carrying heavy clay, water, and lime to make mudbricks and lime plaster. But the hardest work at Abu Hureyra involved preparing grain for cooking. Every day, villagers (mostly women) knelt for hours with their toes curled under and their bodies bent, dehusking dried kernels and grinding the grain on querns set into the ground. The pounding and grinding left them with two distinctive physical conditions: heavily developed arm and shoulder muscles, and arthritic and deformed toes.[13]

Diet

Paleopathologists also study bones and teeth for clues about exactly what Neolithic people ate. Bones are particularly useful because bone collagen (a fibrous tissue that connects the cells) retains a precise record of a person's diet. Plant species metabolize carbon isotopes in different ratios, and the ratios are stored in the collagen. Because most Neolithic diets were low in variety and largely plant-based, analyzing skeletal collagen can reveal which plants were eaten, and also identify radical changes in a population's diet. For example, isotope analysis was used to verify the date when North Americans began eating maize. Teeth don't provide the same kind of direct information about diet, but they provide clues. When people process grain using soft, coarse grinders, tiny grits fall into the flour and get cooked along with it. People who eat grit-filled food eventually wear down the chewing surfaces of their teeth, sometimes all the way to the roots, so the badly worn teeth found at many Neolithic sites are evidence of a diet high in ground grains. Another indication of the Neolithic dependence on cereals is the universal appearance of caries (popularly referred to as cavities or tooth decay). Caused by acids that form in the mouth and dissolve tooth enamel, caries are directly linked to high-carbohydrate diets. (They're rarely seen in pre-farming populations: hunter-gatherers may not have perfect teeth, but they don't have cavities.) Caries are so clearly tied to the advent of farming – about a third of Neolithic farmers in Iran and Iraq had caries[14] – that some archaeologists consider tooth decay as proof of agriculture, even when there's no other physical evidence.[15]

Artifacts, especially tools, can also provide information about diet. The

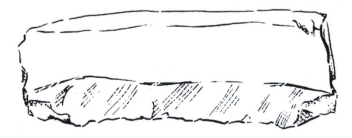

Figure 8.5 When chipped stone tools are used to cut grass, reeds, or clay, silica builds up on the cutting surface and causes "sickle sheen."

most basic measure is simply shape: people use arrows and spears to hunt, and hoes and adzes to clear fields, but even all-purpose shapes like blades and scrapers contain important clues. Because different materials leave distinctive marks on the working edges of chipped stone tools, microscopic examination can identify the last task a tool was used for. Other evidence, like blood, is visible with the naked eye. The most easily recognized residue is "sickle sheen," a high gloss that looks like a layer of clear nail polish. When it was first discovered, archaeologists assumed it was caused by silica transferred from grass stems to the tools during the harvest (hence its name), and that it was a clear indication of cultivation or domestication. But microscopic analysis has proved that scraping or cutting clay and other mineral-rich substances creates a similarly high gloss,[16] so while sickle sheen sometimes provides useful information about what people ate, it doesn't automatically point to a high-cereal diet.

Disease

As we've seen, paleopathologists studying skeletal material can recognize the results of malnutrition, and they can also see the effects of disease. Stored food attracts vermin, and as vermin populations established themselves in the new farming communities, their feces and dead bodies began to accumulate. Human waste also accumulated, and so did rotting garbage, and as a result, new health threats emerged including hemorrhagic fevers carried by rats and fecal-oral infections transmitted by flies and mosquitos. Villagers also became hosts for lice (which can carry typhus), fleas, hookworms, and other intestinal parasites,[17] some of which carried the protozoa that cause malaria and schistosomiasis. People's general resistance dropped as they did more of their work indoors, away from the sunlight (a natural disinfectant) and the fresh air that helped reduce air-borne infections. And they began to catch diseases from their domestic animals.

Some animals actually improve the environment: pigs and dogs are scavengers, so they clean up human waste and garbage, and cats reduce the rodent population. But, because animal diseases can spread to humans, living in close quarters with animals can make people sick. In fact, almost all the major human diseases crossed species during the Neolithic. Dogs gave the villagers rabies and (perhaps) measles; cats gave them toxoplasmosis; they caught the common cold from horses, and tetanus from pigs, horses, cattle, and dogs. Influenza spread to humans from pigs or chickens (scientists aren't sure which); and diphtheria, tuberculosis, and measles all came from cattle. And to make it worse, diseases that were chronic in animals, and therefore particularly dangerous, sometimes became virulent in humans. Cowpox evolved into smallpox; and brucellosis – which causes spontaneous abortions in animals – became a recurring and serious human condition sometimes called undulant fever.

Figure 8.6 Living in close proximity with animals like rats introduced new diseases to humans.

As the agricultural population increased, the new diseases spread. The few parasites and infections that survive in small populations usually don't kill their hosts but instead become chronic.[18] But when populations become large enough to provide a steady supply of new victims, epidemics (which use their hosts for transmission and then kill them) begin to appear. Sometimes they destroy the entire host population and die out, but more commonly there are a few victims who survive and become carriers, and spread the epidemics far beyond their original locations. This is exactly what happened as Neolithic communities grew larger and people began to have more contact with one another.

Neolithic skeletons record the presence of a number of epidemic diseases including tuberculosis, which often destroys the lower vertebrae, and leaves characteristic marks on the ribs; venereal syphilis, endemic syphilis, and yaws which show up the forehead and shin bones; and smallpox, which leaves patterns on bones in the forearm. Three cases of tuberculosis are reported at ʿAin Ghazal in Jordan, and the disease was chronic throughout most of pre-Columbian Peru and Chile.[19] In the Lower Illinois Valley, more than 50 percent of the Middle and Late Woodland people were affected by endemic syphilis; and the bone lesions caused by pulmonary syphilis are so common in Mississippian period skeletons that almost the entire population seems to have been infected.[20] In Neolithic Britain, where the average age at death was less than 30 years, skeletons show signs of polio, sinusitis, tetanus, tuberculosis, and arthritis along with spina bifida and tooth abscesses.[21] And some archaeologists working in the Levant believe that the decline in health seen in later Neolithic populations there was caused by epidemic disease, not malnutrition.[22]

There are adverse medical conditions that don't leave marks on bones, among them constipation, high cholesterol, appendicitis, and obesity, so paleopathologists can only guess that they became more common as the diet changed (although a study of coprolites – human feces – can sometimes be helpful). Similarly, short periods of illness are generally invisible, as are infections of the soft tissues except when they're so severe that they attack the bones. Still, there's plenty of indirect evidence that diseases like these were a serious problem for Neolithic populations.

One of the side-effects of domestication is that many plants develop reduced fiber: seed coats and the skins on fruits, for example, are thinner in domesticated species. Early farmers encouraged these changes – which made it easier to process food – but they paid a high price for this decision. Diets rich in fiber prevent constipation, lower cholesterol, slow the onset of diabetes, and (because bulky food that can't be broken down in the small intestine moves into the large intestine where it stimulates intestinal activity) may discourage obesity, appendicitis, and cancers of the colon, rectum, and large intestine. Low-fiber diets, on the other hand, speed up the rate at which food leaves the stomach: this causes people to feel hungry more often, raises blood sugar levels, encourages the formation of gall stones, and increases the time the stools stay in the large intestine – and therefore the amount of time the intestinal wall is exposed to microbes associated with decay. Another side-effect of domestication was an increase in the fat people ate: domesticated animals have more body fat than their wild cousins, and domesticated plants have higher fat levels, too. Once again, early farmers encouraged these changes, probably because their ancestral diet was sometimes dangerously low in fat. But as we all know, when you consume more fat than your body can burn, it's stored and your weight rises. While it's very unlikely that obesity was a problem in the Neolithic, higher-fat diets may have indirectly raised human fertility rates, because sedentary mothers (who wean their children at an earlier age) regain their pre-nursing weight more quickly and are able to conceive more frequently. Based on numbers of sites and their sizes, archaeologists have suggested that the population of southwest Asia increased from a hundred thousand to five million in the Neolithic.[23]

Even the most seemingly benign aspect of daily life, processing food, created new health risks. Drying cereals and vegetables before storage made them less likely to spoil, but unlike food that's harvested and immediately consumed, stored food can grow bacteria or become moldy (although the latter is not always bad since mold growing on food is a source of antibiotics like tetracycline and penicillin[24]). These dangers didn't exist before agriculture. Another preservation technique, pickling in brine, discourages the growth of most microbes, and sometimes actually increases the vitamin content in the food, but also adds unneeded sodium to the diet. Fermentation, a third processing technique, lowers the pH content of food which makes it harder for bacteria to grow and multiply, increases the length of time food can be stored, and as a result of its anti-bacterial nature is especially important when clean water's difficult to find. And fermented drinks are highly caloric, and can become an important source of nutrition when fresh food is scarce. But, as we all know, alcohol consumption can cause health problems.

The transition to agriculture, far from creating a healthier life for people, initiated a severe decline in human health that has only recently began to reverse itself – and only in some parts of the world. At the beginning of the twenty-first century, much of the world's population continues to suffer episodic, if not chronic, hunger; tuberculosis, arthritis, and other endemic health problems afflict millions; and the threat of new zoogenic diseases is always with us (as is all too clearly illustrated by recent appearance of the Ebola virus and avian flu).

Ceramics and cooking

Ceramic containers allowed farmers to keep their stored grains dry and relatively vermin-free, and because they could be sealed, clay pots made pickling and fermentation much easier. But pottery's major impact on the health of Neolithic populations was in the realm of cooking. Arch-aeological evidence suggests that before the invention of pottery, there were two common ways to prepare food: cooks could broil or roast it over an open flame, or they could heat it by dropping hot stones into a container (usually a clay-lined basket, a skin bag, or a pit). Anyone who's roasted marshmallows on a stick knows the problems associated with the first of these options: food cooked over open fires has a ten-dency to char or even catch on fire while on the broiling stick, it's liable to fall into the flames, and the cook is in constant danger of being burned while trying to rescue it. Indirect moist cooking or "stone boil-ing" requires the cook to heat a group of stones in an open fire, drop them into the container where they transfer their warmth to the food, heat another group of stones, fish out the first group, drop in the second group, and repeat the process. Not only is this laborious, but it's almost impossible to control the temperature of the food being heated, and both the hot stones and the hot food can cause burns. Further-more, these two cooking methods require constant attention: a moment's distraction can ruin a meal.

Cooking in pottery containers is a completely different story. The cook fills a pot with raw food and water, puts it directly on the fire, and then all she has to do is keep the fire going and make sure the pot doesn't boil dry. Food cooked this way is delicious: meat juice and fat don't drip away, so the meal is easier to chew and much more tasty; bone marrow melts and enriches the stewing mixture; and fish bones soften and dissolve. Clams, almost impossible to cook in a fire, open automatically in a cooking pot, and snails and periwinkles can be

---

Inhibits absorption

• Soybean (vitamin D)   • Kidney bean (vitamin E)

Binds zinc, manganese, copper, and maybe iron

• Peas   • Soybean

Inhibits cell metabolism
(Cellular respiraton inhibitors)

• Bamboo • Beans • Cassava • Maize • Millet
• Peas: black-eyes & garden • Sugar cane
• Sweet potato • Yams

Causes edema and blood clots
(Hemagluttinins)

• Beans: black, broad, Jack, red, kidney, lima, runner, & soya
• Lentils • Peas: field, garden, & sweet

Inhibits calcium metabolism

• Common bean

Causes neurological lesions of the spinal cord
(Lathrogen neurotoxin)

• Chick pea • Flat podded vetch • Spanish vetchling

Inhibits metabolism of proteins
(Protease inhibitors)

• Barley • Maize • Oats • Potato • Peanut
• Rye • Various beans

Causes allergic reactions
(Allergens)

• Banana • Barley • Carrot • Celery • Chocolate • Coffee
• Green pea • Mustard • Pineapple • Potato • Rice
• Rye • Squash • Wheat • Yeasts & molds

Figure 8.7 Many common foods are toxic unless they are cooked.

turned into tasty broths. Fruits cook down into easily stored concentrates, leafy plants come out of the pot tender and juicy, and it's easy to add seasonings and develop new recipes.

At the same time, soaking and prolonged cooking make a whole range of foods more digestible or more nutritious. Soaking beans and peas softens the seed coats and reduces the tannins that impede digestion.

Cereals like wheat and barley can be made into porridge which is not only more easily digestible than roasted grains (it's often used as a weaning food) but also causes less wear on teeth. Soaking and boiling maize concentrates the carbohydrates, which slows down digestion and allows more nutrients to be absorbed.[25] The nutritional value of starchy foods like potatoes increases during cooking because moisture swells the starch particles and makes them more soluble in the digestive tract; and, as an added bonus, when tubers like yams and potatoes and cereals like rice are soaked, some of the starch flows into the soaking water and can be strained out and used.

Cooking also makes many foods safer to eat by killing bacteria and dangerous fungi, but also by neutralizing the natural toxins found in plants. Oats, barley, rye, maize, and various beans, for example, contain protease inhibitors which stop enzymes from breaking down protein, but these toxins are reduced or eliminated by heat. Edema and blood clots can be caused by the hemagglutinins in beans, lentils, and peas: soaking and then heating them eliminates the problem. Beans, peas, yams, millet, and maize contain cynogenic glucoside, which inhibits cellular respiration, but chopping them up, soaking them in water, and heating them destroys the toxins. Raw soybeans interfere with the body's ability to metabolize vitamin D, kidney beans inhibit vitamin E, and the common bean interferes with calcium metabolism. Cooking takes care of all of these problems. And many foods (including peas, wheat, rice, barley, carrots, squash, celery, and bananas) contain allergens that are lessened by heat.

The fact that pottery makes controlled fermentation possible also had a significant impact on the Neolithic diet. In many foods, B-complex vitamins are increased by fermentation, and fermenting some legumes – like beans and peas – makes them more easily digestible. Perhaps the most important characteristic of fermentation, however, is that when legumes are fermented the vegetable proteins degrade into amino acids, and the fermented beans can be eaten in place of meat. Tofu, made from fermented soybean paste, is probably the best-known modern example.[26]

It's quite possible that foragers took advantage of the fact that fruit fermentation occurs naturally in nature. But before the invention of pottery, winemaking wouldn't have been possible because in order to keep wine from turning into vinegar it has to be sealed so that no oxygen can get in. It shouldn't surprise us that the first clear evidence for deliberate fermented drinks made from fruit comes from Neolithic sites. Infrared spectrometry of residues on a sherd from Hajji Firuz Tepe in Iran has revealed a combination of terebinth tree resin with tartaric acid and calcium tartrate from grapes. The resin was probably added to preserve the wine and cover up any unpleasant taste, a practice reflected in modern retsina. This sherd has been entered into the *Guinness Book of Records* as the world's oldest wine jar.[27] Wine residues have also been found in jars from Shulaveris-Gora in Georgia and from Jiahu in Henan province, China.[28] The Neolithic wine-makers were probably using wild grapes, because while morphologic-ally domestic pips have been found at a few Neolithic sites including Shulaveris-Gora, and at Shomu-Tepe in Azerbaijan, the earliest solid evidence for domestic grapes is found in the later Chalcolithic period.[29] Archaeologists speculate that beer was also made in the Neolithic period, but so far no clear evidence has been found.[30]

9

POWER AND PRESTIGE

The Neolithic transition was accompanied by unprecedented changes. Agriculturalists had to adjust to new living conditions, new workloads, new diets, new cooking methods, and new diseases. At the same time, new social and economic relationships emerged. Scholars don't agree about the sequence of events: some believe the new relationships developed as a result of settling down, others think the changes came first, and were a major reason for the adoption of agriculture. But no matter how or in what order they appeared, the effects have been long lasting. Modern social, economic, political, and belief systems all developed from patterns first seen in the Neolithic.

Social categories

Before I consider societal developments in the Neolithic, we should take at quick look at social categories in general. All cultures, including our own, define people by categories, some of which are ascribed (biological) while others are achieved (the results of actions taken during life). Your age, for example, is ascribed – it's biologically determined and although you can lie about it, you can't change it – and the same is true of your sex. Your level of education, on the other hand, is the result of your own actions, so it's achieved, and so is your gender, which is not the same thing as your sex. Gender, which is often used incorrectly as a synonym for sex, is an anthropological term referring to the accepted roles the two sexes play in society. While gender-roles may seem to be determined by biology (because women bear children, it's natural for them to be care-givers; because men are strong and aggressive, it's natural for them to be warriors) ethnographers report that gender-roles vary considerably from culture to culture. In general, men and women adhere to their culture's gender-roles, but sometimes they elect to step out of them: in some cultures this is accepted, in others it's severely punished.

Gender-roles help people define themselves and define how they should act. Kinship, which is a broad term encompassing all types of family relationships, consists of both ascribed and achieved categories. In America, for example, your family can include your parents, sisters and brothers, and

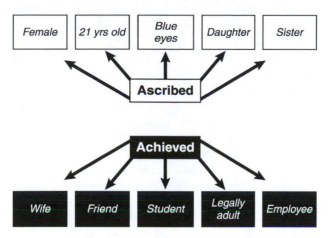

Figure 9.1 Everyone belongs to several social categories, some of them ascribed and others achieved.

children (all related to you biologically); your spouse, your brothers- and sisters-in-law, and your nieces and nephews (all related to you by marriage); and your adopted children, your god-children, your life partner, and your uncle's wife, none of whom is related to you by biology *or* marriage. Kinship rules structure most societal interactions, but their main function has to do with marriage: specifically, they define who you can and cannot marry. Some cultures require marriage outside the group (exogamy) while others allow marriage only within the group (endogamy): the groups can be as small as an extended family or as large as a major religion. Neither marriage pattern is based on a knowledge of genetics. In fact, ethnographers report that cultures that choose exogamy usually do so because it helps build alliances, and those that prefer endogamy use it to maintain social distinctions.

Regardless of the aspect of society they address, the overall function of social categories is to make it possible for people in a community to get along with one another. So they also define a culture's leadership structure: who makes decisions, who enforces them, and who is most respected (in other words, who has power, who has authority, and who has prestige). The most common (but not universal) pattern is that men have more power and authority than women, and that age carries more prestige than youth.

Social systems

Together, all of a culture's social categories define its social system. The social systems of cultures at the same stage of economic development are amazingly similar, and at the same time, consistently different from the social systems connected with other economic stages. For example, everywhere in the world, hunter-gatherer social systems are egalitarian, the basic social unit is the band – a group that can include up to 100 extended family members – and since most bands are too small for endogamous marriages, spouses usually come from the outside. People live in nuclear family groups, and kinship relationships are extremely important because decisions are made by consensus and enforced through social pressure. Because individual members of a band aren't interested in power, leadership is temporary and based on specific talents like hunting, telling stories, or healing; and although men and women have slightly different roles (men fish and hunt and women gather) the rules are loose: men collect plants on their way home from hunting and women trap and snare small game as they gather. Resources, especially food, are pooled and shared without keeping track of who gave the most (or least) – an economic practice called general reciprocity that, given the uncertainty inherent in their lifestyle, is probably the main cultural practice that ensures hunter-gatherer bands' survival.

In contrast, pastoralists and simple agriculturalists have much more structured social systems. Their primary social unit is the tribe, which like the band is organized according to kinship. But because tribes include several extended family groups or clans, they're much larger than bands, and this allows their members to marry distant relatives (i.e. they're endogamous). Tribal societies are strongly stratified – men are the leaders because they have more power and prestige than women – but while the role of headman is prestigious, it doesn't involve much real power or authority, and headmen have to lead by example and solve interpersonal conflicts through diplomacy rather than coercion. In a few places, like the American Northwest and New Guinea, headmen developed a system of competitive feasting during which they won prestige by giving away their wealth, but there's no evidence that this custom was universal or even widespread.

Some tribal groups are pastoralists who depend on their herds for most of their food, and who move seasonally from pasture to pasture (a custom called transhumance). Pastoralists exchange goods and services of equal value (they practice balanced reciprocity), probably because it's an efficient system in their circumstances: the animals belong to individual families or family members but they move as a single herd, and everyone pitches in when it's time to assist with births or butcher unwanted animals. Other tribal groups are farmers. Like the pastoralists, the farmers practice balanced reciprocity, again probably because it's efficient: they own their land jointly, and activities like building houses, harvesting, and preparing new fields are shared. Both tribal farmers and tribal pastoralists need access to large tracts of land. Transhumance is impossible without it, and because the soil in their fields is depleted after a few years, and only about 5 percent of the available land is under cultivation at any time, tribal farming villages have to be small and widely separated.

Chiefs, powerful hereditary leaders who regulate all aspects of life, control communities of agriculturalists who practice mixed farming (that is, they both farm and raise animals). Chiefdoms are much more rigid societally than tribes, and every member of the village fits into a hierarchy that determines wealth, power, and prestige. As you might expect, men generally have more power and prestige than women, but high-ranking women have more power and prestige than low-ranking men, and low-ranking women have more power than male slaves. Because they control the community's resources, chiefly families have more wealth than anyone else. They can pass that wealth on to their heirs, and the hierarchies are perpetuated generation after generation by requiring children to marry into their own social class. Unlike tribal villages, mixed farming communities are often large and densely populated. Villagers own their fields, which they cultivate by themselves, so they need as many children as possible to help with the work; and because they can't move their fields, they add animal fertilizer to the depleted soil, and use terracing and irrigation to create more usable land.

It's undeniable that reconstructing the social systems of Neolithic people is much more speculative than identifying the marks of disease on their bones or tracing the origins of domesticated plants and animals. But if the patterns described above are universal – as they seem to be – it's not an unreasonable exercise. Archaeologists start with a series of assumption about prehistoric social systems: that the first proto-agriculturalists lived in egalitarian bands; that when they began to settle down and domesticate plants and animals, their social systems became tribal and included the characteristic extended families, gender hierarchies, and endogamous marriages; and that as agricultural surpluses became common and people began acquiring wealth, chiefdoms, with their hereditary social inequality, appeared. By extension, finding physical evidence of any of these social systems should point to the stage the culture has reached in its transition from foraging to farming.

Architecture

The distribution of buildings in a community, and their size and shape, reflect the social values of their builders. You have only to compare traditional New England villages with their small houses on large plots clustered around a village green and twenty-first-century "McMansion" developments with their oversized houses squeezed onto small lots in neighborhoods without any community focus to see that this is true. By ethnographic analogy, Neolithic architecture also reflected the social organization and values of the villagers.

Kinship structure is often reflected in architecture, because nuclear families and extended families need very different kinds of living spaces. Archaeologists study both house plans and placement as they try to decide which social system was in place on the site. The earliest Neolithic villages were small clusters of randomly dispersed buildings, and although some had

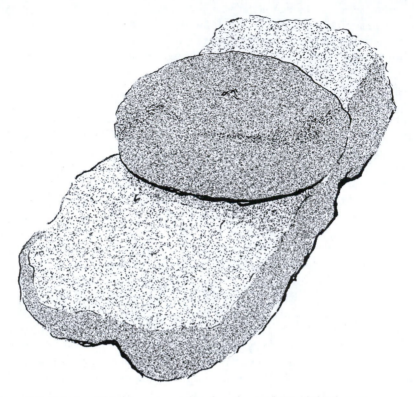

Figure 9.2 Grinders like this one are often found outside Neolithic houses.

internal features like hearths, storage bins, and mortars, they were so small –
in general they had only one room – that it's hard to imagine how people
could have worked in them. In fact, the many grinders, ovens, and similar
remains found in courtyards and open areas imply that people spent most
of their time outside. Because all the houses are small, they seem to reflect
an egalitarian system of nuclear families; in other words, a social system
characteristic of proto-agriculturalist bands.

Over time, the nature of Neolithic villages changed. Houses became more
complicated, developing into many-roomed and multi-storied structures
organized around or near clearly delineated public areas, and divided into
areas dedicated to specific tasks. Without a strong central authority people
tend to place their houses haphazardly, while strong leadership encourages a
structured environment, so it may be that the more organized arrangement
reflects the development of more powerful leaders. In some villages, a few
houses were considerably larger and better constructed than the rest: they
may also be evidence of the growth of hierarchies because members of
social elites usually live in larger, finer houses than lower-ranking families.

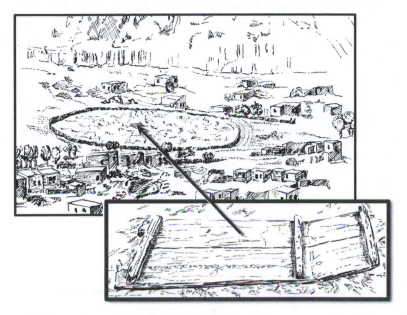

Figure 9.3 As can be seen in this Anatolian village with its communal threshing ground and traditional threshing sledge, the principles of village organization invented in the Neolithic are still followed today.

However, while archaeologists feel comfortable making general statements about social systems based on architectural remains it's not easy to be specific, and turning to ethnographic analogy, which should be extremely helpful, sometimes results in conflicting information. The best example is probably the issue of the Linearbandkeramik culture's social organization. Their longhouses are found in southeastern, central, and western Europe, and because longhouse cultures world-wide have been thoroughly studied ethnographically, it should be simple to extrapolate social patterns from them. Unfortunately (for archaeologists studying the European Neolithic, at least) ethnographers have identified a number of quite different social systems present in longhouse cultures. In some, one family lived in each structure, which also contained work areas, stables, and granaries; in others, longhouses were dormitories housing single-sex groups; in still others, each longhouse sheltered several nuclear families, perhaps related by lineage; and in a few cultures the longhouses were public buildings and the people lived in smaller structures nearby. The only way to differentiate between these various social models is through the artifacts and features found inside the structures. But since all that's left of most Linearbandkeramik longhouses are the postholes, there's no way to do that, which means that all the models are equally possible.

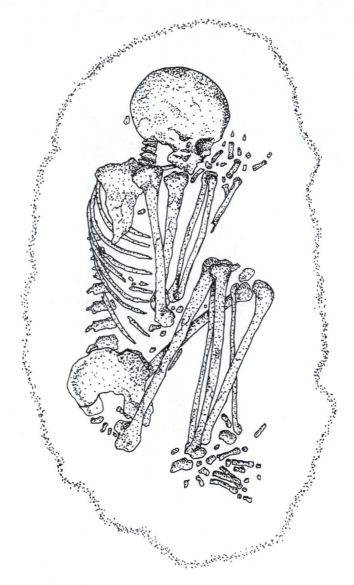

Figure 9.4 Prehistoric people were often buried with their arms and legs bent in a flexed or fetal position.

Burials

Because the act of burial implies social organization, emotional connection, and some sort of spiritual belief system, it seems reasonable to assume that like architecture, Neolithic burials reflect early agricultural social systems.

But while Neolithic village organization seems to develop in similar ways around the world, even within small regions, Neolithic funerary practices varied widely. Some people practiced what we might call traditional burial, inhuming their dead with their bodies intact, while others cremated the dead and either buried or scattered the ashes and burnt bones. Among the cultures that practiced inhumation, some placed each body or set of cremains in a separate grave while others buried their dead in groups. A few cultures buried the dead sitting up, but most bodies were stretched out face up (or in some rare cases face down) or else on the side with their knees drawn up, usually with the heads oriented in a specific direction. Some villages developed separate funeral traditions for men and women: at the Romanian site Parța, for example, men lay on their left sides and women on their right sides.[1] All of these traditions involved placing the bodies or cremains directly into their final resting places as soon as possible after death, a custom anthropologists call primary burial. But many Neolithic cultures practiced secondary burial – they stored the bodies until the flesh had decayed, and then moved them to their graves. There are several types of secondary burial: you can keep each set of bones together by wrapping them in cloth or matting, you can group the bones by type (long bones, skulls), or you can simply add the dry bones to an existing deposit. Neolithic villagers used all three types.

Neolithic burial sites are no more consistent than the burial customs. Sometimes the dead were buried in the ground in graves and cists (stone-lined pits). But in other places, they were interred in rock-cut tombs, caves, and rock shelters, or placed in jars or baskets (a custom originally used for fetuses, babies, and children but later expanded to include adults). Some villages built complex above-ground structures for their dead, others marked the graves by covering them with mounds of stones and earth,[2] and in some regions the burials from several communities were grouped together in mortuary centers. Kfar HaHoresh, a mortuary complex in the lower Galilee is a good example of this.[3] But at the same time, many bodies were dumped in ditches, garbage pits and other casual holes; hidden under house floors and in courtyards; placed in reused pits beside house walls; or stuck into the ground under village streets.

This extensive list of funerary customs may give you the idea that Neolithic burials are plentiful, but as I've mentioned before, they're relatively rare. Still, enough burials have been excavated to allow archaeologists to make some generalizations about Neolithic social relationships. Since ethnographers report that most agriculturalists bury their dead according to family groups, archaeologists assume this was the case in the Neolithic, and so they tend to interpret a woman and infant buried together as mother and child, an adult male and an adult female found in one grave as husband and wife, and any children buried with them as their sons and daughters. Similarly, archaeologists interpret the way graves are arranged in a cemetery as reflections of social relationships. Most commonly, multiple burials in one location

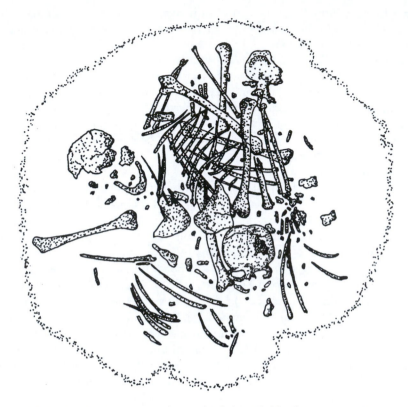

Figure 9.5 Archaeologists assume that multiple burials like this one contain members of a single family or kinship group.

are assumed to hold the graves of family members: a Neolithic cemetery in China with the graves laid out in two groups of three rows each is seen as housing two different clans, and graves in Germany separated into distinct groups within a cemetery are believed to hold the bodies of different local communities that were, perhaps, tied together by lineage.[4]

Occasionally, a surprising piece of evidence like a genetically based dental pattern found at Abu Hureyra supplies some scientific evidence to support the assumptions.[5] In fact, a study of DNA in the bones from a single cemetery or deposit might result in some broader kinship data – exogamy, for example, would be indicated if the women came from a series of different genetic lines – but at most sites too few well-preserved skeletons survive for this kind of analysis to be possible. Instead, archaeologists examine the objects buried with men and women. Grave goods aren't particularly common in the Neolithic, but among the more typical items are flint and obsidian tools, polished stone axes and adzes, stone vessels and figurines, stone beads and pendants, ceramic vessels and figurines, clay spindle whorls and loom weights, stone loom weights, and shells, shell beads, and pendants. Copper and gold objects are rare, but they have been found, and so have a few textiles or textile impressions. Grave goods can provide a surprising range of information, but it's not always easy to decide what the information is. If the grave goods in a woman's tomb are exotic (non-local), they may indicate that she came from outside the group, or that she was high-ranking. Similarly, a cache of fine ceramics in a woman's grave could reflect her wealth and high status, or they could reflect her role as a potter, or they could refer to her responsibilities for cooking and serving food during her life, or they could have contained food for her journey to the afterlife. A beautiful stone axe buried with a man could mean that he was a warrior, or that he was wealthy, or that he was a member of an elite class, or that he was its maker. Almost the only time archaeologists feel reasonably certain about the meaning of grave goods is when they find children's graves filled with fine objects. Because children generally don't achieve much in their short lives, the rich grave goods probably refer to the wealth and prestige of their parents, and to a family-based inheritance system.

In the end, it's often more useful to study the burials on a site as a group rather than individually. If all of them contain similar grave goods (or no grave goods at all) the culture was probably egalitarian (or, to be more accurate, hierarchies weren't reflected in their funerary practices). On the other hand, if some burials are accompanied by fine objects and others aren't, the grave goods probably reflect some sort of social hierarchy. Similarly, exotic items widely distributed throughout the burials indicate that the culture emphasized trade, but if they're restricted to a few graves they probably reflect social prestige. One of the richest Neolithic cemeteries in the world illustrates these points. At the Varna cemetery on the Black Sea coast in Bulgaria, most of the almost 200 burials were accompanied by modest grave goods (the men with a few tools and pottery, the women with pottery) but a few burials were unusual. One man was placed in his grave with 990 objects, 320 of which were made of gold. Weighing a total of more than three pounds, they included a gold shaft for a stone hammer, gold arm bands, earrings and breastplates, small gold discs, beads, tubes, and other clothing ornaments, and a gold penis cover; there were also graphite-and-gold-painted ceramics, copper chisels and awls, copper and stone axes, flint blades, and shell and stone beads. Clearly, Varna was a hierarchal society, and equally clearly this man was a high-ranking person.

Social ranking can also be indicated by the location of the graves themselves. One of the most complex examples of this was found at the Mississippian site of Moundville in Alabama, where almost 30 burial mounds surround a central square. The people of Moundville were buried in these mounds based on social hierarchy. Archaeologists report that the highest-ranking men were buried in mounds, while slightly less high-ranking men, high-ranking women, and high-ranking children were buried in or near the mounds. Another fairly high-ranking group was interred in cemeteries near the mounds, and the lower-ranking people were relegated to their own cemeteries or buried in the village.[6] Of course, not all unusual burials reflect prestige. In both Greece and Jordan, archaeologists have found communities that buried most of their dead off-site, but threw a few bodies into on-site garbage pits. Some of the pits had been cleaned out before the burial, but in others the bodies were deposited along with the trash. These trash pit burials must have some social significance, but what can it be? Suggestions include that the dead were foreigners, low-status people (slaves or servants), or disenfranchised for some reason such as committing crimes or being unable to repay their debts. In one case, the dead person appears to have been the victim of violence, leading the excavator to wonder if murdered people were ineligible for normal burial.[7]

War

War – socially sanctioned group violence that focuses on protecting or increasing resources, and is led by people with power and prestige – is at one end of a range of interpersonal conflicts that starts with fist fights and escalates through murder and feuds to organized battles.[8] Archaeologists don't know when warfare first arose. There's evidence of occasional interpersonal violence among hunter-gatherers, which is not the same as warfare, and in any case it's hard to see why hunter-gatherers would go to war since they don't own property, their ethos of reciprocity discourages fighting, and the part-time leadership that

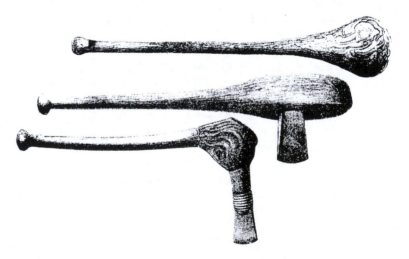

Figure 9.6 Although they have been described as weapons, these artifacts were more likely axes and flax-making tools.

characterizes bands isn't appropriate for military actions. But when people became sedentary, the situation changed. Agriculturalists are bound to their land, and they have a lot at stake when they're threatened because their fields, their animals, their seeds, their processing equipment, and their houses all represent personal wealth and years of hard work. Another important difference is that the centralized political control in tribes and chiefdoms means that people owe allegiance to their leaders. So it's conceivable that war first appeared in the Neolithic, but is there any proof that it did?

Archaeologists know that Neolithic individuals fought with one another. Among the more dramatic examples of violence are Ötzi, the European "Ice Man," who had an arrowhead lodged in his back under his left shoulder, and a stab wound in his right palm;[9] and a man buried in a trash pit at 'Ain Ghazal, killed when a thin blade was thrust into his head with enough force to push a one-inch piece of his skull into his brain.[10] A few cases of traumatic fractures were found at Jericho, and there are scattered examples of violence elsewhere in southwest Asia, but it's not clear that they were caused by war.[11] In North America, there are reports of violence at sites in the Ohio River valley, along the Red River, and in the central Mississippi valley, but again, they don't seem to be the result of wars.[12] In Europe and East Asia, the evidence is more suggestive of warfare: mass burials at a few European sites, including Roiax in the south of France, where 100 people were hastily buried; and in China, where excavations at one Neolithic site found headless and footless corpses stuffed down a well.[13] There are also a few examples of people shot from behind: the remains of 34 people, ten of whom had been shot in the back of the head, were thrown into a pit at Talheim in the Neckar valley; and in one case in Britain, a man shot in the back had fallen forward into a ditch, smothering a child he was clutching.[14] But arrowheads embedded in bones and mass graves don't necessarily mean the victims died because of sanctioned group violence. You need battlefields to prove people died in war.

Battlefields usually have remains from at least two different cultures, dead that were left where they fell, and bodies marked by signs of violence. No Neolithic sites like this have been found so far, and without the typical confirming evidence, how can archaeologists tell the difference between a deadly fight and a deadly war? One way is to look for weapons. Tools/weapons found at European sites include segment and long bows made of yew and elm, arrow shafts almost 30 inches long, arrow smoothers and wrist guards, flint and bone points, one wooden shield, flint daggers, and ground stone axes and adzes; and at Late Neolithic sites some daggers, axes, and points were made of copper. But there's no evidence for the manufacture and trade of artifacts specifically crafted for battle, and residue analysis confirms that most of these "weapons" were multipurpose implements used for hoeing and chopping, and for killing and butchering animals (and only maybe for killing people).[15] European battleaxes were too small to be weapons – they were probably ceremonial[16] – so-called maces and clubs are found only in domestic contexts, and in Greece the so-called "sling bullets" made of unfired or partially fired clay were probably used for herding sheep.[17] And while it's true that axes, daggers, and points often appear in men's graves, they may well indicate that the deceased were high-ranking rather than warriors.

What about defensive architecture? Fortified settlements are found at European sites like Dölauer-Heide in central Germany, Nea Nikomedeia in northern Greece (although this interpretation of the features has been challenged), and at scattered sites in other regions. Excavators tend to assume that villages are only walled to keep out aggressors, and this certainly seems to have been the case in China,[18] but walls can also define the perimeter of the community (as they do today); or separate the outside (non-domestic) sphere from the inside (domestic) sphere; or to keep sacred space and profane space from overlapping. Walls can control animals at night, and keep predators away or, as may have been the case at Jericho and Beidha, they can provide protection from floods.

Did Neolithic people invent war? The most that can be said is that they could have, because they had the necessary technologies and – in some places – the social organization that's needed. But unless unambiguous evidence is found, most archaeologists will continue to believe that warfare was created by urban societies, not by Neolithic farmers and herders.

10

TECHNOLOGY AND TRADE

In egalitarian hunter-gather groups, although some people are better than others at hunting, or healing, or making containers, everyone learns all the skills necessary for survival. But when foragers became farmers this kind of general training wasn't practicable. Food production is time-consuming and complicated: raising wheat isn't like raising radishes, sheep are quite different from pigs, and even the most efficient farmer doesn't have time to make everything he needs. Luckily, as farmers became more successful and food surpluses developed, new ways of acquiring needed goods and services – that is, new systems of economic exchange – emerged.

The first exchanges were undoubtedly informal and reciprocal. But as people began to specialize, reciprocity became more difficult to maintain. Helping your neighbors bring in their crops in exchange for their help with your harvest is one thing, but sharing your food with someone who doesn't farm – and gives you chipped stone tools in exchange for your grain – is a different matter because there's no guarantee that the exchange will be fair. At first, Neolithic villagers seem to have developed redistribution systems (one theory about the monumental wall at Jericho, remember, is that the site was a regional collection and redistribution center). According to the ethnographers who have studied them, redistribution systems work because people contribute goods to a central storage area, and take what they need in exchange based on a formal system of equivalencies set up by the officials in charge: a farmer knows that he can take a sickle as long as he deposits a standard measure of grain.

Simple redistribution systems like these were probably part of early agricultural society, but they disappeared when Neolithic cultures developed social and political hierarchies. Members of elite social classes prefer to make individual exchanges with one another, because then they can cement alliances and amass personal wealth and prestige. As Neolithic society became more complex, so did the systems of exchange. Four new patterns appeared. In the simplest system, traders from neighboring villages met and traded locally produced goods (which may have included stone tools, ceramics, and textiles; meat crops, dried fish, fruit, nuts, cheese, and yoghurt; drinks,

133

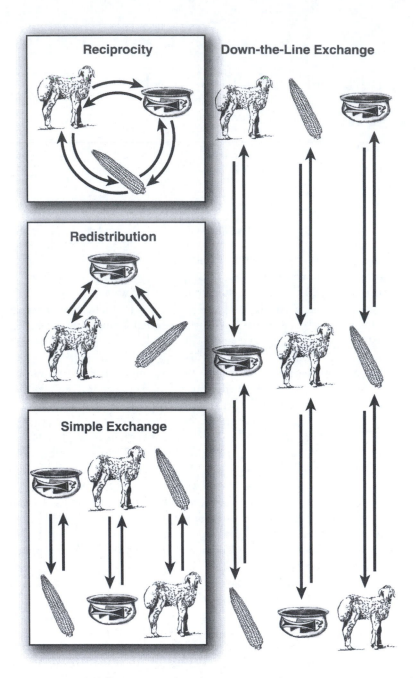

Figure 10.1 Several different patterns of economic exchange first appeared in the Neolithic.

drugs, and medicines; young animals; fur, feathers, antlers, and tusks; baskets, bags, and other containers; and salt).[1] The second, more complex system – down-the-line trading – moved some of the products beyond the local area. For example, a potter might exchange his wares for stone tools in one village, and then exchange some of the stone tools for woven cloth in another village. Down-the-line trading had an unintended, but important result: it spread new technologies beyond the initial trading partners. Linearbandkeramik pottery probably moved westward through down-the-line trading, and a similar pattern probably brought the first ceramics to the Ertebølle culture in Denmark.[2] In the third exchange system, middleman trading, salesmen acquired products and traveled from village to village, trading for new products at each location. And in the fourth model, specialist craftsmen took their raw materials from village to village, making goods to order as they encountered customers. All modern economies are based on a combination of these four systems.

Although archaeologists assume that all of these systems were used by Neolithic traders, it's almost impossible to prove that they were because the probable exchanges are invisible archaeologically. Helping your neighbors build a barn doesn't leave distinctive material remains, nor does swapping the jars you make for a neighbor's woven blankets (although excavators may be able to establish that you have a kiln and your neighbor has a loom). Archaeologists are unlikely to locate and excavate sites that were trading partners, and even if they do, most of what was traded – raw materials, surplus food, and specialized skills related to farming and herding – has disappeared. Down-the-line and middleman trading, however, may leave recognizable evidence, especially if exotic or prestigious objects were part of the exchanges or if the result of trading was technology transfer.

Stone tools

Stone tools were among the most commonly traded items in the Neolithic. They were the first human technology – chipped stone tools were invented more than two million years ago – and since they're still being made, the longest-lived. Surgeons use chipped stone blades in some special procedures,

Figure 10.2 Stone tools with serrated blades like this one were traded over long distances.

traditional hunters use chipped stone points as arrow- and spearheads, and farmers from the Middle East to East Asia process grain using traditional threshing sledges. (A threshing sledge is a heavy platform with sharp chipped stone flakes on the bottom side that's pulled by oxen or donkeys back and forth over piles of harvested grain until the kernels are separated from the chaff. See Figure 9.3.)

Stone-knapping – the technical term for making chipped stone tools – was invented independently all over the world, and the basic technology has never changed. The piece of stone that knappers start with is called the core. The first tools were shaped cores (or core-tools), but as the technology developed, stone-knappers began to make tools from the flakes that came off the core. This was a much more efficient use of the raw material, and once invented, flake tools rapidly replaced most core tools, although a few cultures continued to use core tools for their axes, adzes, and hoes.[3] There are dozens of different flake tools, from arrows, spearheads, and knives to scrapers and borers, and the first reaping tools were fashioned from flakes. Many were hafted (i.e. set with bitumen, mastic, or lime plaster into wooden or bone handles) and some, like those found in the earlier levels of Jericho, were serrated. The Jericho blades were originally identified as sickles for harvesting grains but recent ethnographic studies suggest they were more likely used for cutting reeds.[4]

Almost any kind of stone can be knapped, but the best raw material breaks with a conchoidal fracture pattern. Conchoidal fractures are curved, and this feature allows a stone-knapper to make complex shapes with thin sharp edges. The finest chipped stone tools are made from obsidian – volcanic glass formed during volcanic eruptions that has all the basic properties of manmade glass, although it's slightly harder than most glass in common use – but tools crafted from flint and chert (glassy hard sedimentary

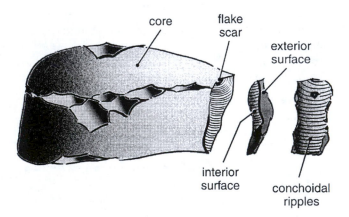

Figure 10.3 The best stone-knapping materials break with a conchoidal, or shell-shaped, fracture.

Figure 10.4 Ground stone tools like these are a hallmark of the Neolithic.

rocks) and chalcedony and jasper (crystalline forms of quartz) are almost as good.

Chipped stone tools are wonderful for precision cutting, but they need constant resharpening, and because they're brittle, they break when they're used to fell trees or hoe heavy soils. Neolithic farmers needed more resilient implements, so they adapted an existing technology used to make containers and ornaments and began shaping ground stone tools from dense igneous rocks like basalt and granite. The earliest ground stone tools were made by Jōmon craftsmen in Japan,[5] but the technology was independently invented by many cultures. Tool-makers shaped the raw material by pecking and grinding, and then polished it using a rubbing stone or sand, and water (as a lubricant). This process created a smooth, lustrous surface that was visually beautiful and pleasant to hold: ground stone tools with a particularly high gloss found on Neolithic sites in China may have been polished using diamonds.[6] Because they have great tensile strength, ground stone tools don't chip or break easily. Hafted into wood or antler, they make excellent woodworking tools: the axes (their blades set at a 90 degree angle to the handle) are useful for cutting trees and splitting wood, while the adzes (their chisel-like blades set horizontally) are perfect for stripping off small branches and shaping logs and planks. These tools – along with ground stone hoes for breaking up the heavy soil – were as essential to the success of Neolithic farmers in heavily forested Europe as their modern versions are to small farmers today.

Stone containers and ornaments

The ground stone containers and implements made by Neolithic craftsmen ranged from mortars and grinders to fine stone dishes. The aceramic Khirokitia culture in Cyprus is famous for a wide range of beautifully made and decorated andesite basins, bowls, dishes, and ladles, some of which were exported to the Levant. Locally made stone bowls with eggshell-thin sides have been found in southeastern Turkey at Hallan Çemi, Çayönü and Cafer Höyük; and in Syria finely finished hemispherical bowls were fashioned out of alabaster or colored limestone.[7] Craftsmen also made ornaments. Some of the smaller ground stone tools, including some from flint and obsidian, were probably ornamental, and so were the "maces," "batons," and phalluses discovered at some Neolithic sites. Stone beads, pendants, and bracelets were common as grave goods, and in China, craftsmen began a long tradition of carving elaborate jade vessels.

Textiles

The term "textile" comes from Latin *texere* (to weave) and technically, it refers only to cloth woven on looms. It's yet another technology that first appeared in the Neolithic. Like many Neolithic innovations, it was based on earlier technologies, in this case net- and mat-making, and spinning. Mats are made by braiding or interlacing stiff plant materials, while nets are made by braiding thin twisted fibers. Spinning, the process of twisting

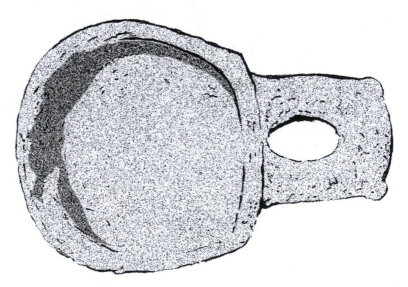

Figure 10.5 Before they invented or adopted ceramic technology, some cultures used ground stone bowls, platters, and cups.

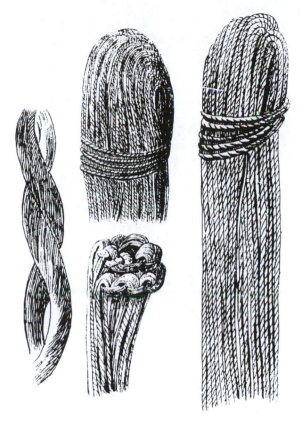

Figure 10.6 Textile historians have identified several types of spinning twists in the flax skeins from Robenhausen.

single fibers into continuous lengths that are strong and flexible, is essential to textile-making because in their natural state, wool, hair, and vegetable fibers are too short to be useful, reeds and grasses are too stiff, and silk, which has the longest filament known, is too fragile. Neolithic weavers spun using hand spindles. The most common type were sticks with a weight (the whorl) at one end to help keep it turning smoothly, a system still used today.

Weaving – the process that turns spun thread into cloth – requires a mechanism to hold one set of threads (the warp threads) stretched tight so that a second set (the weft threads) can be interlaced at right angles. The simplest kind is the band loom, made by tying one end of the warp threads to a tree or post and the other end around the weaver's waist. Neolithic weavers used band looms to weave narrow strips of cloth (some examples were found at Çatalhöyük)[8] but for larger pieces they needed more complex

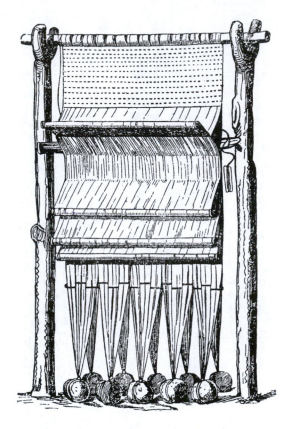

Figure 10.7 Before the Industrial Revolution, most of the cloth that women wove was made on vertical looms like this one.

mechanisms, and they invented two different systems. The first was the horizontal ground loom, which is still used by weavers around the world. It's simple to set up: the warp threads are tied on to two straight pieces of wood, stretched tight, and the wood is pegged into the ground. The weavers sit or squat on the ground beside the warp threads and push the thread-filled shuttle back and forth. The second invention – the warp-weighted loom – is the ancestor of modern looms. Here, the warp threads hang vertically, attached to a piece of wood supported by two uprights, with the free ends weighted to keep them straight. Weavers using vertical looms sit in front of the hanging warp threads and pass the shuttle from one side to the other. Although both designs probably originated in Turkey, the ground loom and the warp-weighted loom are so different that they must have been invented independently. The ground loom spread south and east to Egypt, the Sudan, and India, perhaps because in those climates most of the work is done outside. The warp-weighted loom spread north and west through Europe where the weather forces weavers to work inside.[9]

Very little is known about the appearance of the earliest Neolithic textiles (few very early examples have survived) but they seem to have been plain, although there was variety in the weaves. Two small balls of clay bearing impressions of different but equally finely woven cloth were found at Jarmo in the Zagros foothills; and several pieces of varying weaves were found associated with secondary burials at Çatalhöyük, most wrapped around the bones but in one case, stuffed into a skull.[10] These textiles were probably made of flax, as were most of the numerous fragments of netted cloth excavated at Nahal Hemar in the Judean desert (a few of which were woven using human hair).[11]

Some scholars think the southwest Asian linen was painted, and while there's no real evidence for dyeing or decoration on any of these finds, at Çatalhöyük beads were strung on red-dyed string, and clay stamp seals that could have been used to create patterns on cloth were found.[12] In contrast, textile historians know that the well-preserved cloth from the Neolithic lake villages in Switzerland and a few Neolithic passage graves in Germany was heavily decorated.[13] The workmanship was sophisticated and the textiles were elaborately patterned with woven and embroidered triangles, stripes, and checkerboards. Some pieces had decorative beading using seeds, and ribbed and fringed borders. Although the color hasn't survived, the patterns suggest that it was an important element of the design.

Metalworking

Like pottery-making and weaving, metalworking first appears at Neolithic sites in southwest Asia and the Levant. Archaeometallurgists report that

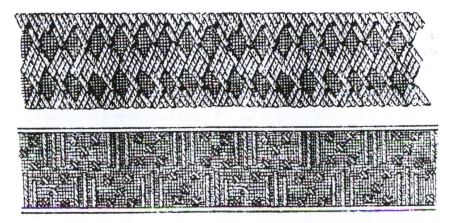

Figure 10.8 The weavers at Robenhausen were highly skilled, and produced many intricate patterns.

most of the examples are hammered from native copper: pins and beads were excavated at Çayönü, and hammered copper rings, pins, and pendants made of folded sheets of metal were found in the oldest levels at Tell Ramad. At Çatalhöyük, the metal grave goods include lead and copper beads, pendants and tubes, copper rings, and copper-sheathed wooden pins. Although early excavators reported evidence of smelting on the site, the grave good were all made by hammering.[14]

Evidence for trade

And now we return to Neolithic economic systems, and specifically to the exchange of obsidian tools. Of the over 750 known obsidian sources in the world,[15] only a few are suitable for tools, and even fewer were actually mined in the Neolithic. Because each volcano produces glass with distinctive trace elements, archaeologists are able to trace obsidian found on sites back to their original sources and the results have been surprising. On most sites all the obsidian comes from a single source, and in many cases the source is hundreds of miles away. Obsidian tools in the Levant, for example, came from two volcanoes in central Turkey (Göllü Dağ Çiftlik and Nenezi Dağ) and one in eastern Turkey (Nemrut Dağ). The obsidian found at Kalavassos-Tenta in Cyprus also came from central Turkey,[16] but almost all of the obsidian found in the Mediterranean comes from islands: Melos supplied most of the obsidian used in Neolithic Greece, volcanic glass from Sardinia, Pantelleria, Palmarola, and Lipari supplied most of Italy (over 90 percent of the obsidian in Calabria came from Lipari), and Lipari obsidian has been found as far west as southern France and as far east as Croatia.[17] In North America, despite the hundreds of possible sources, most of the obsidian traded by the Hopewell culture came from a single site (Obsidian Bluff, Wyoming).[18]

Because archaeologists can identify the sources of obsidian tools, because obsidian was traded over long distances, and because stone tools survive in good condition on most sites, the obsidian trade is often used as a model for Neolithic trade in general. In most of the source regions, people living near volcanoes collected raw material for their own use, and in their villages the percentage of obsidian tools is very high. But as the obsidian was traded and re-traded from village to village, it became both progressively less common,[19] as well as smaller and thinner,[20] while flint tools become progressively more common – a pattern that seems to reflect down-the-line trading. One of the most interesting discoveries about trading in southwest Asia is that in many cases, neither finished tools nor rough raw material were exchanged. Instead, traders carried preformed cores (ready for a customer to knapp) or unfinished blades (ready for a customer to finish). A bundle of 56 large obsidian blades struck from the same core and found fitted together at Tell Sabi Abayad II may be an example of this.[21] In Greece, on the other hand, a different pattern can be seen. Most of the chipped stone tools on Greek sites were poorly knapped – probably by the villagers – using local raw materials. But tools made from imported stone (obsidian from Melos, jasper from Liguria, "chocolate jasper" from northern Greece, and chert from Cyprus) were beautifully made.[22] There are several different methods flint knappers use to remove flakes from cores, some of which are quite easy to master, while others – especially those which produce finely shaped tools – require great skill (and a great deal of practice). When most of the fine-quality tools on a site are made of locally available raw materials, archaeologists assume that they were made by high-skilled local craftsmen. But when the fine tools are made from exotic stone, they were probably imported as part of an exchange system or trading network, and it follows that the local craftsmen were less likely to have made them. So the evidence suggests that in Greece the traders who imported the exotic stone were also craftsmen who used it to make special tools to order.[23]

Obsidian is a remarkable material, but it's hard to know why it was so popular. It's sharper than flint – it's sharper than modern surgical steel, for that matter, which is why it's used for certain heart and eye surgeries – but much more brittle, and the edges dull easily. While a fresh obsidian blade produces an amazingly close shave (I'm told that newly knapped obsidian blades are far easier on the skin than commercial razor blades) that hardly seems a sufficient reason for importing it across seas and deserts and over mountains. And there seems to be even less reason for importing raw materials like chocolate and yellow jasper, because tools made from them aren't significantly better than those made of local flint. This brings us to the last aspect of Neolithic trade – the question of whether it involved prestige (as opposed to practical) goods.

How do archaeologists differentiate between practical and prestige items? By one definition, practical objects are those that can be made quickly and efficiently, while prestige items take a long time to produce.[24] This distinction is not terribly useful: North American pioneer women spent hundreds of hours making quilts, often creating elaborate patterns, but their work was seen as entirely practical. Another definition is that practical goods are necessities, while prestige items aren't. But who decides what's a necessity? How you view air-conditioning depends on who and where you are, and in any case, the dichotomy between utilitarian and luxury goods is a modern concept arising from capitalism and may not be applicable to Neolithic societies at all.[25]

Still, in most cultures, rare items, especially those that come from far away, represent some sort of social differential, and since archaeologists know that some Neolithic cultures included social hierarchies, it's likely that some of the trade goods represented prestige. In many cultures, ceremonial axes are symbols of male authority: the small polished chisels found in Syria mentioned above could have been used for fine work, but they were pierced as pendants and probably never used as tools.[26] Small, roughly triangular celts (stone axe heads) found in Cyprus are made of polished greenstone, quartzite, and steatite (soapstone) and are too soft to be used as tools. The dozens of gold objects that accompanied the male burial at Varna certainly point to prestige (or at least wealth) and so do the fine stemmed cups found at Dawenkou in the Yellow River valley, and the carved jades characteristic of Lonshan culture burials in northern China.

It seems clear that trade in the Neolithic, like buying and selling in the modern world, involved both necessities and luxuries and so it represents one more aspect of Neolithic life that survives to the present day.

Women's work

We all know how hard it is to avoid applying our own cultural standards to other societies (as is clearly reflected in the American response to almost any other culture's plumbing), and archaeologists are no different from the rest of us. But during the past thirty years, archaeologists have begun asking themselves a pointed question – "to what extent are my own cultural beliefs shaping my reconstruction of ancient life?" This question is particularly significant for prehistorians because without contemporary descriptions, they're forced to fall back on their own assumptions about how Neolithic life "must have been."

Until very recently, for example, most prehistorians believed that Neolithic men had more power and prestige than Neolithic women. Although this assumption was largely a reflection of the gender hierarchy in nineteenth- and twentieth-century industrialized societies, archaeologists had consulted texts from the earliest civilizations and read ethnographic reports about prehistoric cultures, and these sources seemed to establish the universality of male supremacy. As a result, most reconstructions of Neolithic life described the men as engaged in high-status activities like making tools, controlling the food supply, trading, and going to war. Women, on the other hand, stayed at home, raising children, milking cattle, sheep and goats, and producing butter, yoghurt, and cheese. They tended kitchen gardens, fetched water and firewood, washed dishes, wove cloth and sewed clothing, and made pottery. All of these activities were assumed to be low-status occupations just as they are in modern western society, where many people continue to assume that ceramics and sewing are middle-class hobbies and housekeeping is nasty but necessary menial labor.[27]

But this picture of Neolithic life was based on seriously flawed sources. The ancient texts described state societies, not small tribes and chiefdoms, and they were largely written by men from a male point of view. Unfortunately, the ethnographic reports were equally suspect,

Figure 10.9 Like this modern villager, Neolithic weavers using hand spindles probably spun as they went about their daily chores.

because most of them reflected the experiences of male researchers who had no idea that talking with women might give them another point of view. The ethnographers aren't entirely to blame. In many cultures, female society is separate from male society, and it would be inappropriate for a male researcher to intrude. But when women ethnographers began using women informants, the view of status changed. Women may have been responsible for household tasks, but their work wasn't necessarily low-status. In fact, because they were the potters and the textile-makers, in many cultures women were among the most respected craftsmen.

It's easy to see why weaving and pottery-making were women's work. As any mother of young children knows, when you're concentrating on their care there's not much else you can do (unless it's mechanical, repetitive, can be interrupted and then resumed, doesn't endanger the family, and can be done at home).[28] Both pottery-making and textile manufacture fit this description because they can easily be done in the presence of small children. They're extremely repetitive, which means they don't require much conscious thought. Each technology consists of a series of discrete stages: a weaver prepares fibers, spins and dyes thread, strings the loom, weaves the cloth, and then fashions clothing; potters prepare clay, form pots, load and fire kilns, and then unload the finished work. At most of these stages the process can be stopped and started again without damaging the finished products and, except for dyeing thread in boiling liquid and firing the kiln, the work isn't dangerous. A final point is that weaving and pottery-making complement each other in terms of time management. They can be done year-round, of course, but it's definitely best to make pottery during the warmest, driest part of the year, and in temperate climates at least, spinning and weaving are usually winter chores, which means that one person in a family could be responsible for both.

Is it fair to assume that in the Neolithic the women were potters and weavers, and that those crafts conferred high status? Archaeologists don't know. Women were often buried with ceramic vessels – but as I explained in Chapter 9, no one knows what these grave goods actually represent – and at many sites pottery kilns were built next to bread ovens. But there's no proof that women were solely responsible for baking bread and firing clay, or that these tasks were prestigious. Most of the evidence for Neolithic textile manufacture (mainly in the form of spindle whorls and loom weights) comes from inside houses or from work areas near them, and there are no help in determining who the weavers were or how the cultures viewed textile-making. There are many ethnographic parallels, including some with living cultures, but once again that doesn't prove anything about Neolithic gender-roles or status.

For the moment, most archaeologists continue to assume that women's work included spinning and weaving and firing pottery, and many suspect that those activities were as important as tool-making and trading. But no one knows if that's true.

11

ART AND RELIGION

Art and religion are cultural universals – anthropologists have never found a human society without them – so it's fair to assume that Neolithic people made art and had religious beliefs. But of all the aspects of Neolithic life, art and religion are the hardest to reconstruct. You may have had the confusing

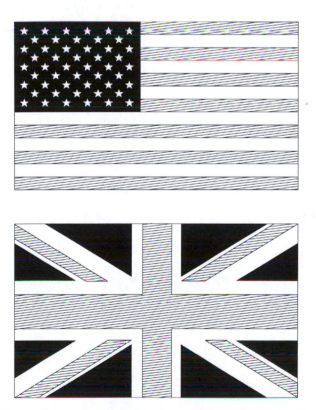

Figure 11.1 Physically, a country's flag is a rectangle of cloth decorated with colored shapes. Iconographically, it represents the nation and by extension its people, as well as everything they do.

experience of looking at art that you know means something to the people who made it, but not to you. I was certainly confused the first time I entered a Shinto shrine in Japan, because while I knew how a church worked, and what Christian painting and sculptures represented, I'd never studied Shinto art. In a sense, I was just like an archaeologist trying to reconstruct Neolithic belief systems. The difference is that while I could find books that explained Shinto, the archaeologist can't read up on Neolithic symbolism because nobody really knows how to interpret it.

Defining art

Art is a form of symbolic communication, and until the modern era all artists used standard sets of symbols that the public understood. These artistic languages, or iconographies, like all forms of communication, have to be learned. Excavators working in historic periods can do what I did in Japan: they can look up the meaning of a culture's iconography. Archaeologists dealing with Neolithic art, on the other hand, have nowhere to turn for help as they try to figure out what the symbols mean. Even ethnographic analogy isn't useful, because the same symbols (the sun and the moon for example) mean different things in different cultures. And there's an added problem. Some art is purely decorative rather than meaningful, but an outsider may not be able to tell which is which: few non-Scots can tell if a specific tartan pattern represents a clan or was created for the tourist trade. So, while archaeologists may recognize that a small sculpture depicts a sheep, they have no way of knowing why the artist made it or what it meant to the person who owned it.

Defining religion

It's slightly easier for archaeologists to reconstruct Neolithic religion. Religion plays several essential roles in society, most of them entirely practical. On its most basic level, religion reduces anxiety by explaining the unknown and by teaching people the correct way to contact supernatural beings. But religious systems do much more than that. It may not be obvious in modern western societies, but religion is the glue that holds cultures together. Religion provides a common identity that transcends family and tribal allegiances; maintains societal morality by establishing rules on how to behave, and then encouraging people to abide by those rules; and gives leaders their authority by affirming that supernatural beings approve of them and will come to their aid. In a few societies, like the United States, where the political system is formally separate from any religion, the philosophy of the founders of the state provides the official ethical guidelines and group identity.

What about religion's role as a bridge to the supernatural? All religious systems assume that supernatural beings, while they're unknowable and uncontrollable, will help people if they're contacted in the right way, and that religious practitioners know how to do that. Supernatural beings fall into three broad categories: non-human spirits, ancestor spirits, and gods and goddesses. Each type is reached through a specific kind of activity, ranging from trancing to sacrificing animals and plants to reciting religious texts, praying, dancing, and singing, all of which take place in spaces that are fundamentally different from the rest of the world because supernatural beings are able to interact with humans there. These sacred spaces are often decorated with art.

Non-human spirits animate animals, plants, and natural features like rivers and mountains. They're close to people, actively involved in daily affairs, and easily reached, although some people are more skilled at it than others. Their worship is called shamanistic, after the name (shaman) given by Siberian hunter-gatherers to band members who specialize in contacting the supernatural. Like all band leaders, shamans work part-time, and they usually work alone. The second category of supernatural beings, ancestor spirits, are different. They look like people, but they're not nearly as easy to reach as the non-human spirits, and in some cultures they're only available once or twice a year. The original significance of Halloween was that on All Hallows Eve (the night before All Saints' Day) barriers to the spirit world dissolved and the ancestors could be contacted. Ancestor worship, or veneration, is typical of small farming societies where it's usually described as communal because the shamans contact the ancestors during public ceremonies that involve the entire population.

Gods and goddesses, the third type of supernatural being, are remote, in charge of the universe, and impersonal. Their worship is usually ecclesiastical, which means that they're supported by centralized bureaucracies that train and certify full-time religious specialists (priests and priestesses) who then perform ceremonies that the population – or congregation – simply observes or participates in minimally. Ecclesiastical systems seem to have developed at about the same time as state societies.

Art in the Neolithic

Excavators have found a surprising amount of Neolithic art, ranging from geometric shapes painted on the floors and walls of houses and carved on stone slabs – there are over a hundred different motifs on the walls and ceilings of passage graves in Brittany and the British Isles[1] – to wall paintings and sculptures depicting people, animals, and fantastic creatures. In addition, potters painted, burnished, and incised pots, tool-makers incised and carved their creations, weavers used colored thread, beading, and fringing to decorate cloth, and leather-workers and basket-makers must have ornamented their work, too, although no evidence of this has survived.

Neolithic sculptors made both free-standing and relief sculptures (free-standing sculptures aren't attached to a background, but relief sculptures,

Figure 11.2 The famous spiral from Newgrange is only one of the many geometric
motifs carved into megalithic monuments in Europe and the British Isles.

like the heads on coins, are). Both in number and geographical distribution,
free-standing sculptures are the single most common type of Neolithic art.
They vary in size from larger-than-life-sized to tiny, and in media from clay,
plaster, and plaster-over-reeds, to stone, bone, clay, and wood. Neolithic
sculptors made models of buildings, ovens and loaves of bread, domestic
objects, and carts,[2] but their most common subject was people. The anthropomorphic representations include men, women, children, hermaphrodites,
and asexual beings as well as some human forms that were abstracted
into cross-shapes and triangles. There are human heads and busts with faces
ranging from realistic to entirely schematized, and cups shaped like human
heads that have been found from southwest Asia to central Europe. There
are also symbolic (and probably sexual) representations of phalluses, breasts,
and breast-and-phallus and buttocks-and-phallus combinations. Most of
the anthropomorphic figures are nude, but they're often decorated with
geometric patterns, and some of them have sculpted clothes and hair, while
others probably wore removable wigs and clothing. Some are multi-media,
with inlaid eyes or detachable heads made of different materials (some
examples have sets of heads with faces showing a range of emotions[3]). The
figures stand, sit on the ground or on furniture, and recline; some are
alone, some are in pairs or groups, and some (perhaps) are engaged in sexual
activities. Female figures are depicted giving birth, holding children or

150

Figure 11.3 This standing nude woman touching her breasts was found at ʿAin Ghazal in Jordan.

domestic objects, and a few are shown working. Many of them have extremely fat bellies, thighs and buttocks, some touch their genitals, and others support their breasts. Some of the male figures touch their phalluses, which are often depicted erect. Sculptors also depicted animals (sheep, cattle, goats, equids, dogs, lions, bears, and unidentifiable quadrupeds); birds and reptiles; and composite animal-human figures. Some potters created animal-shaped vessels: particularly fine zoomorphic jars were made in the Balkans, and at Hacilar in Turkey.

Relief sculptures are much less common. Engraved pebbles decorated with schematic faces are found at sites like 'Ain Ghazal in Jordan and Sha'ar Hagolan in the Jordan Valley, and at a few other places in southwest Asia human faces and anthropomorphic figures (some wearing headdresses or elaborate hairstyles) appear on larger stone slabs. Other relief figures are found on anthropomorphic vessels. In Greece, some jars have schematized faces applied to the neck, in other parts of Europe potters made cremation urns with applied eyes and noses and stubby upturned handles on the shoulders that resemble arms, and there are many vessels with nothing more than bumps on the shoulders representing breasts that archaeologists believe are also anthropmorphic. Animals are depicted more frequently in relief sculpture than humans. Among the species carved on stone slabs or modeled in plaster on walls are bulls, felines, birds, unidentified quadrupeds, reptiles, snakes, and what may be reptile-human composites. The sculptures at Göbekli Tepe in southeastern Turkey, for example, include reptiles with swollen bellies standing upright with their arms raised: one has a long snout and prominent teeth, another has a prominent tail.[4] And there's a unique carinated jar from the Wadi Raba culture of the southern Levant decorated with what may be a person wearing an animal headdress.[5]

The rarest type of Neolithic art is wall paintings. They're intrinsically fragile, and although a handful are preserved inside European passage graves

Figure 11.4 The potters at Hacilar created graceful and complex animal-shaped vessels.

and some fragmentary examples appear on house walls in various regions, very few have survived. For this reason, the well-preserved paintings at Çatalhöyük are particularly surprising. Dozens of cream-colored plastered walls covered with paintings have been unearthed at the site. The paint was mostly mineral-based and quite colorful: shades of red, pink, red-orange, yellow, and brown made from iron oxides, cinnabar, and hematite; bright blue from copper ores; mauve from magnesium; lead grey from galena; and organic black paint, made from soot.[6] The motifs include geometric shapes and hand-prints, human and animal figures (bulls, birds including vultures, leopards, and deer), and a scene that seems to show a volcano erupting with the village of Çatalhöyük, seen from above, in the foreground. If this interpretation of the scene is correct, it's the earliest known landscape painting.

The meaning of Neolithic art

A great deal of effort and creativity went into making Neolithic art. But for what purpose? Archaeologists have been arguing about this for a century, and – like so many aspects of the Neolithic – it's unlikely they'll ever know for sure, but that doesn't mean they can't make educated guesses. Although no one can ever be certain which motifs are purely decorative and which have meaning, archaeologists assume that most of the Neolithic art was iconographic, depicting sacred images, totems, or important societal figures. While this may be true, it has led to some unfortunate interpretations. The most famous was the tripartite assumption that all prehistoric female figurines were related to sexuality, that fat or seemingly pregnant figures were depictions of fertility goddesses, and that all European and southwest Asian fertility goddesses were actually the same deity. The idea was most famously articulated in *The White Goddess* by Robert Graves. Graves was a reputable Classicist, but this work (particularly the revised version published in the 1960s) gave rise to the notion that all prehistoric people worshiped a mother goddess (the Great Goddess) who was displaced by later male deities brought into Europe by Indo-European warriors on horseback. Among the archaeologists who initially embraced the theory were James Mellaart who in 1967 suggested that Çatalhöyük was an ancient pilgrimage center for Great Goddess worship. Despite the fact that he moderated his views less than a decade later, the site continues to be sacred for neo-pagan Goddess worshipers.[7]

Today, this simplistic interpretation is (finally) no longer accepted, and most archaeologists believe that Neolithic figurines had several functions. There's quite a bit of ethnographic evidence about the four main roles small sculptures play in living cultures: one type of figurine is used in communal rituals where it represents the supernatural, a second type is a teaching aid used in puberty ceremonies, a third type helps shamans practice sympathetic

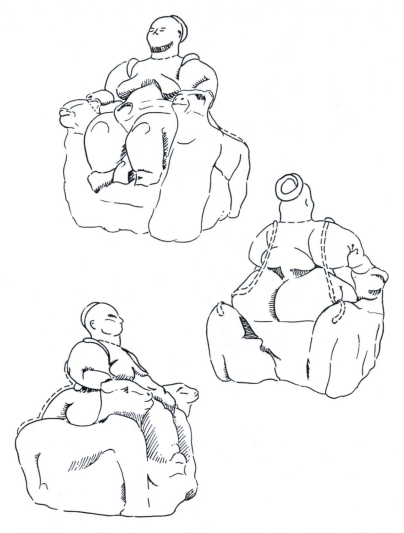

Figure 11.5 Figurines like the famous "Mistress of the Animals" from Çatalhöyük are difficult to interpret. Her head is reconstructed.

magic (these are sometimes called fetishes), and a fourth type is either purely decorative or made for children (in other words, they're either art objects or toys).[8] But knowing this doesn't really help archaeologists, because it's their function, not their appearance, that differentiates them. For example, an unusual figurine with a mounded stomach added after she was made was found in a trash pit at the site of Gritille. She has been interpreted as a charm for ensuring a safe pregnancy,[9] but figures of pregnant women aren't necessarily about pregnancy *per se* because they're often used in female puberty rites as teaching tools.[10] The Gritille figurine may be a magic fetish or a ritual teaching aid, or maybe it was just a toy for a child whose mother was pregnant.

Non-human figurines are equally difficult to interpret. At 'Ain Ghazal, excavators found more than 150 animal figures, most of them unidentifiable in terms of species. Among them was a pair of small clay cattle pierced with tiny blades that had been added before firing. While these two animals may represent a ritual killing, what are archaeologists to make of the rest of them? A few have the marks of string around their necks, so they may have been connected with domestication, and the excavator writes that some may have been toys (but puts the word in quotation marks).[11]

Most Neolithic relief sculptures, on the other hand, seem to be icono-graphic, and are most likely sacred images. The richest collection comes from Çatalhöyük, where the reliefs include a few anthropomorphic figures, very schematized, with their arms and legs outstretched and their hands and

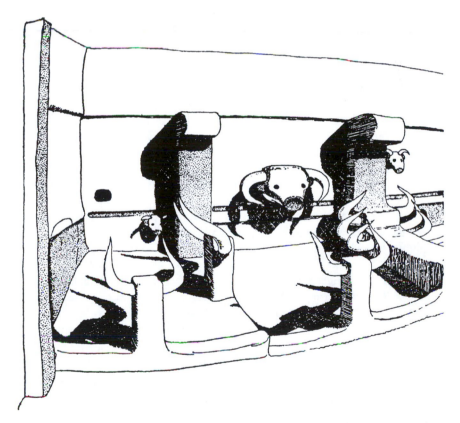

Figure 11.6 Buchrania, horn cores, and sculpted bulls' and rams' heads are found in some rooms at Çatalhöyük.

feet pointing up that were originally interpreted as goddesses giving birth,[12] but more recently reinterpreted as dancers. This theory is quite reasonable. At sites from west Pakistan to the Danube archaeologists have excavated dozens of images of dancers painted on pottery and walls, carved in stone, and modeled in clay. Many of them are from ritual contexts, and their presence suggests that dance was an important aspect of Neolithic religion just as it is in modern prehistoric cultures.[13] But the most common subject of the relief sculpture at Çatalhöyük is animals. Bulls, stags, and leopards are depicted in profile on the walls. Horned cattle and sheep heads, many of them modeled over skulls, protrude from interior walls in horizontal or vertical groups: often they were painted with complex geometric patterns. In some rooms, rows of partial skulls with horns attached are set along low platforms, in others the lower jaws of wild boars are embedded in the walls, and in still others the skulls and jaws of felines, foxes, weasels, and vultures are set into conical shapes that protrude above the platforms in the rooms. This assemblage is unparalleled, and no one has been able to come up with a coherent explanation for it.

Another interesting (and equally inexplicable) example of Neolithic art that may be considered a form of relief comes from Kfar HaHoresh in the lower Galilee, where ash-filled pits beneath plaster floors contained three figures outlined in human bones. One is simply a circle made of human long bones, and another is too fragmentary to identify. But the third is an animal in profile, constructed from skeletal material from at least four people. The mouth is formed by an upturned human skull and mandible, and the tail is an articulated human leg and foot. The excavators suggest that it may represent either a carnivore or an aurochs and the only possible parallels seem to be animal outlines made of small stones found in the Sinai and the Negev.[14]

It's more difficult to generalize about the function of the last category of Neolithic art, wall paintings, because the most complete examples all come from one site, Çatalhöyük. Most of the Çatalhöyük paintings seem to be decorative rather than religious, and many appear to depict normal activities like hunting: even the landscape appears to be "real" as opposed to symbolic. But in three rooms the scenes are different. They show vultures, some with human legs, attacking headless bodies: in one scene a man with a sling seems to be trying to chase the vultures away. Based on the secondary burial practices at Çatalhöyük, these paintings have been interpreted as depictions of the practice of allowing vultures can strip away the flesh before the bones are gathered for burial.[15] Another suggestion is that the scenes are connected with the ritual practice of postmortem skull removal.

Archaeological evidence for religion

Archaeologists are usually careful about hypothesizing that an artifact or feature is ritual in nature. On historic sites, temples and shrines are often

Figure 11.7 The "Vulture Shrines" at Çatalhöyük are decorated with wall paintings, human skulls, and animal heads.

significantly bigger or more complex than other buildings, and many are located in special areas, but on prehistoric sites – unless there's clear evidence that ritual activities took place in a building (and this is rarely the case) – it can't be identified as sacred just because it's unusual. While the large round building at Kalavassos-Tenta in Cyprus (Figure 6.4) is often referred to as a shrine, the excavator carefully describes it as a village leader's house.[16] And the same is true of unusual artifacts – the fact they're unusual doesn't automatically mean that they're connected with religion. Occasionally, however, the evidence of ritual practices is so striking it can't be denied: one example is the custom of skull removal, characteristic of Neolithic cultures in the Levant and, to a lesser extent, Greece and Turkey.

Postmortem skull removal has a long history in southwest Asia: it originated several millennia before the Neolithic and was still being practiced by Iron Age Phoenicians.[17] It may seem horrible to us, but ethnographers report that skull removal is usually connected with heroism or honor or pride, and that there have been a number of cultures in which the skulls of ancestors were displayed, revered, and consulted. This suggests that the skull removal found at sites like Hacilar, Çatalhöyük, Çayönü, Nevali Çori, Köşk

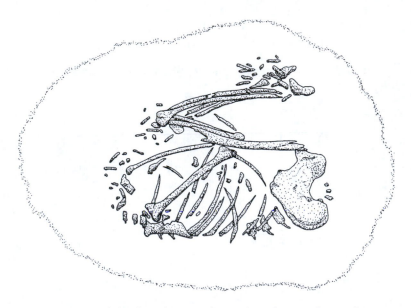

Figure 11.8 Many Neolithic burials in southwest Asia show evidence of postmortem skull removal.

Höyük, Cafer Höyük, and Tell Aswad was probably a ritual act.[18] In southwest Asia, Neolithic adults of both sexes were buried without skulls, and so were some children and infants, but the practice wasn't universal. Archaeologists have found primary burials in single graves with intact skulls, primary burials in single graves that later had their skulls removed, leaving behind the lower jaws, secondary burials (with or without skulls) in group graves, secondary burials of skulls either singly or in groups that are sometimes referred to as "skull caches," and skulls displayed in public and private areas. At many sites, several of these options appear.

The tops and backs of many of the detached skulls were painted or covered with resin or bitumen which may have been meant to represent hair – or may have held removable wigs in place. Some skulls have faces modeled in colored plaster (at Jericho, Kenyon describes "a fine ruddy flesh-colour"[19]) and their eye sockets filled with white plaster or with cowrie or bivalve shells. In appearance they range from naturalistic to very abstract. Many were found in domestic contexts under house floors or in courtyards outside houses. At Hacilar two skulls of adults kept upright by pebbles were placed in the courtyard of a house, and a baby's skull was hidden behind a wall; at Nevali Çori five skulls and other bones were buried under one house, and nine skulls were placed under another. At Çatalhöyük a subfloor burial of an adult woman included a plastered skull and lower jaw held in her crossed arms. But other locations were decidedly ritual in nature. In the

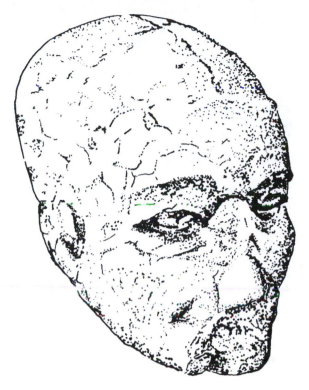

Figure 11.9 Sometimes skulls, like this famous example from Jericho, were plastered and displayed.

"skull building" at Çayönü, the bones of about 400 people were piled haphazardly under the floor, and ninety adult and infant skulls were stored on shelves in a small room.[20] In that same building the excavators found a stone slab with traces of human, sheep, and cattle blood, and a flint dagger with human and cattle blood on it; and in a later structure on the site, traces of human blood were found on the stone rim of a round depression in one corner, and on a limestone slab with a human face. At Çatalhöyük, one room included four skulls: two placed beneath sculpted bulls' heads, and the others on a platform near the vulture paintings (Figure 11.7).

There are also artistic depictions of decapitated skulls: one grave at Hacilar held a clay cup in the shape of an upside-down skull that had been wrapped in cloth and partly burned, and is interpreted as symbolic decapitation. Male, female, and asexual clay figures with removable heads are found at many sites in southeastern Turkey. At Höyücek, for example, an asexual figure with a bone tube between its shoulders was found next to several small bone faces; and Hacilar produced a group of clay figures, probably female, with

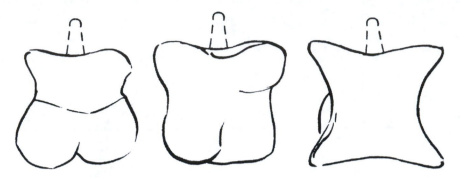

Figure 11.10 Figurines with detachable heads like these from Hacilar may be connected with the practice of skull removal.

wooden heads attached by pegs that were originally described as ritual but are now seen as teaching aids.[21] Many of the figurines at Çatalhöyük may have had detachable heads, and the most famous of the statues, the "Mistress of the Animals," may well depict skull removal, too (see Figure 11.5). The now headless figure is seated, flanked by two large standing felines. Her hands – also missing – originally rested on their heads, their tails curve over her back and rest on her shoulders, and a human head lies face-upward between her feet. Mellaart originally described her as giving birth,[22] but archaeologists now think that the head is, in fact, a skull.

The presence of so many skulls in southwest Asia, along with paintings of headless bodies and figurines with removable heads, indicates that whatever it meant, skull removal was a ritual activity. The ceremonies surrounding it probably reflected the basic beliefs of the people, and those beliefs included ancestor veneration. The question is, did ancestor veneration involve the supernatural? Or to put it another way, are the skulls sacred, or totemic? In some cultures, ancestor cults reflect ideas about how life changes into death, and based on this model, one interpretation is that Neolithic skeletons were decapitated to help the dead to leave the world of the living.[23] Another is that since the head was where the spirit resided, severing and displaying it kept the ancestor nearby and easy to contact.[24] In other cultures, ancestor cults involve lineages, and the skulls are used as totems; so another interpretation of the Neolithic skull removal practice is that the skulls were displayed in public places or secondarily buried in caches as part of ceremonies designed to reaffirm the social and political ethos of the culture.[25] The fact that only a small percentage of burials received this special treatment may reflect the rise of social elites.

As we have seen, Neolithic art is rich and varied, and if the art reflects cultural practices, Neolithic religion was, too. It's entirely possible that the seeds for the major world religions were sown during the Neolithic.

The monumental statues from 'Ain Ghazal

The discoveries in 1983 and 1985 of caches of monumental plaster and reed statues at the Jordanian site of 'Ain Ghazal was of major importance to the study of both Neolithic art and Neolithic religion. In contrast to fragmentary remains of similar figures excavated at Jericho and Nahal Hemar, the thirty-two statues at 'Ain Ghazal, found carefully placed in two pits dug into the floors of abandoned houses, were remarkably well preserved. One burial pit contained thirteen full-sized statues and twelve one-headed busts, and the other included two full-sized statues, three two-headed busts, and two fragmentary heads. Although more than 200 years separates the two caches, the statues are remarkably similar. They were all made in the same way, with heads, torsos, and legs made of separate bundles of reeds that were then assembled, tied together, and plastered. Given their fragile nature, it's surprising that the 'Ain Ghazal figures are so tall (the largest is over 3 ft in height) and so flat (about 4 in at the thickest). It's also surprising that despite their tall thin proportions, they seem to have been designed to stand up on their own, probably anchored through the floor inside enclosed areas, and (probably) seen only from the front.

The statues' heads are outsized and their faces are somewhat crude, with small upturned noses, vertical slash nostrils, and lipless incised lines for mouths. But the predominant features, the eyes, were carefully made. Large and wide-set, the sockets are outlined by a v-shaped incision filled with black bitumen and highlighted with green pigment,[26] and filled with rounded white plaster eyeballs inlaid with bitumen irises. The eyes make the statues come to life, and their gaze is direct. In the older statues the irises are round, but in the later figures they're diamond-shaped, which gives them "an eerie, alien, or almost feline look."[27] Some of the faces are painted (one has sets of three stripes on the forehead and each cheek) but there's no indication of hair, although the high foreheads step back slightly near the top which may mean that there were attached wigs or headdresses.

The bodies are even more schematized than the heads. One has vertical lines of red paint from the waist to the ankles and similar lines around the shoulders which may represent clothing, but the rest are nude. On the earlier statues, the arms are small, and by the later period they've entirely disappeared – if the later statues were dressed in real clothing the sleeves may have taken the place of the arms.[28] Fingers and toes, when they appear, are simply slashes in the plaster. The number of fingers and toes is interesting: one statue has four fingers on one hand and five on another; and another statue's hand has seven fingers; while one foot from the first cache has six toes. This has caused

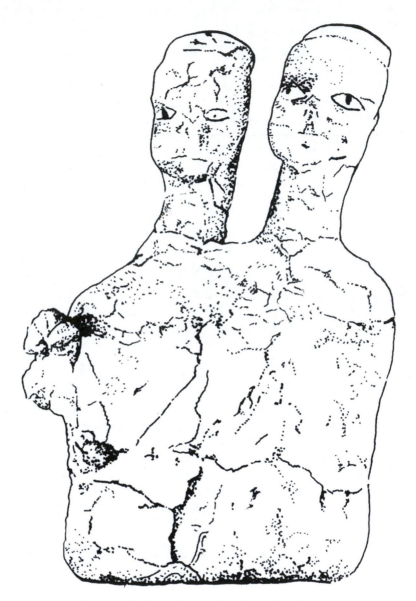

Figure 11.11 The double-headed busts from ʿAin Ghazal may represent a god and a goddess, or may be totemic figures.

some scholars to suggest that the ʿAin Ghazal figures depict the biblical Rephaim or "giants" – primordial people at least one of whom had six fingers and toes.[29] But a more likely explanation is that when they built their villages the Israelites accidentally uncovered Neolithic statues

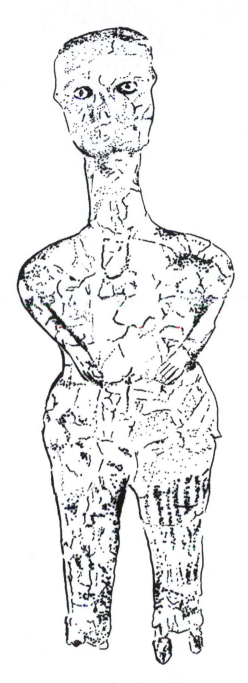

Figure 11.12 The standing figures from ʿAin Ghazal have no genitals, but archaeologists assume that the ones without breasts are male.

like the ones at 'Ain Ghazal, which then inspired the mythological figures in the Hebrew Bible.[30]

The 'Ain Ghazal statues were buried in good condition, and their manufacture suggests that they were never meant to last. So why were they made and then buried? Since skull burial was practiced at the site, and stylistically the statues resemble some plastered skulls, they may have been associated in some way with ancestor cults. Another possibility is that they're divine figures (perhaps representing fertility or the changing seasons, or the primeval pairs so common in later mythology) but this suggestion is weakened by the fact that while the excavators report that the figures include men, women, and children, their sexuality isn't emphasized: a few figures have breasts but none has genitals. A third possibility is that they're fetishes associated with magic ceremonies in which they represented specific characters – evil spirits, ancestors, or the like – who were stripped of their power through burial.[31] And the excavator thinks that they're totems: the smaller busts depicting mythical lineage or clan founders, the larger figures the mythical ancestors of groups of clans, and the double-headed figures representing the merger of two or more related lineages.[32] But the most important aspect of the 'Ain Ghazal statues, aside from their extraordinary preservation, isn't the role they played in Neolithic culture on the site. It's that they were publicly displayed. And this makes them one of the earliest possible indications in the world of the development of communal religion.

12

WHAT CAUSED THE NEOLITHIC TRANSITION?

And now we come to the most contentious, and for many scholars the most interesting, aspect of the Neolithic transition – why did it happen? Why, after millions of years of hunting-gathering, did people build villages, create new social systems, and most importantly, begin to produce their food? No one knows for sure. For almost a hundred years scientists have tried to figure out what launched the Neolithic, and during the past fifty years many excavations have been specifically organized to address the question, but rather than providing consensus, this explosion of research has produced a plethora of conflicting theories. There are a number of reasons for the lack of agreement, most of which I've already mentioned. They include the fragmentary condition of the evidence in general, and the fact that since domestication isn't visible in the archaeological record until the process is well underway, if an archaeological team uncovered evidence from the earliest stages of the Neolithic transition they probably wouldn't recognize it. Another problem is the lack of cultural analogies: anthropologists have never found foragers in the process of spontaneously altering the genetics and morphology of a local species (i.e. taking the very first steps toward domestication) so prehistorians don't have models for the beginning of the process. The basic nature of academic discussion plays its part, as well. But the most significant stumbling block is that while archaeological evidence can usually reveal *what* happened on a prehistoric site, it's much less useful at explaining *why*.

As we've seen, scientists have had considerable success in reconstructing *what* happened at the beginning of the domestication process. They've learned that the advent of the warmer, wetter, and more stable environmental conditions early in the Holocene made successful agriculture possible, but that this climate change by itself didn't cause the invention of agriculture. They've figured out that successful domestication was extremely rare, because while many groups undoubtedly experimented with cultivation and taming, unless there were domesticable plants and animals in the region, and unless they had already developed the basic technologies necessary for agriculture, foragers couldn't become farmers. Excavations have revealed that even in areas where the invention of farming was possible, the transition was slow and faltering, and that in most cases, only one village or a group of neighboring villages actually succeeded in creating a domestic species.[1] Archaeologists now understand that foragers couldn't have consciously set out to domesticate plants and animals, because they didn't know what domestication was. And finally, ethnographic studies reveal that in almost all parts of the world, once people stopped moving seasonally and began to farm and herd, their dependence on food production became irreversible.[2] But despite all this knowledge, archaeologists don't know *why* a few people in a very small number of places felt compelled to create an entirely new way of life, or *why* some were successful and some weren't, or *why* most groups tended to focus on a single species, or *why* they selected for certain traits over and over again until the species was no longer wild.

Almost all of the serious theories that attempt to explain *why* the Neolithic transition occurred are focused on southwest Asia. They range from simple (the Dump-Heap Theory, which argued that women tending wild plants growing in garbage dumps accidently domesticated them) to abstruse (the co-evolution theory, which posits as the cause parallel evolutions resulting in hunter-gatherers becoming farmers and wild species becoming domesticates). Some of these explanations – the Dump-Heap Theory for example – don't fit the scientific evidence and have been discarded,[3] but many others can't be proved or disproved scientifically. No single explanation is entirely satisfactory, but several are worth considering if only because they reflect a century of scholarly thinking.

There's no consensus about a logical way to discuss the theories. Many authors divide them into groups, but (again) there's no agreement about the best way to do that. They can be divided into primal cause and multicausal theories: primal cause theories posit a single initiating factor for the rise of agriculture, while multicausal theories propose more complicated scenarios. Another common division is into push theories, pull theories, and social theories. Push theories assume that human societies evolve because they're forced to adapt to environmental changes; pull theories see human behavior as the primary force in cultural change, and environmental factors as secondary; and social theories concentrate on increasing social complexity as the main motivation for cultural change. But the simplest way to address the theories is in roughly chronological order.

Childe's Oasis Theory

The earliest formal attempt to explain domestication was proposed by V. Gordon Childe in 1928.[4] Childe believed that culture progressed through a series of economic revolutions (an idea first articulated in 1904 by Raphael Pumpelly, director of an archaeological expedition to central Asia) and that these revolutions occurred when people were forced to innovate in order to survive. Childe believed that people made rational and conscious decisions

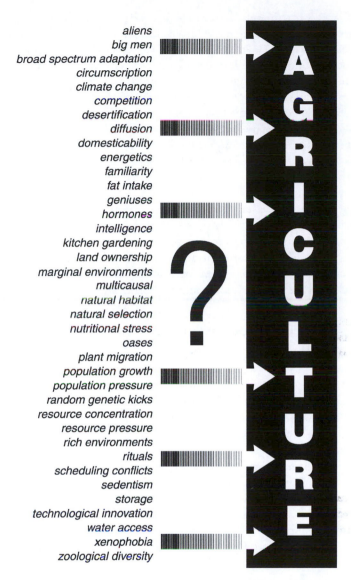

Figure 12.1 Over the past century, all of these explanations for the Neolithic transition have appeared in print.[5]

to invent new production techniques; and that the Neolithic Revolution – during which people invented food production – was the first and most important example. Because he assumed that one revolution inevitably led to the next as society advanced (thus, agriculture led to state societies) he focused his attention on Mesopotamia, the region of the first Urban

Revolution. Unfortunately, before the invention of irrigation, farming was impossible in the region, and Childe was hard pressed to explain why domestication would have arisen there. He suggested that drastic climate change at the end of the last glaciation created an increasingly hot, dry environment, forcing people, plants, and animals to congregate in Mesopotamian river valleys and oases where water was readily available. Under these circumstances, the invention of agriculture was logical and inevitable because food production is inherently superior to foraging.

When Childe proposed his Oasis Theory there was no way to test its validity, but by the 1940s and 1950s scientific research had refuted his assumptions: there had been no sudden climatological crisis at the end of the Pleistocene, and therefore no reason for people, plants, and animals to congregate in oases. In fact, recent studies seem to show that despite fluctuation in weather patterns, at the beginning of the Holocene southwest Asia was slowly becoming more temperate.[6] Furthermore, none of the wild ancestors of the first domestic species – neither plants nor animals – lived in Mesopotamian river valleys. Their wild ranges were all in mountain uplands. Clearly, a new theory was needed, and Robert Braidwood provided one.

Braidwood's Nuclear Zones Theory

Like most of his contemporaries, Braidwood assumed that plant and animal domestication took place in the same places at the same time. He was familiar with the work of Vavilov and other botanists on the natural habitats of the wild ancestors of domestic crops, and agreed with their theory that the first experiments in agriculture must have taken place in regions where wild wheat, barley, sheep, goats, and cattle all lived. The unusual abundance of resources in such areas, he wrote, had allowed foragers living there to develop sedentism, which then led to agriculture. Braidwood thought that the most likely locations for early domestication would be found in what he called the "hilly flanks of the Fertile Crescent" (i.e. the grassy slopes below the Zagros, Taurus, and Lebanon-Amanus mountain ranges which curve across the northern and western edges of the Levant and Mesopotamia). To test his Natural-Habitat or Nuclear Zones Theory, Braidwood put together a multidisciplinary team – he knew he would need botanists and zoologists along with his archaeologists – and began looking for likely sites in the foothills of the Zagros mountains of northern Iraq. He found one in the early agricultural site of Jarmo, and the team spent from 1950 to 1955 excavating there, researching the origins of domestication, and collecting an enormous number of scientific samples including some of the first to be radiocarbon-dated. Among the finds were the remains of domesticated emmer and einkorn wheat and barley, and domesticated dogs, sheep, and goats. Braidwood's work at Jarmo confirmed the theory that the earliest transitions to food production took place where potential domestics were plentiful. He didn't ask why the transitions took place because, like Childe, he assumed that farming was more secure and less time-consuming than foraging, and that all foragers would choose to farm if they could.

By the mid-1960s, however, several problems with Braidwood's theory had emerged, all related to his assumption that abundant wild resources automatically encouraged sedentism and domestication. Botanists discovered that natural stands of wild grass produce almost as much grain as the fields of subsistence farmers, and that wild grains are more nutritious than domestic varieties. Experiments in harvesting wild einkorn wheat using a flint sickle produced almost 1 kg of grain per hour of work, which meant that a family of four or five could have collected a year's supply of wild grain in only few weeks.[7] Why, archaeologists asked, would people living in the midst of wild wheat fields have any incentive to begin cultivation? At the same time, biologists and botanists pointed out that Jarmo was on the edge of the wild ranges of early plant domesticates rather than in the center where they would have been most abundant. And in-depth ethnographic studies of one of the few remaining hunter-gatherer groups, the !Kung San of the Kalahari Desert in Africa, revealed that they had much more leisure time than farmers, and had no desire to change their way of life. Far from being drawn into agriculture by a surplus of potential domesticates, it began to appear that foragers would turn to farming only if something destabilized their culture and forced them to. In response to this new information, the focus of discussion shifted from where agriculture originated to what destabilizing forces had caused its invention.

Population Pressure theories

Between 1968 and 1977 a series of scholars focused on population as the main destabilizing factor. Louis Binford was the first of these, and also the first to propose an hypothesis that wasn't specific to southwest Asia. He believed that foraging maintained a balance between population size and natural resources, but that this balance could be disturbed by environmental or demographic change. Binford focused on demographics, arguing that when population increases made it more and more difficult to hunt and gather enough food, foragers – no matter where they lived – would move in the direction of plant domestication.[8] At about the same time, Kent Flannery, who was studying sheep domestication in western Iran, refined Binford's hypothesis by suggesting that food production originated when foraging groups faced with dwindling resources split in half. Those forced into the more marginal areas, he theorized, would have had to invent agriculture in order to survive.[9] A third scholar, Mark Cohen, reported that while the diet in the marginal zones was adequate, the foods weren't particularly palatable, which he thought might have encouraged the inhabitants to import cultivated and tamed (and more tasty) species and to become farmers.[10] Unlike

Braidwood's theory, these Marginal Zone/Edge Zone or Population Pressure theories propose that a lack of resources, rather than an abundance of them, caused foragers to turn to agriculture. For the scenarios to be credible, archaeologists would have to prove that forager populations increased either before sedentism or in its earliest stages, with the result that food resources became scarce. But hunter-gatherers don't live in year-round settlements, and they don't bury their dead in community-wide cemeteries, so there's no way to extrapolate their population figures from the archaeological record. Although the work of some archaeologists provides supporting evidence, or at least supporting hypotheses (one scholar believes that in southwest Asia the population increased from 100,000 to 5 million during the transition to agriculture; another suggests that the world population increased from 10 million to 50 million; and a third posits an increase in Japan from 75,000 at the end of the Jōmon to 5.4 million after rice cultivation was introduced[11]), there's no way to test the validity of the Population Pressure theories.

Social Prestige and Social Complexity theories

Although the causal factors are different, the theories I've mentioned so far assume that environmental conditions pushed or pulled people into inventing agriculture. Over the past fifteen years, however, quite different scenarios have emerged: far from being coerced into agriculture, these more recent theories suggest, people were active participants in the transition.[12] One set of hypotheses, the Social Prestige theories, assumes that sedentism inevitably leads to social inequality and affluence, and that as social systems develop, acquiring and redistributing wealth becomes increasingly important. Social Prestige theorists argue that agriculture was invented, not in reaction to the relative abundance or lack of food, but as a way to create and control food surpluses. The most prominent advocate of this approach, Bryan Hayden, believes that the driving force behind food production was rivalry among leaders who wanted to amass wealth – that is, food – and then gain status by giving it away at competitive feasts.[13] His hypothesis is based on ethnographic studies, especially those describing the redistribution systems of some northwestern American groups, and the Big Man cultures in New Guinea mentioned in Chapter 9. Hayden argues that all societies, regardless of their environment, pass through a redistribution stage in which their leaders' prestige is based on the amount they can give away. It follows, he says, that the earliest crops were grown as luxuries to be redistributed, not as staples needed for survival. Recently he suggested that in southwest Asia, wheat and barley (which were certainly staples) were first domesticated in order to make beer for competitive feasts.[14] Hayden admits there's no archaeological evidence to support his ideas and, while his Social Prestige theory is interesting, many archaeologists remain unconvinced.

Another group of scholars believes that the invention of agriculture was an unintentional side-effect of the development of sedentism. Their Social Complexity theories suggest that as people became sedentary, the birth rate increased and communities began to grow. In the face of ever-larger populations, the old egalitarianism failed and more complex (and hierarchical) social systems replaced it. For a number of different reasons, leaders needed to control the food supply and food production was invented to help them do that. Charles Heiser, for example, suggests that people began planting crops as a way to appease the gods after wild plants had been harvested,[15] and that a similar situation might pertain to animal domestication. One of the best developed theories is Ofer Bar-Yosef's Levantine Primacy Theory. Bar-Yosef and his colleagues think that, in the Levant at least, agriculture arose in reaction to a series of mild fluctuations in the climate. During the wetter periods, foragers responded to the increased resources by settling down, and their populations increased. Drier periods caused stress as the sedentary foragers struggled to find enough food, and eventually they were forced into food production. As society became more complex and food production more entrenched, animal husbandry was added to the mix. Bar-Yosef writes that he has found archaeological evidence for this pattern of repeated periods of stress giving rise to new technologies, and that ethnographic studies support his conclusions.[16]

Co-evolution

Yet another set of recent theories is based on the premise that the domestication process was symbiotic or co-evolutionary. Co-evolution is commonly found in nature, where symbiotic organisms evolved together: one example is that certain plants and insects co-evolved so that the insects became specifically adapted to help cross-pollinate the plants. Co-evolution theorists believe that over long periods of time, as people and wild species interacted, the people evolved culturally into farmers while the plants and animals evolved genetically and morphologically into domestic species. This view was most notably set forth by David Rindos,[17] who proposed three stages of concurrent evolution of wild plant species and human behavior. The first stage, incidental domestication, appeared millions of years ago when early humans began gathering plants selectively. The second stage occurred when people and preadapted plants began to influence one another more directly – for example, in the earliest stages of cultivation. The third stage appeared with full-scale domestication, when people and plants could no longer survive without one another. Other scholars have proposed a similar scenario for animal domestication. Co-evolution presupposes that Darwinian selection, rather than conscious decisions, drove the process of domestication, pointing out that (as is the case with all radical change) people could hardly have imagined farming before it was invented. This is not a new idea – as a specialist in early agriculture writes: "I think Rindos is merely emphasizing the rather obvious point that an agricultural economy could not have been foreseen, let alone consciously and instantaneously created or invented, by one or a small group of prehistoric human beings"[18] – but before Rindos no one had addressed it so directly. Co-evolutionists understand that as early farmers took full control of food production, personal choices rather than natural selection began to guide the process, so their theories are applicable only to the earlier stages of the domestication process. None of this can be proved archaeologically, and there's a problem of timing: domestication, especially agriculture based on grains, was a very rapid development, while natural selection – by definition – is a very slow process.

Why did people invent agriculture?

It should be obvious by now that despite the many experts who have advanced theories, no entirely satisfactory answer to the question of *why* foragers became farmers has emerged. One problem is that all the theorists assume that (in some way at least) human behavior is predictable. But current research in a number of fields suggests that human behavior is almost the opposite, and that many human decisions are illogical and unexpected. Trying to explain why people responded to particular challenges – particularly when the challenges don't exist in the modern world, and can't be replicated and studied – is an extremely speculative business. The domestication of plants and animals, and the societal changes that appeared as a result, required a mixture of serendipity, necessity, and ingenuity, and that mixture varied from place to place. The only explanation that could encompass the entire world – Renfrew's suggestion that humans beings are simply preadapted for change[19] – begs the issue, although it may well be the truth.

And it's important to keep in mind that despite its astonishing success, the transition from foraging to farming was surprisingly uneven. In some regions life seems to have changed almost overnight, but in others there was a long period of slow adaptation. Some people appear to have embraced agriculture willingly, adding their own local domesticates to the agricultural assemblage. Others became agricultural only when they were colonized or conquered. Quite often, foragers adopted some aspects of Neolithic culture but rejected others, and a few groups of foragers simply refused to change and lived for millennia alongside the farming cultures until modern colonialism forced them to settle down.

In the end, there are more questions than answers when we discuss the Neolithic transition. Archaeologists don't know what caused people to abandon hunting and gathering – a cultural strategy that had worked for millions of years – and invent a radically different way of life. They haven't identified the first experiments in planting seeds or taming animals or making ceramic vessels. They haven't figured out why social inequality appeared, or why some cultures chose to mark it with megalithic architecture and others with elaborate burials. They can't reconstruct Neolithic gender-roles or religious beliefs or political systems with any degree of certainty.

Until the second half of the twentieth century most of the world's population was essentially Neolithic (although not, of course, prehistoric), and even today, millions of people live in small farming communities not all that different from the first sedentary villages. After all, the basic rhythms of agriculture haven't changed over the last 10,000 years: farmers prepare their fields; sow seeds or plant seedlings; fertilize, weed, and water the plants; harvest their crops and take them to market. If they raise animals they give them food and water, control their reproduction, and use their meat, milk, fleece, and skins. It's no wonder that Neolithic life seems so familiar to us. Archaeologists may not know why or how it began, but they all agree about the importance of the Neolithic transition. Without it, our modern world would not exist.

APPENDIX I

A note about the dates in this book

Archaeologists generally report dates in terms of the Christian calender, although increasingly the traditional abbreviations BC (before Christ) and AD (*anno Domini* or in the year of our Lord) are being replaced with culturally neutral terms: BCE (before the Common Era) and CE (Common Era). Many prehistorians prefer to use ya (years ago). Radiocarbon dates, on the other hand, are expressed in years before present (bp), and because "present" is always changing, radiocarbon scientists have established a convention to be used only for radiocarbon dates: they define "present" as 1950.

Unfortunately, many published radiocarbon dates – especially the older ones – have not been recalibrated based on the dendrochronological correction factors (see Chapter 1). This has created a confusing situation for everyone, and has led to such bewildering phrases as "2,500 radiocarbon years," and to a host of conflicting dates. A particular piece of Neolithic evidence, for example, may be variously dated to 10,500 bp, 10,550 ya, 8,550 BCE or c.8,000 BC. Many technical sources routinely explain whether they are using recalibrated dates, but popular books usually not, and the reader left wondering where the dates came from. Even when an author identifies his dates as uncalibrated or calibrated, it can be confusing. One common (but not universal) convention is to use bc/bce for radiocarbon dates and BC/BCE for their recalibrated equivalents, while another uses BC and BP for uncalibrated dates, and BC and CAL BP for calibrated dates. Unless the author explains this the reader will not understand. And when both calibrated and uncalibrated dates are used in a publication, it's particularly frustrating, because few readers can convert the dates in their heads.

With two exceptions, dates in this book are expressed in years ago, and they've been rounded up or down: for example, I've reported a published date of 9,325 BP, as about 9,300 years ago. I feel comfortable with this system for three reasons. First, as I mentioned in Chapter 1, published dates are rarely accurate to the year, the decade, or even the half-century. Second, it's often difficult to figure out if the dates mentioned in a publication are the result of tests run by more than one radiocarbon lab; and as I mentioned in Chapter 1, different labs consistently produce dates that are a little high or a little low. And third, some authors average the dates reported by radio-carbon testing while others don't. In the discussion of radiocarbon dating, however, I have left the dates in the more familiar BCE/CE format. I have also chosen not to convert the well-known nineteenth-century date for the creation of the earth, 4004 BC.

If you're interested in more precise figures, the primary sources listed in the bibliography are good places to look.

APPENDIX II
Geographical place names

The earliest experiments in agriculture took place in an area some scholars call the Fertile Crescent. Others refer to it as the Middle East or the Near East, while some prefer to use the names of ancient or modern political entities. Many prehistorians working in the area prefer to use regional designations like southwest Asia (roughly equivalent to Turkey, northern Syria, northern Iraq, and Iran) or the Levant (Lebanon, western Syria, Israel, the West Bank, and Jordan) pointing out that prehistoric cultures didn't recognize modern boundaries, and that some modern names can be seen as inflammatory. In this book I use both systems: for aspects of the Neolithic that were widely spread I use regional names, but when I talk about specific sites I use the modern political names.

The following is a list of the geographical designations found in this book:

Africa: the African continent

The Balkans: the peninsula north of Greece, including Albania, Bulgaria, Croatia, Bosnia, Romania, and Serbia

Central America: Guatemala, Belize, El Salvador, Honduras, Nicaragua, Costa Rica, and Panama

Central Asia: Afghanistan, Turkistan, Uzbekistan, Tadzhikistan, Kazakhstan, and Kirgizstan

Central Europe: the region from the Baltic Sea to the Alps, including Eastern Germany, Austria, Poland, Czechoslovakia, and northern Hungary

East Asia: China, Korea, and Japan

The Levant: Lebanon, western Syria, Israel, the West Bank, and Jordan

The Mediterranean: southern France, Italy, Cyprus, Sardinia, Malta, and the Iberian Peninsula

Mesoamerica: central and southern Mexico and the adjacent areas of central America

North America: the continental United States and Canada

Southeast Asia: Thailand, Myanmar, Laos, Vietnam, Cambodia, the Malaysian Peninsula and the Philippines

Southwest Asia: Turkey, northern Syria, northern Iraq, and Iran

Transcaucasia: the area between the Black Sea and the Caspian Sea, north Turkey, including Georgia, Azerbaijan, and Armenia

Western Europe: northern France, Germany, the British Isles, Benelux, and Switzerland

APPENDIX III
Sites mentioned in the text

Abu Hureyra   The cultivated and perhaps domesticated rye found at this site in the Euphrates River valley in northern Syria establishes it as the earliest known farming village in the world.

Agia Sophia   This Neolithic site in Greece is known for its rammed earth architecture.

ʿAin Ghazal   Located near Amman, Jordan, ʿAin Ghazal is one of the earliest farming villages in the Levant. It is best known for the discovery of two caches of large-scale twig and plaster statues which seem to have been publically displayed. If this is true, they may provide the earliest evidence we have for communal religion.

ʿAin Mallaha   This Natufian-period village in the Levant is located between the Galilean hills and Lake Hula. The pit-houses there had walls lined with stone slabs.

Alepotrypa Cave   Located in one of three spectacular caves at Diros, just south of Areopolis in Greece, the late Neolithic community at Alepotrypa was destroyed by an earthquake. The numerous remains of the victims make up one of the largest collections of Neolithic skeletons in the world.

Argissa-Magoula   A Neolithic site in Greece with early faunal remains of domesticated sheep which must have been imported from southwest Asia.

Balsas River Basin   The region in southern Mexico where farmers manipulated mutant teosinte and produced the first maize.

Banpo Ts'un   A village in Henan Province, China. The well-preserved architecture and many distinctive artifacts found at the site illustrate the complexity of Chinese Neolithic culture.

Beidha   This early Neolithic site near Petra in Jordan was surrounded by a terrace wall that may have served the same purpose as the monumental wall at Jericho.

Bouqras   An early Neolithic village in Syria where morphological changes in the faunal remains indicate that the domestication process was underway. The site is atypical because paintings decorate some of the walls.

Brześé Kujawski An early farming village northwest of Warsaw in Poland known for the remains of its trapezoidal longhouses and for its diverse substance strategy which included farming and hunting-gathering. The villagers hunted, fished, collected shellfish, and probably gathered wild plants, and at the same time, raised emmer wheat, cattle, sheep, goats, and pigs.

Cafer Höyük A village in southeastern Turkey known for skull-removal and beautiful stone bowls. It was also an important transit site in the obsidian trade. Villagers at Cafer Höyük had cultivated, but not fully domesticated, einkorn wheat.

Cahokia This Mississippian culture site in Ohio is located near the junction of the Mississippi, Missouri and Illinois Rivers. It includes over 120 mounds, including a rammed earth monument that is the largest prehistoric structure in the United States.

Çatalhöyük An extraordinary Neolithic site with a unique architectural plan located on the Anatolian plateau in Turkey near the modern city of Konya. It has produced the richest collection of Neolithic art in the world.

Çayönü Farmers in this village on a tributary of the Tigris River in southeastern Turkey cultivated einkorn wheat and may have domesticated it. The site is best known for a red terrazzo floor inset with two pairs of parallel white terrazzo lines and a "skull building" in which dozens of bones and skulls were stored.

Dawenkou This type site for the eastern Yellow River Valley Dawenkou culture in China is known for its elaborate grave goods that point to the presence of social hierarchy.

Dhali Agridhi A site in southern Cyprus where the remains of morphologically domesticated grapes have been found.

Dölauer-Heide A fortified late Neolithic complex in central Germany surrounded by a series of ditches and banks.

Dolní Věstonice A Paleolithic site in the Czech Republic where the first known experiments in intentional firing of clay objects took place.

Ertebølle The first pottery-producing culture in Scandinavia, it was located mainly in Denmark.

Ganj Dareh A Neolithic village in western Iran that has produced the earliest known remains of domesticated goats.

Göbekli Tepe An early Neolithic site in the Urfa region of southeastern Turkey with particularly interesting ritual sculpture.

Gritille An early Neolithic village on the Euphrates River in southeastern Turkey that has produced a series of interesting figurines.

Guilá Naquitz A Mexican site in the Valley of Oaxaca with important botanical remains. Early in the site's history, the people domesticated a single crop (squash) rather than the typical assemblage of plants; and in later levels, archaeologists have found the earliest known corn cobs.

Hacilar A late Neolithic site in southern Turkey which has produced examples of Neolithic art second only to those from Çatalhöyük.

Hajji Firuz Tepe A site in Iran with the earliest known evidence for wine production.

Hallan Çemi One of the earliest Neolithic villages in southeastern Turkey, the site is known for unusual architecture (including pisé platforms) and for fine stone bowls.

Hemudu At this extraordinarily well-preserved site near the Yangtze River in Zhenjiang Province, China, the remains included wooden architecture, lacquer artifacts, and evidence of very early rice cultivation.

Höyücek A village in southwestern Turkey with cultural remains similar to those found at Hacilar.

Jarmo An early farming village in Iraqi Kurdistan that was excavated by Braidwood in an attempt to validate his Natural Habitat theory of domestication.

Jericho A site on the west bank of the Jordan River that has been occupied continually since the Neolithic period. Archaeologically, Jericho is best known for its monumental city wall and articulating tower.

Jiahu Wine residues were found in vessels from this Neolithic site in Henan Province, China.

Kaido A Middle Jōmon site in central Honshu.

Kalavassos-Tenta An early Neolithic village in the Vasilikos Valley in southern Cyprus. The round mudbrick structures at the site include a large building that has been variously interpreted as the house of a headman or as a shrine.

Karanovo A farming village with wattle and daub architecture located in central Bulgaria.

Kfar HaHoresh A mortuary complex in the lower Galilee that seems to have been a regional collection center for burials.

Khirokitia A village of stone, mudbrick and pisé beehive-shaped houses in southern Cyprus known for its fine ground stone artifacts. The villagers there may have experimented with pottery and then rejected it.

Köşk Höyük A Neolithic site near Niğde in central Turkey where evidence of skull removal has been found.

Kuk A site in highland New Guinea where taro may have been independently domesticated. Bananas were also an early domesticate here.

Linearbandkeramik Pioneers from this culture in central and western Europe, named for its distinctive ceramic decoration, facilitated the rapid diffusion of ceramic technology across the continent. Linearbandkeramik sites are characterized by timber longhouses with wattle and daub walls.

Mehrgarh A village site in northeastern Pakistan. During the Neolithic period, farmers at the site seem to have independently domesticated zebu cattle along with sheep.

Moundville   A site in Alabama noted for its elaborate funerary customs based on social hierarchy.

Nahal Hemar   A Neolithic site in the Judean desert near the Dead Sea. Archaeologists have found netted flax, some interwoven with human hair, at the site, as well as fragments of large plaster statues like those from 'Ain Ghazal in Jordan.

Nea Nikomedeia   This site in Macedonian Greece is one of the earliest known farming settlements in Europe. The only Early Neolithic village in Greece to have been extensively excavated, it was once described as fortified, but recent interpretations suggest that the features were for water control not defense.

Neveli Çori   A village in southeastern Turkey with domesticated einkorn wheat, known for its ritual building containing skull burials.

Ohalo II   This well-preserved Upper Paleolithic site near the Sea of Galilee has produced a flood of ecofacts, leading excavators to believe that it was occupied year-round.

Ozette   The excellent preservation at this northwest American Makah culture site, located in the Olympic Peninsula of Washington State, is the result of a landslide.

Parţa   A Neolithic site in Romania where the differing funerary customs for men and women may reflect gender status.

Poverty Point   This Late Archaic ceremonial site and trading center in northeastern Louisiana is known for some of the largest rammed earthworks in the Americas.

Ramat Harif   The type-site of the pre-Neolithic Harifian culture in the Negev Desert, this village has some good examples of early pit-houses.

Robenhausen   The location of one of the Neolithic Swiss lake villages, famous for their extraordinary preservation of wood, textiles, and plant material (including opium poppy capsules and seeds).

Roiax   A Neolithic mass grave in the south of France which may be evidence for the presence of warfare.

Sha'ar Hagolan   A Yarmulkian culture settlement in the Jordan Valley south of the Sea of Galilee where archaeologists have found both free-standing and relief sculpture.

Shomu-Tepe   The remains of morphologically domestic grapes have been found at this Neolithic site in Azerbaijan.

Shulaveri-Somutepe-Group culture   The people of this Neolithic culture in the Republic of Georgia built complex houses with semi-domes added to circular domed structures and rectangular additions added to semi-circular flat-roofed structures.

Shulaveris-Gora   A Neolithic site in the Republic of Georgia where archaeologists have found morphologically domestic grapes and wine residues in jars.

Snaketown   This Hohokam village located by the Gila River near Phoenix, Arizona has well-preserved wattle and daub architecture.

St Kilda Island   The feral Soay sheep found on this island in the Hebrides were imported during the Scottish Neolithic.

Stonehenge   One of the most famous Neolithic monuments in the world, this circular megalithic structure on Salisbury Plain in Wiltshire was probably both a sacred site and an astronomical calculator.

Talheim   This site in the Neckar valley in Germany is noted for a pit holding over 30 people, some shot in the back of the head.

Tell Ramad   This village in the Damascus basin in Syria is known for White Ware vessels, red-plastered house walls, and plastered skulls.

Tell Sabi Abayad II   A Neolithic site in Syria where the presence of fifty-six large obsidian blades struck from the same core and then fitted together may point to down-the-line trading.

Varna   A burial ground in Bulgaria near the Black Sea, this site produced rich graves attesting to the presence of a wealthy social elite.

Wadi Raba culture   A culture in the southern Levant that produced, among other finds, a unique jar with a relief sculpture of a man wearing an animal headdress.

Watson Brake   A site in Louisiana noted for its rammed earth architecture.

Zawi Chemi Shanidar   A small site in the Zagros Mountains of north-eastern Iraq where archaeologists have found early remains of domesticated sheep (the identification is based on demographics rather than morphology).

GLOSSARY

Absolute date   A date expressed in terms of a calendrical system. Archaeologists use the western (Christian) calendar, although radiocarbon dates are expressed as BP (before present) with "present" defined as CE 1950.

Aceramic Neolithic   The Neolithic period before the invention of pottery.

Achieved status   Social ranking or prestige based on individual decisions or actions. If you graduate from college you gain status, which is the result of your own talents and efforts, so that status is achieved.

Adaptive trait/adaptive strategy   Any biological or behavioral trait or behavior that increases a species' chance of survival. Shattering is an adaptive trait in wild grains.

Agglomerate architecture   A plan in which buildings are connected by party walls. A modern townhouse complex is an agglomerate structure.

Aggression or territorialism   Because they're unwilling to share their living quarters with other species, including humans, aggressive or territorial animals are almost impossible to control. Zebras are aggressive and often territorial, which is why they've never been domesticated.

Agriculture   The practice of producing food by raising domesticated plants and animals. Agriculture was invented in the Neolithic period.

Amino acid   Amino acids are the building blocks of protein in the human body. Animal protein contains all the amino acids that people need, but plants are usually missing one or two. When cereals and legumes are eaten together they provide the needed amino acids.

AMS (accelerator mass spectrometry)   A method of radiocarbon dating that allows the testing of very small samples such as single pollen grains.

Ancestor cult   A religious system centered on a community's ancestors. Ancestor cults are communal, and not all are the same. In some, the ancestors are deified and worshiped, in others the ancestors aren't gods, but they're venerated and asked for advice.

Animal husbandry   The term used for raising and breeding animals.

Anthropological culture   In Anthropology, culture is defined as learned behavior that is passed down from generation to generation, resulting in shared beliefs, values and ways of doing things.

183

Anthropology   The academic discipline that studies human biology, evolution, and culture. In the United States, archaeology is sometimes considered to be a branch of anthropology.

Archaeobotany   The study of plant remains (such as pollen, seeds, and stalks) found in archeological contexts.

Archaeological culture   A group of artifacts, features, and structures common to a group of sites. In other words, the physical signs of shared beliefs, values, and behaviors.

Archaeology   The academic discipline that studies the past 2.5 million years by excavating and analyzing material remains.

Archaeometallurgury   The study of metal artifacts (such as beads, cups, and axe-heads) found in archaeological contexts.

Archaeozoology   The study of animal remains (such as bones, teeth, and dung) found in archaeological contexts.

Arcikjowski, A.W.   A Russian archaeologist who, in the late 1940s, proposed that animal demographics could be used to distinguish among subsistence strategics on archaeological sites. He theorized that the slaughtered animals on hunter-gatherer sites would differ demographically from those on agricultural sites, and that flocks raised for meat could be differentiated from those raised for milk or for wool.

Arnold, J.R.   An American physicist who, along with W.F. Libby, invented the first scientific absolute dating technique – radiocarbon dating. Their research was first published in 1949.

Art   A form of symbolic communication. Before the modern period, artists transmitted specific cultural messages through their art.

Artifact   Any portable object found in an archaeological context that was made or modified and used by people. A pottery jar is an artifact.

Artificial selection   The process of selecting and encouraging certain characteristics in plants and animals so they are more useful to people. Also known as selective breeding.

Ascribed status   The social status or prestige that comes to you as a result of your birth. Your age, sex, and position within your family are ascribed.

Aurochs (pl. aurochsen)   The extinct wild ox (*Bos primigenius*) that is the ancestor of all western breeds of cattle.

Balanced reciprocity   An exchange of goods or services that have roughly the same value, as determined by the leaders of the community. Balanced reciprocity is commonly found in tribes.

Band   The social organization of hunter-gatherers. Bands usually have fewer than 100 members, all of whom are related, and leadership is part-time and based on ability rather than age or sex.

Bar-Yosef, O.   Israeli archaeologist who developed a Social Complexity hypothesis for the Levant. He suggests that agriculture arose in reaction to a series of mild fluctuations in the climate that forced the hunter-gatherer populations into food production. As society became more complex and food production more entrenched, animal husbandry was added to the mix.

Barley (*Hordeum vulgare*) An annual, self-pollinating, flowering grass that originated in southwest Asia and was an early domesticate.

Belyaev, D.K. A Russian geneticist whose mid-twentieth-century breeding experiments with red foxes provided a model for the development of neotony in early domesticated animals.

Binford, L. An American archaeologist who was the first to propose a Population Pressure theory about the origins of agriculture. This theory, formulated in the late 1960s and 1970s, was the first discussion of the Neolithic transition not specific to southwest Asia.

Binomial nomenclature The use of two Latin taxonomical categories (genus and species) to identify all living things. Barley is known scientifically as *Hordeum vulgare*, and sheep are known as *Ovis aries*.

Biomechanical stress Physical stress to the body caused by repeated mechanical actions. Biomechanical stress is most obvious in joints and bones, and a common result of biomechanical stress is osteoarthritis.

Bitter vetch (*Vicia ervilia*) One of the four southwest Asian founder legumes, today it's grown mainly as an animal feed.

Bitumen A naturally occurring tar sometimes referred to as natural asphalt. Bitumen was used by Neolithic cultures in southwest Asia to waterproof containers and to emphasize facial features in sculpture.

Braidwood, R. An American archaeologist whose excavations in the 1950s led him to develop his Natural-Habitat or Nuclear Zones Theory in which he suggested that the earliest domestication occurred in regions where abundant resources allowed foragers to develop sedentism and then agriculture.

Breed A group of domestic animals that has been created by people through artificial breeding.

Burnish Some Neolithic potters burnished the surface of their vessels by rubbing the leather-hard clay with a stone, stick, bone, or cloth. Burnishing aligns the clay particles and makes the surface hard and glossy.

Caprovines Because the skeletons of sheep and goats are almost identical sometimes the two species are lumped together as caprovines.

Cereal Annual flowering grasses grown for their kernels or grains, cereals provide most of the calories in the human diet.

Chaff The husks and stalks of cereals that are separated from the kernels by threshing.

Chickpea (*Cicer arietinum*) One of the southwest Asian founder crops, chickpea is a legume. Its importance in the Classical world is reflected in the prestigious Roman surname Cicero.

Chiefdom A socio-political system with a hereditary leader (the chief) who makes and enforces decisions for the community.

Childe, V.G. A British archaeologist who in 1928 proposed the Oasis Theory, the first formal hypothesis about the rise of domestication.

Chipped stone tool A chipped stone tool is made by removing flakes from a piece of raw material, or core.

Chloroplast DNA/ctDNA A type of DNA found in plants, ctDNA is inherited only through the maternal line.

Co-evolution Co-evolution is a symbiotic process during which two or more organisms evolve together. Some plants and insects co-evolved so that the insects became specifically adapted to help cross-pollinate the plants.

Cohen, M. An American archaeologist whose late 1970s Marginal Zone/ Edge Zone theory, based on his research in Peru, proposed that although the inhabitants of marginal zones had enough to eat, the food wasn't palatable, so they imported species and became farmers.

Conchoidal The fracture pattern found in flint and obsidian. Conchoidal fractures form shapes resembling sea shells.

Coprolites Fossilized or dried feces. Analysis of human coprolites gives archaeologists information about diet and disease.

Core The piece of raw material used by stone tool-makers.

Core tool A chipped stone tool made by shaping the core.

Cremation A funerary custom in which the body is burnt and then the bones and ashes are buried.

Crick, F. An English scientist who, along with James Watson, suggested a model for the structure and function of DNA and was awarded the 1962 Nobel Prize for Medicine.

Cross-pollination Many plants combine genetic material by cross-pollination in which the pollen is carried from one plant to the next by the wind, insects, and animals.

Cultivation The long process of people–plant interactions that results in fully domestic crops.

Darwin, C. A British naturalist whose 1858 publication on his theory of evolution through the mechanism of natural selection laid the foundation for modern scientific research into biological diversity.

Dendrochronology An absolute dating system based on tree rings. Annual alterations in climate cause trees to lay down growth rings that vary from year to year. Dendrochronology compares the growth rings of wood found in archaeological contexts with a master sequence and pinpoints the year the tree was cut down or died.

Diffusion Ideas that are spread from one culture to another are referred to as diffused. Diffusion can take place through trade, the movement of people, or conquest.

Dispersed architecture Dispersed architecture consists of free-standing buildings.

DNA (deoxyribonucleic acid) The material in cells that carries the genetic code or instructions for all living organisms.

Domestication The use of artificial selection to change both the genetic and the morphological (physical) characteristics of plants and animals so that they will be more useful to people. The domestication process results in new species of plants and animals, some of which can no longer survive without human help.

Domestication process The long continuum of interactions between people and plants and animals, which begins with cultivation and taming, and ends with full domestication.

Dominance hierarchy A behavioral patterns seen in some animals in which the members of the group follow a dominant leader. Dominance hierarchy is one factor in successful domestication.

Down-the-line trading A trading pattern in which goods move from one location to another through successive exchanges.

Ecofacts Non-artifactural plant and animal remains (such as burned wood in a hearth) found in archaeological contexts.

Einkorn wheat (*Triticum turgidum*) One of the two southwest Asian founder cereals, einkorn is an ancestor of modern bread wheat.

Emmer wheat (*Triticum monococcum*) One of the two southwest Asian founder cereals. A variety of emmer called durum wheat is still used to make pasta.

Endemic diseases Diseases that are chronic and constantly present in a population. Endemic diseases rarely kill their hosts.

Endogamy The social practice of marrying members of the same social or kinship category. Endogamous marriages help maintain cultural stability.

Epidemic diseases Diseases that suddenly appear and spread rapidly through a population. Usually, epidemics kill the available hosts and then disappear.

Ethnographic analogy Because they assume that human behavior in the past was the same as it is today, archaeologists working on prehistoric sites turn to ethnographic studies to help them interpret the function of the artifacts, features, and structures they find. That is, they make use of ethnographic analogy.

Ethnography The study of specific human groups through participant observation. Ethnographers live with the people they study, and describe all aspects of the culture.

Evolution The process by which living organisms change and diversity is created. According to Darwin, evolution is caused by natural selection, a process during which individuals better adapted to the environment survive and pass on their genes, while those not as well adapted do not. Evolution is a long process, populations (not individuals) evolve, and what is adaptive is determined by nature.

Exogamy   The social practice of marrying people from different social or kinship categories. Exogamous marriages cement ties between communities and are often used for political gain.

Fabric   The technical term for fired clay.

Faunal remains   Bones, teeth, horns, and antlers found in archaeological contexts.

Feature   Immovable objects found in an archaeological context that were made or modified and used by people. A hearth is an example of a feature.

Fetish   An amulet that contains magical power. A rabbit's foot is a good-luck fetish.

Flake tool   A chipped stone tool made from flakes struck from a core.

Flannery, K.   An American archaeologist whose Marginal Zone/Edge Zone Theory, formulated in the 1970s and based on his research in Mesoamerica, suggested that agriculture originated when some foraging groups were forced into less fertile areas where they had to produce food in order to survive.

Flax (*Linum usitatissimum*)   A southwest Asian founder crop grown for its oil (linseed oil) and as a source of fiber.

Flint/Chert   Flint is a glassy hard sedimentary rock found in limestone and chalk beds. Technically, flint is a type of chert, and the two words are sometimes used interchangeably.

Food production   The end result of domestication. Technically, food production is reached when a culture produces more than 50 percent of its food.

Foragers   People who have no permanent settlements, and move throughout the year. Foragers rely on wild plants and animals for survival.

Founder population   The domesticated plants and animals in an area of primary domestication are called founder populations, because they were the foundation of early agriculture.

Free-standing sculpture   Sculpture that is not attached to a background. Free-standing sculptures are designed to be seen from more than one angle.

Gender   Gender (unlike sex, which is determined by biology) is an artificial category, set by society.

Gender roles   The different behaviors that a culture assigns to men and women.

Gene pool   All of the genes available to a population make up its gene pool. Through natural selection, gene pools are slowly changed over time.

General reciprocity   An informal exchange of goods or services without expecting an equal return. General reciprocity is commonly found within families.

Genus   The first of the two taxonomical categories referred to in binomial nomenclature. A genus is composed of a group of species that belong to the same family or subfamily, and resemble one another more than they do other members of the family.

Glycemic index   A measure of the amount of glucose found in the blood.

Grain   The word grain is sometimes used interchangeably with the word cereal (annual flowering grasses grown for their kernels) and sometimes interchangeably with the word kernel (the fruit of cereals).

Grave goods   Many funerary customs involve artifacts that are left in the grave with the body. Grave goods often indicate the social rank of the deceased.

Graves, R.   A British Classicist whose mid-twentieth-century work in comparative religions led to the idea that all prehistoric people worshiped a mother Goddess (the Great Goddess) who was displaced by later male deities.

Gregariousness   Gregarious animals live in groups and exist comfortably in tight quarters.

Ground stone tools   Ground stone tools are a cultural marker of the Neolithic. They're made by pecking and grinding, and then polishing and grinding dense igneous rocks like basalt and granite. Ground stone tools are useful for felling trees and hoeing heavy soils.

Half-life   The amount of time it takes half of the radioactive isotopes in a sample to decay. The half-life of ^{14}C is roughly 5730 years.

Harris Lines   Dark lines caused by nutritional stress that form across long bones when their linear growth is interrupted.

Hawkins, G.   An English astronomer who in 1965 suggested that the main function of Stonehenge was astronomical.

Hayden, Brian   An American archaeologist who is the main Social Prestige theorist. He believes that food production arose in reaction to rivalries among leaders who wanted to amass food and then gain status by giving it away at competitive feasts.

Heiser, Charles   An American archaeologist and Social Complexity theorist who suggested that domestication originated in religious rituals.

Hillman, G.C.   One of the directors of the Abu Hureyra rescue project.

Holocene   The current geological epoch, the Holocene began about 11,500 years ago when a rise in world temperatures caused the glaciers covering much of the northern hemisphere to retreat.

Hughes, D.   A British astronomer who in 2005 supported Hawkins' theory that Stonehenge had an astronomical function, although he disagrees about what that function actually was.

Hunter-gatherer   Another term for forager.

Hypoplasias   Visible lines and pits of thinner enamel on the tooth surface caused by nutritional stress or disease.

Iconography   The content or subject of a work of art. Iconography refers to what a work means, not what it looks like.

Independent invention   Ideas or technologies that arise within a culture without any outside influence are said to be independently invented.

Inhumation   A funerary custom involving the burial of bodies or cremated remains.

Kemps   The hairs in the stiff outer coats of sheep and goats.

Kenyon, K.   A British archaeologist who excavated the Neolithic levels at Jericho in the early 1950s, and discovered the fieldstone wall and articulating tower for which the site is famous.

Kernel   The fruit of cereals.

Kiln   An oven designed for firing pottery.

Kinship systems   The definition and organization of kin groups in a culture.

!Kung San   The popular name for the Paleolithic "bushmen" who live in the Kalahari Desert in southern Africa. The most heavily studied of any prehistoric people, most of the !Kung no longer follow their ancestral traditions – except for the tourists.

Lamarck, J.-B.   A nineteenth-century French naturalist who proposed the Theory of Acquired Characteristics which stated that when natural conditions forced animals to adjust the way they used various muscles, their bodies would change physically in response, and the physical changes would then be passed on to their offspring.

Legge, A.J.   One of the directors of the Abu Hureyra rescue project.

Legume   An annual plant grown for its seeds and pods. Some legumes, like snow peas, are eaten pods and all, and others, like green beans, are shelled.

Lentil (*Lens culinaris*)   One of the four legumes that are southeast Asian founder crops. The importance of lentils is reflected in the prestigious Roman surname Lentulus.

Libby, W.F.   An American physicist who, along with J.R. Arnold, invented the first scientific absolute dating technique – radiocarbon dating. Their research was first published in 1949, and Libby was awarded the 1961 Nobel Prize in Physics for it.

Linnaeus, C.   An eighteenth-century Swedish botanist who invented the first biological classification system or taxonomy. Linnaeus' categories form the basis for modern taxonomies.

Lubbock, J.   A nineteenth-century English nobleman who subdivided the Stone Age into two phases: the Paleolithic when only chipped stone tools were made; and the Neolithic during which ground stone tools were invented.

Magoula, *tepe*, *tel*, and *höyük*   Terms used for settlement mounds found from Greece to Iran. *Magoula* is a Greek term, *tepe* and *höyük* come from Turkish, and *tel* (sometimes spelled *tell*) comes from Arabic.

Maize (*Zea mays mays*)   An annual grass grown for its seeds. Maize (called "corn" in North America) is the most important New World cereal.

Maladaptive trait   Any biological or behavioral trait that decreases the chance of survival. A tough rachis is a maladaptive trait in wild grains.

Marginal Zone/Edge Zone or Population Pressure theories   Theories proposing demographic changes as the cause of the Neolithic transition.

Material remains   The physical remains studied by archaeologists. Artifacts, ecofacts, features, and structures are all material remains.

Megalith   Literally, large stone. In the European Neolithic, some cultures created megalithic monuments.

Mellaart, J.   A British archaeologist who discovered the site of Çatalhöyük in 1958 and oversaw the first excavations there in the early 1960s.

Mendel, G.   A mid-nineteenth-century Moravian monk and botanist who developed the explanation of the biological inheritance of traits.

Middleman trading   A trading pattern in which a salesmen (or middleman) travels from village to village, trading his products at each location.

Mitochondrial DNA/mtDNA   A type of DNA found in mitochondria located in the nuclei of cells, mtDNA is inherited only through the maternal line.

Mixed farming   Farming that includes both raising crops and breeding animals.

Monumental architecture   Buildings that are larger than the typical structures on a site are referred to as monumental.

Moore, A.M.T.   One of the directors of the Abu Hureyra rescue project.

Morse, E.   An American archaeologist who first identified the Jōmon culture in the late nineteenth century when he explored the Ōmori shell mound near Tokyo.

Naked seeds   Seeds that have evolved without hulls. A naturally occurring mutation resulted in naked barley, which is much easier to thresh than hulled varieties.

Natufian   A culture in the southern Levant that immediately preceded the first Neolithic settlements.

Natural-Habitat or Nuclear Zones Theory   Robert Braidwood's theory which posits that agriculture developed in areas where the natural habitats of several domesticable species overlapped.

Natural selection   According to Darwin, biological diversity is the result of natural selection, a process during which individuals better adapted to the environment survive and pass on their genes, while those not as well adapted do not.

Neolithic   The "New Stone Age." A cultural stage that first appeared about 12,000 years ago. Neolithic people are farmers and herders, live in settled communities, and rely on domesticated plants and animals for their survival.

Neolithic Revolution   A term coined in the early twentieth century for the change in human subsistence strategies from foraging to food production.

Neolithic transition   The term used in this book for the Neolithic Revolution.

Neotony   The retention of fetal or juvenile features in adult domestic animals.

Oasis Theory   In the first serious attempt to explain the reasons for the Neolithic transition, V. Gordon Childe posited that the end of the Holocene brought drought to Mesopotamia, which forced people, plants, and animals to congregate in river valleys and oases, and caused the invention of agriculture.

Obsidian   Volcanic glass formed during volcanic eruptions. During the Neolithic obsidian was the preferred material for fine chipped stone tools in southern Europe and southwest Asia.

Onager (*Equus hemionus*)   The Syrian onager (*E. hemionus hemippus*), now extinct, was an important food source in prehistory.

Ötzi   The "Iceman." A Neolithic European whose body was preserved in the Austrian Alps for over 5,000 years.

Paleolithic   The "Old Stone Age." A cultural stage that began about 2.6 million years ago when the first recognizable human ancestors began to use stone tools. It ends with the advent of the Neolithic period.

Paleopathology   The study of human remains found in archaeological contexts.

Pea (*Pisum sativum*)   One of the four southwest Asian founder legumes. Its importance in the Classical world is reflected in the prestigious Roman surname Piso.

Phytoliths   Microscopic silica structures that line the stalks and stems of some grasses and give them stability.

Pisé   Rammed earth walls made by tamping a mixture of sand, loam, clay, and other ingredients into forms.

Post-and-lintel construction   A construction technique in which upright posts support the horizontal elements. A rectangular doorway is a good example of a post-and-lintel structure.

Postmortem skull removal   A funerary custom in which the skull is removed and displayed or buried separately from the body.

Preadaptation   Some plants and animals have characteristics that make them preadapted to domestication. Gregariousness and dominance-hierarchy systems are preadaptive traits in animals.

Prehistory   The period before the invention of writing. Human prehistory began over two million years ago, and until about 5,000 years ago, when the first formal writing systems appeared in Mesopotamia and Egypt, every culture on earth was prehistoric.

Primary area of domestication   Areas in which domestication was independently invented.

Primary burial   A funerary custom in which the body is buried intact.

Rachis   The stem or plant umbilicus that attaches the seeds or spikelets to the stalk and through which nutrients pass.

Radiocarbon dating/Carbon-14 or ^{14}C dating   An absolute dating method that measures the decay of a radioactive isotope of carbon (^{14}C or carbon-14) in organic remains.

Redistribution system   A pattern of economic exchange in which a central authority collects goods and then reallocates them to members of the community.

Relief sculpture   Relief sculptures are attached to a background, and can only be seen from the front. The head on a coin is in relief.

Religion   Beliefs and rituals designed to contact supernatural beings or powers.

Rindos, D.   An American archaeologist and famous proponent of co-evolution as the cause of the Neolithic transition.

Ritual   Repeated formalized actions and words that are intended to influence supernatural forces. A mass is a religious ritual.

Sacred emblem   An image that identifies membership in a religious group. A Star of David is a sacred emblem.

Secondary area of domestication   An area where people learned about domestication through diffusion, and then applied that knowledge to the domestication of local plants and animals.

Secondary burial   A funerary custom in which the bones are stripped of their flesh (usually through natural decay), stored until they're clean and dry, and then buried.

Selective breeding   The process of selecting and encouraging certain characteristics in plants and animals so they become more useful to people. Also known as artificial selection.

Self-pollination   In self-pollinating species, the pollen and ovule are from the same plant. Self-pollinating plants make good crops, because they breed true (the characteristics are unchanging in generation after generation).

Sexual dimorphism   The physical differences between males and females of a species. Human dimorphism is seen in the differently shaped pelvises of men and women.

Shaman   A part-time religious specialist who contacts the supernatural on behalf of his community. Shamans are typically found in bands and tribes.

Shattering   Plants that shatter have rachises that become extremely brittle as the seeds mature, allowing the ripe seeds to fall off at the slightest touch. An adaptive trait in wild plants, shattering is maladaptive in crops.

Sherd   A piece of broken pottery.

Shuttle   Weavers wind their weft thread onto shuttles, and use them to help pass it back and forth across the warp threads.

Sickle sheen   A high gloss on a chipped stone tool that looks like a layer of clear nail polish.

Site   A site is any place where there is physical evidence of human activity. A stream is a stream, but a stream with a swimmer in it is a site.

Slip   A dilute solution of clay and water used to prepare the surface of ceramic vessels before they're fired.

Social Complexity theories   A series of theories that suggest that the Neolithic transition took place when foragers settled down and developed complex and hierarchical social systems, and the new leaders needed to control the food supply.

Social hierarchy   A system for organizing a society based on prestige, which may be the result of birth, wealth, or power.

Social Prestige theories   Social Prestige theories assume that sedentism inevitably leads to social inequality and affluence, and that when acquiring and redistributing wealth becomes important, agriculture is invented as a way to create and control food surpluses.

Social ranking   A hierarchical system that identifies the level of prestige of all members of the community.

Social system   The sum of all of a culture's social categories. Prehistoric peoples at roughly the same level of economic and political development usually have parallel social systems.

Species   The second of the two taxonomical categories referred to in binomial nomenclature. The members of a species can interbreed and produce viable offspring.

Spikelet   A small group of grass flowers that ripens into a seed cluster on an ear.

Stone-knapping   The process of making chipped stone tools.

Strata   Sequential layers of deposit in an archaeological context.

Stratigraphic dating   A relative dating method based on the fact that the older strata on a site lie beneath the younger strata. In stratigraphic dating, material remains are recorded according to their stratigraphic position, and described in relation to one another as "older than" and "younger than."

Structures   Buildings found in archaeological contexts.

Taming   Taming refers to the long process of people–animal interactions that resulted in fully domestic animals.

Taxonomy   A classification system in which the categories move from the broadest to the most specific. Developed by Linnaeus.

Temper   Material that is added to clay to reduce shrinking and cracking during the drying process. In the Neolithic, temper was first used in mudbrick architecture and was later adopted by potters.

Teosinte (*Zea mays parviglumis*)   An annual wild grass native to southern and western Mexico, teosinte is the wild progenitor of modern maize.

Theory of Acquired Characteristics   Developed in the nineteenth century by Lamarck to explain biological diversity, the theory incorrectly assumed that physical changes developed during an animal's lifetime could be inherited by its offspring.

Tool   Any object that has been altered to make it useful: a stick becomes a tool if someone whittles one end to a point in order to bore a hole.

Totem   An image that identifies membership in a social, political, or religious group. A college seal on a sweatshirt is a totem.

Tournette   A piece of wood or a mat that potters use to slowly rotate a vessel as they construct it.

Transhumance   The practice of moving flocks seasonally, from low pastures in the winter to higher pastures in the summer.

Tribe   Tribes include several extended family groups or clans, and tribal leaders (always men) gain their positions through power and prestige.

Vavilov, N.   A Soviet biologist and plant geneticist. In the 1930s he identified many of the habitats of the wild ancestors of modern domesticates, and suggested that agriculture arose in areas where several of the habitats overlapped.

War   War is socially sanctioned group violence designed to protect or increase resources.

Warp threads   The threads in a woven piece of cloth that run parallel to the edges.

Watson, J.   An American scientist who, with Francis Crick, suggested a model for the structure and function of DNA, and was awarded the 1962 Nobel Prize for Medicine.

Wattle and daub   A construction technique in which walls are made of a series of poles (wattles) interwoven with twigs and branches and then plastered with clay and straw (daub).

Weft threads   The threads in woven cloth that run at right angles to the edges.

Wheat (Triticum)   An annual, self-pollinating, flowering grass with considerably more protein than any other cereal. Two varieties – emmer wheat and einkorn wheat – were among the founder crops in southwest Asia.

NOTES

PREFACE

1 1956: 9.
2 1959: 9f.

1 INTRODUCTION TO THE NEOLITHIC

1 For a more complete discussion see Zohary and Hopf 2000: 4ff.
2 Dickson *et al.* 2005: 4ff.
3 Perlès 2001: 90.
4 Dendrochronology is more complicated than my description suggests. For technical information, along with links to various projects' web sites, check the web site for the World Data Center for Paleoclimatology. A particularly good source for the non-specialist is the Aegean Dendrochronology Project at Cornell University.
5 Keller 1878a: 3ff.
6 Whittle 1996: 217.
7 Whittle 1996: 215f.
8 Heer 1878: 518ff.
9 Zohary and Hopf 2000: 232f.
10 Barber 1991: 13, 95.
11 Heer 1878: 523, 531. Zohary and Hopf report that they represent the cultivated or domesticated species (2000: 232f.).
12 Zohary and Hopf 2000: 135ff.; Merlin 1984: 89ff.

2 THE GENETICS OF DOMESTICATION

1 Sproul 1979: various.
2 Smith, B. 1998: 1651f.
3 Weier *et al.* 1982: 358.
4 Avery *et al.* 1944.
5 Watson and Crick 1953a; 1953b.
6 Zohary and Hopf 2000: 166.
7 Malthus first published his theories anonymously in 1798. A more developed version – An *Essay on the Principle of Population or, A View of its Past and Present Effects on Human Happiness: with an Inquiry into our Prospects Respecting the Future Removal or Mitigation of the Evils which it Occasions* – was produced under his name in 1803 and further revisions appeared in 1806, 1807, 1817 and 1826. A good recent edition was published in 1992.

8 Lewin and Foley 2004: 28.
9 Majerus 1998: 116ff.

3 ARCHAEOLOGICAL EVIDENCE FOR DOMESTICATION

1 Smith, B. 1997: 932ff.
2 A good summary of the argument is found in Bellwood 2005: 142ff. For more detailed information, see Denham *et al.* 2003: 189ff.; and Neumann 2003: 180f.
3 Cowan and Watson 1992: 2.
4 For more information, see Smith, B. 1995: 5f.
5 Zohary 1984: 582. For a summary of the process of genetic analysis of plants see Hilu 1987: 68ff.
6 Heum *et al.* 1997: 1312ff.
7 For an overview of this issue see Clutton-Brock 1999: 211ff.
8 Kislev *et al.* 2006: 1372ff.
9 Smith, B. 1995: 30f. provides a good description of an ideal site.
10 Rosen *et al.* 2005: 2.
11 Davis 1987: 24ff.
12 For an overview of the preservation of animal remains see Davis 1987: 33ff.; and a technical description differentiating lambs' and kids' teeth is found in Payne 1985: 139ff.
13 For information on Kurdish pastoralists, see Davis 1987: 39. The Turkish village statistics are reported in Payne 1973: 301.
14 Bökönyi 1969: 221.
15 Clutton-Brock 1981: 25; Barber 1991: 27.
16 This is the pattern seen today (Payne 1973: 281ff.).
17 This issue is discussed by Rowley-Conwy (1969: 126ff.) and Chaplin (1969: 235).
18 Davis 1987: 46.
19 Hillman 2000: 371.
20 The dates for the earliest domestic rye were obtained by AMS dating (Hillman 2000: 373).
21 Moore *et al.* 2000: 494.
22 Moulins 2000: 400f.
23 Legge and Rowley-Conwy 2000: 471.
24 Moore *et al.* 2000.
25 Moore *et al.* 2000: 38.
26 Hillman 2000: 340.
27 Moore *et al.* 2000: viii.

4 PLANT DOMESTICATION

1 The best discussion of Old World plant domestication is Zohary and Hopf's classic, *Domestication of Plants in the Old World*, now in its third edition. Another excellent source with a wider geographic scope is Bellwood, *First Farmers: The Origins of Agricultural Societies*.
2 The importance of legumes is reflected in Roman family surnames. Four of the most prominent were Cicero (from *cicer*, chickpea), Fabius (from *faba*, faba bean), Lentulus (from *lens*, lentil), and Piso (from *pisum*, pea) (McGee 1997: 249).
3 An excellent short discussion of the nutrients needed for the human diet can be found in Heiser 1990: 27ff.
4 Zohary and Hopf 2000: 92.
5 Kislev *et al.* 2006: 1372ff.

6 Except where otherwise noted, the discussion of these three crops is based on Zohary and Hopf 2000.
7 Hillman 2000: 353ff.
8 Harlan 1999: 22.
9 Hillman and Davies 1999: 146ff.
10 McGee 1997: 235; see also his explanation of beer-making 1984: 455ff.
11 Hillman and Davies 1999: 114; 1999: 72.
12 Bellwood 2005: 154; Iltis 1987: 210.
13 Iltis 1987: 208.
14 Fedoroff 2003: 1158f.
15 Iltis 1987: 195.
16 Wilkes 1989: 444.
17 Piperno 2001: 2260.
18 Piperno and Flannery 2001: 21092f.
19 Hard and Roney 1998: 1661ff.
20 Visser 1986: 30.
21 McGee 1997: 240.

5 ANIMAL DOMESTICATION

1 Clutton-Brock 1999: 73f.
2 Grandin and Deesing 1998: 2f.
3 Meadow 1989: 86f.; Widdowson 1980: 7.
4 Clutton-Brock 1981: 24.
5 A good discussion of Soay sheep can be found in Jewel 1995.
6 Grandin and Deesing 1998: 124.
7 For more on pathologies caused by close confinement see Meadows 1989: 85.
8 Clutton-Brock 1989: 25.
9 Akkermans, P.A. et al. 1983: 355ff.; Clutton-Brock 1981: 56.
10 Larsón et al. 2005: 1618ff.
11 See Hanotte et al. 2002: 336ff.
12 Possehl 1990: 261ff.
13 Clutton-Brock 1999: 87.
14 Haber 1999: 67.
15 Clutton-Brock 1999: 50.
16 Coppinger and Collinger 1998: 197.
17 Clutton-Brock 1999: 54.
18 Vilà et al. 1997: 1687f.
19 Clutton-Brock 1999: 54.
20 Clutton-Brock (1999), for example, discusses cats along with elephants and reindeer in a section entitled "Exploited Captives."
21 Vigne and Guilaine 2004: 249ff.
22 Vigne et al. 2004: 259.

6 ARCHITECTURE

1 Whittle 1996: 25ff.
2 For more information see Davis 1987: 59f.
3 In his catalog to the 1964 exhibition Architecture without Architects, Rudofsky provides interesting photographs of Cappadocian and Chinese subterranean villages.
4 Ian Todd, personal communication.
5 Akkermans and Schwartz 2003: 112ff.

6 Good illustrations of the Transcaucasian structures are found in Mellaart 1975: 202.
7 Akkermans and Schwartz 2003: 50.
8 An excellent discussion of the architecture at Hallan Çemi is found in Rosenberg and Redding 2000: 39ff.
9 Perlès 2001: 189f.; notes 13 and 14.
10 Byrd reports that fired bricks were found at Hatoula in Israel (2000: 74).
11 Kenyon 1957: 55.
12 Based on a rate of 3.3 cu m of wall completed every day, if the wall was 600 m long, 4 m high and 2 m wide (1,200 ft × 13 ft × 6.5 ft); 13,760 workdays or a week's work for 200 laborers would be needed to build it (Ben-Tor 1992: 15).
13 Ben-Tor 1992: 17.
14 Hutton 1991: 71.
15 Trachtenberg and Hyman 1986: 50.
16 Recent excavations at Durrington Walls, less than two miles away from Stonehenge, have uncovered the largest Neolithic village in Britain. The complex is contemporary with Stonehenge, and includes the remains of what may be a smaller wooden version of the monument (Wilford 2007a; 2007b).
17 Hughes 2005: 30f.
18 Hughes 2005: 33.

7 POTTERY

1 Barnett 1995: 79.
2 Most notably by Gimbutas, who suggested that the geometric decoration on Neolithic pottery from what she termed "Old Europe" was, in fact, a pictorial script based on Great Goddess worship (1989: xv).
3 See Chapter 8.
4 Moore 1995: 39ff.
5 Amiran 1965: 240ff.
6 Mellaart 1975: 130.
7 Arnold 1985: 158; Barnett 1995: 82; Vitelli 1995: 62.
8 Orrelle and Gopher 2000: 299ff.
9 Moore and Scott 1997: 83
10 Kidder 1968: 7.
11 Kidder 1968: 13.
12 Kidder 1968: 15.
13 Aikens and Higuchi 1982: 95.
14 Kidder 1968: 15.
15 Aikens 1995: 15.
16 Aikens and Higuchi 1982: 137.
17 Kidder 1968: 14f.
18 Kidder 1968: 16; Aikens 1995: 14f.

8 DIET AND DISEASE

1 In the Levant, however, people were generally healthy throughout the Neolithic (Peterson 2002: 77f.).
2 Rathbun 1984: 140.
3 Cohen 1989: 121.
4 But note that farmers in the Levant were slightly taller than their ancestors (Cohen 1989: 119; Moore 2000: 305).

5 Cohen 1989: 112; Kennedy 1984: 174; Meikeljohn *et al.* 1984: 90; Papathanasiou 2004: 382.
6 Cohen 1989: 121f.
7 Cohen 1989: 107.
8 Papathanasiou 2004: 382; Rathbun 1984: 149.
9 Peterson 2002: 69.
10 Goodman, Martin *et al.* 1984: 20.
11 Molleson 2000: 310.
12 Rathbun 1984: 156.
13 For a full report see Molleson 2000: 302–324.
14 Rathbun 1984: 150.
15 Goodman, Martin *et al.* 1984: 37.
16 Anderson 1994: 62; Perlès 2001: 205.
17 Cohen 1989: 18, 64; Akkermans and Schwartz 2003: 79.
18 Cohen 1989: 32.
19 Akkermans and Schwartz 2003: 79; Allison 1984: 523.
20 Buikstra 1984: 229; Cook 1984: 259.
21 Hutton 1991: 16.
22 Smith, P. *et al.* 1984: 129.
23 Bellwood 2005: 15.
24 Cohen 1989: 45.
25 Crown and Wills 1995: 246.
26 Stahl 1989: 171ff.
27 McGovern 2003: 64ff.
28 McGovern *et al.* 2004: 17593ff.
29 Zohary and Hopf 2000: 156; McGovern 2003: 37.
30 Jennings *et al.* 2005: 279.

9 POWER AND PRESTIGE

1 Whittle 1996: 107.
2 Whittle 1996: 127 ff.
3 Goring-Morris 2000: 114.
4 Barnes 1993: 106; Whittle 1996: 192.
5 Moore *et al.* 2000: 318.
6 Price and Feinman 2005: 288ff.
7 Perlès 2001: 274ff.; Rollefson 2000: 170ff.
8 Christensen 2004: 129.
9 Dickson *et al.* 2005: 4ff.
10 Peterson 2002: 84; Rollefson 2000: 173.
11 Smith, P. *et al.* 1984: 122; Kennedy 1984: 183; Perlès 2001: 7.
12 Perzigian *et al.* 1984: 360f.; Rose *et al.* 1984: 409ff.
13 Christensen 2004: 136f.; Barnes 1993: 113.
14 Whittle 1996: 170; Hodder 1990: 261; Christensen 2004: 137.
15 Christensen 2004: 139ff.
16 Christensen 2004: 140.
17 Perlès 2001: 288ff.
18 Barnes 1993: 113.

10 TECHNOLOGY AND TRADE

1 Robb and Farr 2005: 31.
2 Gebauer 1995: 100, 103.

3 Akkermans and Schwartz 2003: 80; Aikens and Higuchi 1982: 10ff.
4 Kenyon 1957: 56f.; Odell 2000: 306.
5 Aikens and Higuchi 1982: 109.
6 Goho 2005: 116.
7 Mellaart 1975: 132f.; Özdoğan 2002: 156; Akkermans and Schwartz 2003: 81.
8 Mellaart 1967: 219.
9 Barber 1991: 253f.
10 Mellaart 1967: 219 and pls. 94 and 116–118.
11 Barber 1991: 30.
12 Mellaart 1967: 219f.
13 Barber 1991: 141ff. The German fabrics have been lost.
14 Mellaart 1975: 54; Akkermans and Schwartz 2003: 133; Mellaart 1967: 217f.
15 The International Association of Obsidian Studies' lists of known sources include 402 in the United States (139 of them in Oregon), 89 in Eurasia, 62 in Mexico, 55 in Japan, 52 in the Pacific islands (including Hawaii and New Zealand), 40 in South America, 39 in Africa, and 14 in Canada.
16 Todd 1976: 127f.; Carter et al. 2000; 2004; Gomez et al. 1995: 503ff.
17 Barge and Chataigner 2002; Bigazzi et al. 2005: 1ff.; Robb and Farr 2005: 34ff.
18 Odell 2000: 274.
19 Renfrew 1984: 124.
20 Robb and Farr 2005: 37.
21 Karimali 2005: 182; Akkermans and Schwartz 2003: 80.
22 Perlès 2001: 209.
23 Perlès 2001: 201ff.
24 Hayden 1995: 258.
25 Robb and Farr 2005: 39.
26 Akkermans and Schwartz 2003: 131f.; Chauvin in Hayden 1995: 259; Karimali 2005: 200.
27 Bevan 1997: 81ff.
28 Barber 1991: 289.

11 ART AND RELIGION

1 Hutton 1991: 57.
2 Illustrated in Mellaart 1975: 114.
3 See the discussion in Talalay (2004).
4 Voigt 2000: 274.
5 Orrelle and Gopher 2000: 300.
6 Mellaart 1967: 131.
7 Another offshoot is Marija Gimbutas' theory that Neolithic "Old Europe" (basically the Balkans) was controlled by women, and that the Great Goddess was the main deity. Gimbutas assumed that all Neolithic art conveyed specific messages, and she spent years deciphering and published a "sacred script" made up of the geometric and animal motifs on Old European art (1989). Her theories have been largely discredited.
8 The types were proposed by Ucko (1968) and summarized in Voigt (2000: 258).
9 Voigt 1988: 269.
10 Bevan 1997: 84.
11 Rollefson 2000: 167.
12 Mellaart 1967: 101.
13 Garfinkel 2003: 291f.
14 Horwitz and Goring-Morris 2004: 169.
15 Mellaart 1967: 166.

16 Ian Todd, personal communication; Blake 2005: 102f.
17 Chauvin 2000: 113.
18 Talalay 2004: 139f.
19 Kenyon 1957: 62.
20 Talalay 2004: 141f.; Boz and Hager 2004; Chauvin 2000: 89f.; Talalay 2004: 144.
21 Talalay 2004: 141f.; Mellaart 1970a: 175.
22 Mellaart 1967: 137ff.
23 Blake 2005: 110.
24 Kujit 2000: 156.
25 Peterson 2002: 27.
26 Rollefson reports that the bitumen was dusted with a green crystal powder (2000: 172), Schmandt-Besserat writes that the eyes in the first cache had thin line of intense green paint (1998: 6), and Chauvin reports that green paint was added to the grooves below the eyes (2000: 112).
27 Schmandt-Besserat 1998: 6.
28 Schmandt-Besserat 1998: 9.
29 Genesis 14:5; Deuteronomy 2:11; 2 Samuel 21:20.
30 P. Kyle McCarter, personal communication.
31 Schmandt-Besserat 1998: 10.
32 Rollefson 2000: 185.

12 WHAT CAUSED THE NEOLITHIC TRANSITION?

1 Zohary 1996: 142; Anderson 1999: 50; Ladizinsky 1998: 123, 175.
2 Bellwood 2005: 20.
3 Hillman and Davies 1999: 71.
4 Childe 1969: 23ff.
5 Gebauer and Price 1992b: 2
6 Baruch and Bottema 1991: 11ff.
7 Harlan 1967: 197–201; 1989: 80.
8 Binford 1968; 1984.
9 Flannery 1973: 271ff.
10 Cohen 1977a.
11 Smith, P. 1972: 9; Hassan 1981: 125; Hudson 2003: 312.
12 Bender 1978: 204ff.; 1990: 62ff.
13 Hayden 1990: 31ff.
14 Hayden 2003: 458ff.
15 Heiser 1990.
16 Bar-Yosef and Belfer-Cohen 1992: 211ff.
17 Rindos 1984.
18 Watson, P. 1995: 31.
19 Renfrew 2004: 51.

BIBLIOGRAPHY

Aegean Dendrochronology Project Reports. Online. Available HTTP: <www.arts.cornell.edu/dendro> (accessed 9 July 2006).

Aikens, C.M. (1995) "First in the World: The Jōmon Pottery of Early Japan," in W.K. Barnett and J.W. Hoopes (eds) *The Emergence of Pottery: Technology and Innovation in Ancient Societies*, Washington DC: Smithsonian Institution Press.

Aikens, C.M. and Higuchi, T. (1982) *Prehistory of Japan*, New York: Academic Press.

Akkermans, P.A., Boerma, J.A.K., Clason, A.T., Hill, S.G., Lohof, E., Meikeljohn, C., Le Mière, M., Molgat, G.M.F., Roodenberg, J.J., Waterbolk-van Rooyen, W. and van Zeist, W. (1983) "Bouqras Revisited: Preliminary Report on a Project in Western Syria," *Proceedings of the Prehistoric Society* 49: 335–372.

Akkermans, P.M.M.G. and Schwartz, G.M. (2003) *The Archaeology of Syria: From Complex Hunter-Gatherers to Early Urban Societies*, Cambridge: Cambridge University Press.

Allison, M.J. (1984) "Paleopathology in Peruvian and Chilean Populations," in N.M. Cohen and G.J. Armelagos (eds) *Paleopathology at the Origins of Agriculture*, New York: Academic Press.

Amiran, R. (1965) "Beginnings of Pottery-Making in the Near East," in F.R. Matson (ed.) *Ceramics and Man*, Viking Fund Publications in Anthropology # 41, New York: Wenner-Gren Foundation for Anthropological Research.

Anderson, P.C. (1994) "Reflections on the Significance of Two PPN Typological Classes in Light of Experimentation and Microware Analysis: Flint 'Sickles' and Obsidian 'Çayönü Tools'," in *Neolithic Chipped Stone Industries of the Fertile Crescent*, H.G. Gebel and S.K. Kazlowski (eds), Studies in Early Near Eastern Production, Subsistence, and Environments 1, Berlin: ex oriente.

—— (ed.) (1999) *Prehistory of Agriculture*, Institute of Archaeology Press Monograph 40, Los Angeles CA: UCLA Press.

Angel, J.L. (1984) "Health as a Critical Factor in the Changes from Hunting to Developed Farming in the Eastern Mediterranean," in N.M. Cohen and G.J. Armelagos (eds) *Paleopathology at the Origins of Agriculture*, New York: Academic Press.

Arnold, D.E. (1985) *Ceramic Theory and Cultural Process*, Cambridge: Cambridge University Press.

Avery, O.T., Macleod, C.M. and McCarty, M. (1944) "Studies on the Chemical Nature of the Substance Inducing Transformation in Pneumococcal Types," *Journal of Exploratory Medicine* 79: 137–158.

Balter, M. (2005) *The Goddess and the Bull*, New York: Free Press.

Bar-Yosef, O. and Belfer-Cohen, A. (1992) "From Foraging to Farming in the Mediterranean Levant," in A.B. Gebauer and T.D. Price (eds) *Transitions to Agriculture in Prehistory*, Madison WI: Prehistory Press.

Bar-Yosef, O. and Valla, F.R. (eds) (1991) *The Natufian Culture in the Levant*, Ann Arbor MI: International Monographs in Prehistory.

Barber, E.J.W. (1991) *Prehistoric Textiles*, Princeton NJ: Princeton University Press.

Barge, O. and Chataigner, C. (2002) "The Procurement of Obsidian: Factors Influencing the Choices of Deposits," paper presented at Natural Glasses 4 Conference, Lyon, France, August 2002.

Barnes, G.L. (1993) *China, Korea and Japan: The Rise of Civilization in East Asia*, London: Thames & Hudson.

Barnett, W.K. (1995) "Putting the Pot before the Horse: Earliest Ceramics and the Neolithic Transition in the Western Mediterranean," in W.K. Barnett and J.W. Hoopes (eds) *The Emergence of Pottery: Technology and Innovation in Ancient Societies*, Washington DC: Smithsonian Institution Press.

Barnett, W.K. and Hoopes, J.W. (eds) (1995) *The Emergence of Pottery: Technology and Innovation in Ancient Societies*, Washington DC: Smithsonian Institution Press.

Baruch, U. and Bottema, S. (1991) "Palynological Evidence for Climate Changes in the Levant c. 17,000–9,000 B.P.," in O. Bar-Yosef and F.R. Valla (eds) *The Natufian Culture in the Levant*, Ann Arbor MI: International Monographs in Prehistory.

Bellwood, P. (2005) *First Farmers: The Origins of Agricultural Societies*, Oxford: Blackwell.

Bellwood, P. and Renfrew, C. (eds) (2003) *Examining the Farming/Language Dispersal Hypothesis*, Cambridge: McDonald Institute for Archaeological Research.

Ben-Tor, A. (ed.) (1992) *The Archaeology of Ancient Israel*, New Haven CT: Yale University Press.

Bender, B. (1978) "Gatherer-hunter to Farmer: A Social Perspective," *World Archaeology* 10: 204–222.

—— (1990) "The Dynamics of Non-hierarchical Societies," in S. Upham (ed.) *The Evolution of Political Systems*, Cambridge: Cambridge University Press.

Betancourt, P.P., Karageorghis, V., Laffineur, R. and Niemeier, W.-D. (1999) MELETEMATA: *Studies in Aegean Archaeology Presented to Malcolm H. Weiner as He Enters His 65th Year*, Aegaeum 20, Liège: Université de Liège, and Austin TX: University of Texas.

Bevan, L. (1997) "Skin Scrapers and Pottery Makers? 'Invisible' Women in Prehistory," in J. Moore and E. Scott (eds) *Invisible People and Processes: Writing Gender and Childhood into European Archaeology*, London: Leicester University Press.

Bigazzi, G., Marton, P., Norelli, P. and Rozioznik, L. (1990) "Fission Track Dating of Carpathian Obsidians and Provenance Identification," *Nuclear Tracks and Radiation Measurements* 17/3: 391–396.

Binford, L.R. (1968) "Post-Pleistocene Adaptations," in S.R. Binford and L.R. Binford (eds) *New Perspectives in Archaeology*, Chicago IL: Aldine.

—— (1984) *In Pursuit of the Past: Decoding the Archaeological Record*, New York: Thames & Hudson.

Binford, S.R. and Binford, L.R (eds) (1968) *New Perspectives in Archaeology*, Chicago IL: Aldine.

Blake, E. (2005) "The Material Expression of Cult, Ritual and Feasting," in E. Blake and A.B. Knapp (eds) *The Archaeology of Mediterranean Prehistory*, Blackwell Studies in Global Archaeology Vol. 6, Oxford: Blackwell.

Blake, E. and Knapp, A.B. (eds) (2005) *The Archaeology of Mediterranean Prehistory*, Blackwell Studies in Global Archaeology Vol. 6, Oxford: Blackwell.

Bogucki, P. (1995) "The Linear Pottery Culture of Central Europe," in W.K. Barnett and J.W. Hoopes (eds) *The Emergence of Pottery: Technology and Innovation in Ancient Societies*, Washington DC: Smithsonian Institution Press.

Bökönyi, S. (1969) "Archaeological Problems and Methods of Recognizing Animal Domestication," in P.J. Ucko and G.W. Dimbleby (eds) *The Exploitation and Domestication of Plants and Animals*, Chicago IL: Aldine.

—— (1989) "Definitions of Animal Domestication," in J. Clutton-Brock (ed.) *The Walking Larder*, London: Unwin Hyman.

Boserup, E. (1965) *The Conditions of Agricultural Growth*, Chicago IL: Aldine.

Boz, B. and Hager, L.D. (2004) "Human Remains," in *Çatalhöyük, 2004 Archive Report*. Online. Available HTTP: <http://catal.arch.cam.ac.uk/catal/catal.html> (accessed 18 July 2006).

Braidwood, R.J. and Howe, B. (1960) *Prehistoric Investigations in Iraqi Kurdistan*, Chicago IL: University of Chicago Press.

Buchanan, M. (ed.) (1995) *St. Kilda: The Continuing Story of the Islands*, Edinburgh: HMSO.

Budiansky, S. (1999) *The Covenant of the Wild: Why Animals Chose Domestication*, New Haven CT: Yale University Press.

Buikstra, J.E. (1984) "The Lower Illinois River Region: A Prehistoric Context for the Study of Ancient Diet and Health," in N.M. Cohen and G.J. Armelagos (eds) *Paleopathology at the Origins of Agriculture*, New York: Academic Press.

Burenhult, G. (ed.) (1993) *People of the Stone Age*, New York: HarperCollins.

Byrd, B. (2000) "Households in Transition: Neolithic Social Organization within Southwest Asia," in I. Kuijt (ed.) *Life in Neolithic Farming Communities: Social Organization, Identity, and Differentiation*, New York: Kluwer Academic/Plenum.

Campbell, S. and Green, A. (eds) (1995) *The Archaeology of Death in the Ancient Near East*, Oxbow Monograph 51, Oxford: Oxbow Press.

Cappers, R.T.J. and Bottema, S. (eds) (2002) *The Dawn of Farming in the Near East*, Studies in Early Near Eastern Production, Subsistence, and Environments 6, Berlin: ex oriente.

Carter, T., Spasojevic, A. and Underbjerg, H. (2000) "Chipped Stone Report," in *Çatalhöyük, 2000 Archive Report*. Online. Available HTTP: <http://catal.arch.cam.ac.uk/catal/catal.html> (accessed 18 July 2006).

Carter, T., Delerue, S. and Milić, M. (2004) "Chipped Stone Report," in *Çatalhöyük, 2004 Archive Report*. Online. Available HTTP: <http://catal.arch.cam.ac.uk/catal/catal.html> (accessed 18 July 2006).

Chaplin, R.E. (1969) "The Use of Non-morphological Criteria in the Study of Animal Domestication from Bones Found on Archaeological Sites," in J. Ucko and G.W. Dimbleby (eds) *The Exploitation and Domestication of Plants and Animals*, Chicago IL: Aldine.

Chauvin, J. (1994) *Naissance des Divinités, Naissance de l'Agriculture. Les Révolution des*

Symboles au Néolithique; trans. T. Watkins (2000) *The Birth of the Gods and the Origins of Agriculture*, Cambridge: Cambridge University Press.

Cherry, J., Scarre, C. and Shennan, S. (eds) (2004) *Explaining Social Change: Studies in Honour of Colin Renfrew*, Cambridge: McDonald Institute for Archaeological Research.

Childe, V.G. (1928; 4th edn 1969) *New Light on the Most Ancient East*, London: Routledge & Kegan Paul.

—— (1956) *Piecing Together the Past*, London: Routledge & Kegan Paul.

Christensen, J. (2004) "Warfare in the European Neolithic," *Acta Archaeologica* 75/2: 129–157.

Clark, J.E. and Gosser, D. (1995) "Reinventing Mesoamerica's First Pottery," in W.K. Barnett and J.W. Hoopes (eds) *The Emergence of Pottery: Technology and Innovation in Ancient Societies*, Washington DC: Smithsonian Institution Press.

Close, A.E. (1995) "Few and Far Between: Early Ceramics in North Africa," in W.K. Barnett and J.W. Hoopes (eds) *The Emergence of Pottery: Technology and Innovation in Ancient Societies*, Washington DC: Smithsonian Institution Press.

Clutton-Brock, J. (1981) *Domesticated Animals from Early Times*, Austin TX: University of Texas Press.

—— (ed.) (1989) *The Walking Larder*, London: Unwin Hyman.

—— (1999) *A Natural History of Domesticated Mammals*, Cambridge: Cambridge University Press.

Cohen, M.N. (1977a) *The Food Crisis in Prehistory*, New Haven CT: Yale University Press.

—— (1977b) "Population Pressure and the Origins of Agriculture: An Archaeological Sample from the Coast of Peru," in C.A. Reed (ed.) *The Origins of Agriculture*, The Hague: Mouton.

—— (1989) *Health and the Rise of Civilization*, New Haven CT: Yale University Press.

Cohen, M.N. and Armelagos, G.J. (eds) (1984) *Paleopathology at the Origins of Agriculture*, New York: Academic Press.

Colledge, S., Conolly, J. and Shennan, S. (2004) "Archaeobotanical Evidence for the Spread of Farming in the Eastern Mediterranean," *Current Anthropology* 45: S35–S50.

Coppinger, R. and Collinger, L. (1998) "Differences in the Behavior of Dog Breeds," in T. Grandin, (ed.) *Genetics and the Behavior of Domestic Animals*, San Diego CA/London: Academic Press.

Cook, D.C. (1984) "Subsistence and Health in the Lower Illinois Valley: Osteological Evidence," in N.M. Cohen and G.J. Armelagos (eds) *Paleopathology at the Origins of Agriculture*, New York: Academic Press.

Cowan, C.W. and Watson, P.J. (eds) (1992) *The Origins of Agriculture: An International Perspective*, Washington DC: Smithsonian Institution Press.

Crabtree, P.J. and Campana, D.V. (2006) *Exploring Prehistory: How Archaeology Reveals Our Past*, 2nd edn, New York: McGraw-Hill.

Crown, P.L. and Wills, W.H. (1995) "Economic Intensification and the Origins of Ceramic Containers in the American Southwest," in W.K. Barnett and J.W. Hoopes (eds) *The Emergence of Pottery: Technology and Innovation in Ancient Societies*, Washington DC: Smithsonian Institution Press.

Darwin, C. (1859) *On the Origin of Species by Means of Natural Selection, or, The*

Preservation of Favored Races in the Struggle for Life; reprinted (1998), New York: Modern Library.

Davis, S.J.M. (1987) *The Archaeology of Animals*, New Haven CT: Yale University Press.

Denham, T., Haberle, S.G., Lentfer, C., Fullagar, R., Field, J., Therin, M., Porch, N. and Winsborough, B. (2003) "Origins of Agriculture at Kuk Swamp in the Highlands of New Guinea," *Science* 301/5630: 189–193.

Diamond, J. (1999) *Guns, Germs and Steel*, New York: Norton.

Dickson, J.H., Oeggi, K. and Handley, L.L. (2005) "The Iceman Reconsidered," *Scientific American* 15/1: 4–13.

Fedoroff, N.V. (2003) "Prehistoric GM Corn," *Science* 302/5648: 1158–1159.

Flannery, K.V. (1973) "The Origins of Agriculture," *Annual Review of Anthropology* 2: 271–310.

Frazer, J.G. (1890) *The Golden Bough*, reprinted (1993), New York: Gramercy Books.

Garfinkel, Y. (2003) *Dancing at the Dawn of Agriculture*, Austin TX: University of Texas Press.

Gebauer, A.B. (1995) "Pottery Production and the Introduction of Agriculture in Southern Scandinavia," in W.K. Barnett and J.W. Hoopes (eds) *The Emergence of Pottery: Technology and Innovation in Ancient Societies*, Washington DC: Smithsonian Institution Press.

Gebauer, A.B. and Price, T.D. (eds) (1992a) *Transitions to Agriculture in Prehistory*, Madison WI: Prehistory Press.

—— (1992b) "Foragers to Farmers: An Introduction," in A.B. Gebauer and T.D. Price (eds) *Transitions to Agriculture in Prehistory*, Madison WI: Prehistory Press.

Gebel, H.G. and Kazlowski, S.K. (eds) (1994) *Neolithic Chipped Stone Industries of the Fertile Crescent*, Studies in Early Near Eastern Production, Subsistence, and Environments 1, Berlin: ex oriente.

Gebel, H.G.K., Kafafi, Z. and Rollefson, G.O. (eds) (1997) *The Prehistory of Jordan II: Perspectives from 1997*, Studies in Early Near Eastern Production, Subsistence, and Environment 4, Berlin: ex oriente.

Gimbutas, M. (1989) *The Language of the Goddess*, San Francisco CA: Harper & Row.

—— (1991) *The Civilization of the Goddess*, San Francisco CA: Harper & Row.

Goho, A. (2005) "In the Buff," *Science News* 167/8: 116.

Gomez, B., Glascock, M.D., Blackman, M.J. and Todd, I.A. (1995) "Neutron Activation Analysis of Obsidian from Kalavassos-Tenta," *Journal of Field Archaeology* 22: 503–508.

Goodman, A.H., Lallo, J., Armelagos, G.J. and Rose, J.C. (1984) "Health Changes at Dickson Mounds, Illinois (A.D. 950–1300)," in N.M. Cohen and G.J. Armelagos (eds) *Paleopathology at the Origins of Agriculture*, New York: Academic Press.

Goodman, A.H., Martin, D.L., Armelagos, G.J. and Clark, G. (1984) "Indications of Stress from Bone and Teeth," in N.M. Cohen and G.J. Armelagos (eds) *Paleopathology at the Origins of Agriculture*, New York: Academic Press.

Goring-Morris, N. (2000) "The Quick and the Dead: The Social Context of Aceramic Neolithic Mortuary Practices as Seen from Kfar HaHoresh," in I. Kuijt (ed.) *Life in Neolithic Farming Communities: Social Organization, Identity, and Differentiation*, New York: Kluwer Academic/Plenum.

Gosden, C. and Hather, J. (eds) (1999) *The Prehistory of Food: Appetites for Change*, London: Routledge.

Gowlett, J.A.J. and Hedges, R.E.M. (1986) *Archaeological Results from Accelerator*

Dating, Oxford University Committee for Archaeology Monograph 11, Oxford: Alden.

Grandin, T. (ed.) (1998) *Genetics and the Behavior of Domestic Animals*, San Diego CA/London: Academic Press.

Grandin, T. and Deesing, M.J. (1998) "Behavioral Genetics and Animal Science," in T. Grandin, (ed.) *Genetics and the Behavior of Domestic Animals*, San Diego CA/London: Academic Press.

Grant, W.F. (ed.) (1984) *Plant Biosystematics*, Montreal: Academic Press.

Graves, R. (1948; rev. 1966) *The White Goddess*, New York: Farrar, Straus and Giroux.

Haber, A.F. (1999) "*Uywaña*, the House and its Indoor Landscape: Oblique Approaches to, and beyond, Domestication," in C. Gosden and J. Hather (eds) *The Prehistory of Food: Appetites for Change*, London: Routledge.

Hanotte, O., Bradley, D.G., Ochieng, J.W., Verjee, Y., Hill, E.W. and Rege, J.E.O. (2002) "African Pastoralism: Genetic Imprints of Origins and Migrations," *Science* 296/5566: 336–339.

Hard, R.J. and Rooney, J.R. (1998) "A Massive Terraced Village Complex in Chihuahua, Mexico, 3000 Years Before Present," *Science* 279/5357: 1661–1664.

Harlan, J.R. (1967) "A Wild Wheat Harvest in Turkey," *Archaeology* 20: 197–201.

—— (1989) "Wild-grass Seed Harvesting in the Sahara and Sub-Sahara of Africa," in D.R. Harris and G.C. Hillman (eds) *Foraging and Farming: The Evolution of Plant Exploitation*, London: Unwin Hyman.

—— (1992) *Crops and Man*, 2nd edn, Madison WI: American Society of Agronomy/ Crop Society of Agronomy Press.

—— (1999) "Wild Grass Seed Harvesting and Implications for Domestication," in P.C. Anderson (ed.) *Prehistory of Agriculture*, Institute of Archaeology Press Monograph 40, Los Angeles CA: UCLA Press.

Harris, D.R. (ed.) (1996) *The Origins and Spread of Agriculture and Pastoralism in Eurasia*, London: UCL Press.

Harris, D.R. and Hillman, G.C. (eds) (1989) *Foraging and Farming: The Evolution of Plant Exploitation*, London: Unwin Hyman.

Hassan, F. (1981) *Demographic Archaeology*, New York: Academic Press.

Hawkins, G. (1965) *Stonehenge Decoded*, New York: Doubleday.

Hayden, B. (1990) "Nimrods, Piscators, Pluckers and Planters: The Emergence of Food Production," *Journal of Anthropological Research* 9: 31–69.

—— (1992) "Models of Domestication," in A.B. Gebauer and T.D Price (eds) *Transitions to Agriculture in Prehistory*, Madison WI: Prehistory Press.

—— (1995) "The Emergence of Prestige Technologies and Pottery," in W.K. Barnett and J.W. Hoopes (eds) *The Emergence of Pottery: Technology and Innovation in Ancient Societies*, Washington DC: Smithsonian Institution Press.

—— (2003) "Were Luxury Goods the First Domesticates? Ethno-archaeological Perspectives from Southwest Asia," *World Archaeology* 34: 458–469.

Heer, O. (1878) "Abstract of the Treatise on the 'Plants of the Lake Dwellings,' " in F. Keller, *The Lake Dwellings of Switzerland and Other Parts of Europe*, Vol. 1; trans. J.E. Lee, 2nd edn, London: Longmans, Green, & Co.

Heiser, C. Jr. (1990) *Seed to Civilization: The Story of Food*, 3rd edn, Cambridge MA: Harvard University Press.

Helmer, D., Gourichon, L. and Stordeur, D. (2004) "À l'aube de la domestication animale: Imaginaire et symbolisme animal dans les premières néolithiques du nord du Proche-Orient," *Anthropozoologica* 39/1: 143–163.

Henry, D.O. (1995) *Prehistoric Cultural Ecology and Evolution: Insights from Southern Jordan*, New York: Plenum.

Heum, M., Schäfer-Pregi, R., Klawan, D., Castagna, R., Accerbi, M., Borghi, B. and Salamini, F. (1997) "Site of Enkorn Wheat Domestication Identified by DNA Fingerprinting," *Science* 278/5344: 1312–1314.

Higgs, E.S. (ed.) (1972) *Papers on Economic Prehistory*, Cambridge: Cambridge University Press.

Hillman, G.C. (2000) "The Plant Food Economy of Abu Hureyra 1 and 2," in Moore *et al., Village on the Euphrates: From Foraging to Farming at Abu Hureyra*, Oxford: Oxford University Press.

Hillman, G.C. and Davies, M.S. (1999) "Domestication Rate in Wild Wheats and Barley Under Primitive Cultivation," in P.C. Anderson (ed.) *Prehistory of Agriculture*, Institute of Archaeology Press Monograph 40, Los Angeles CA: UCLA Press.

Hilu, K.W. (1987) "Chloroplast DNA in the Systematics and Evolution of the Poaceae," in T. Sodestrom (ed.) *Grass Systematics and Evolution*, Washington DC: Smithsonian Institution Press.

Hodder, I. (1990) *The Domestication of Europe*, Cambridge: Blackwell.

—— (2005) "Women and Men at Çatalhöyük," *Scientific American* 15/1: 34–41.

Holden, C. (2003) "Isotopic Data Pinpoint Iceman's Origins," *Science* 302/5646: 759–61.

Hole, F. (2000) "Is Size Important? Function and Hierarchy in Neolithic Settlements," in I. Kujit (ed.) *Life in Neolithic Farming Communities: Social Organization, Identity, and Differentiation*, New York: Kluwer Academic/Plenum.

Hoopes, J.W. (1995) "Interaction in Hunting and Gathering Societies as a Context for the Emergence of Pottery in the Central American Isthmus," in W.K. Barnett and J.W. Hoopes (eds) *The Emergence of Pottery: Technology and Innovation in Ancient Societies*, Washington DC: Smithsonian Institution Press.

Horwitz, L.K. and Goring-Morris, N. (2004) "Animals and Ritual During the Levantine PPNB: A Case Study from the Site of Kfar HaHoresh, Israel," *Anthropozoologica* 39/1: 165–178.

Hudson, M. (2003) "Agriculture and Language Change in the Japanese Islands," in P. Bellwood and C. Renfrew (eds) *Examining the Farming/Language Dispersal Hypothesis*, Cambridge: McDonald Institute for Archaeological Research.

Hughes, D.W. (2005) "Neolithic and Early Bronze Age Skywatchers and the Precession of the Equinox," *Journal of the British Astronomical Association* 115/1: 29–35.

Hutton, R. (1991) *The Pagan Religions of the Ancient British Isles: Their Nature and Legacy*, Oxford: Blackwell.

Iltis, H.H. (1987) "Maize Evolution and Agricultural Origins," in T. Sodestrom (ed.) *Grass Systematics and Evolution*, Washington DC: Smithsonian Institution Press.

International Association of Obsidian Studies Source Catalog (2005). Online. Available HTTP: <http://www.obsidianlab.com/sourcecatalog/s_home.html> (accessed 3 August 2005).

Isaac, E. (1970) *Geography of Domestication*, Englewood Cliffs NJ: Prentice-Hall.

Jaenicke-Després, V., Bucjler, E.S., Smith, B.D., Gilbert, M.T.P., Cooper, A., Doebley, J. and Pääbo, S. (2003) "Early Allele Selection in Maize as Revealed by Ancient DNA," *Science* 302/5648: 1203–1206.

Jenkins, R.M. (2005) "You Hear About New Ears of Corn?" *The Baltimore Sun*, August 17: 3F.

Jennings, J., Antrobus, K.L., Atencio, S.J., Glavich, E., Johnson, R., Loffler, G. and Luu, C. (2005) "Drinking Beer in a Blissful Mood," *Current Anthropology* 46/2: 275–303.

Jewel, P. (1995) "Soay Sheep," in M. Buchanan (ed.) *St. Kilda: The Continuing Story of the Islands*, Edinburgh: HMSO.

Johannessen, S. and Hastorf, C.A. (1994) *Corn and Culture in the Prehistoric New World*, Boulder CO: Westview Press.

Jones, R.F.J. (1979) "Why Pottery," in M. Millet (ed.) *Pottery and the Archaeologist*, Occasional Publication No. 4, London: London University Institute of Archaeology.

Kanowski, M. (1987) *Old Bones: Unlocking Archaeological Secrets*, Melbourne: Longman Cheshire.

Karimali, E. (2005) "Lithic Technologies and Use," in E. Blake and A.B. Knapp (eds) *The Archaeology of Mediterranean Prehistory*, Blackwell Studies in Global Archaeology Vol. 6, Oxford: Blackwell.

Keller, F. (1878a) *The Lake Dwellings of Switzerland and Other Parts of Europe* Vol. 1, 2nd edn, trans. J.E. Lee, London: Longmans, Green, & Co.

—— (1878b) *The Lake Dwellings of Switzerland and Other Parts of Europe* Vol. 2, 2nd edn, trans. J.E. Lee, London: Longmans, Green, & Co.

Kennedy, K.A.R. (1984) "Growth, Nutrition, and Pathology in Changing Paleo-demographic Settings in South Asia," in N.M. Cohen and G.J. Armelagos (eds) *Paleopathology at the Origins of Agriculture*, New York: Academic Press.

Kenyon, K.M. (1957) *Digging Up Jericho*, New York: Praeger.

—— (1981) *Excavations at Jericho*, ed. T. Holland, British School of Archaeology in Jerusalem.

Kidder, J.E. (1968) *Prehistoric Japanese Arts: Jōmon Pottery*, Tokyo: Kodansha.

Kislev, M.E., Hartmann, A. and Bar-Yosef, O. (2006) "Early Domesticated Fig in the Jordan Valley," *Science* 312/5778: 1372–1374.

Kokkinidou, D. and Nikolaidou, M. (1997) "Body Imagery in the Aegean Neolithic: Ideological Implications of Anthropomorphic Figurines," in J. Moore and E. Scott (eds) *Invisible People and Processes: Writing Gender and Childhood into European Archaeology*, London: Leicester University Press.

Kottak, C.P. (1999) *Mirror for Humanity: A Concise Introduction to Cultural Anthropology*, 2nd edn, New York: McGraw Hill.

Kramer, S.N. (1959) *History Begins at Sumer*, New York: Doubleday.

Kuijt, I. (ed.) (2000) *Life in Neolithic Farming Communities: Social Organization, Identity, and Differentiation*, New York: Kluwer Academic/Plenum.

—— (2000) "Keeping the Peace: Ritual, Skull Caching, and Community Integration in the Levantine Neolithic," in I. Kujit (ed.) *Life in Neolithic Farming Communities: Social Organization, Identity, and Differentiation*, New York: Kluwer Academic/Plenum.

Ladizinsky, G. (1998) *Plant Evolution Under Domestication*, Dordrecht: Kluwer.

Lamarck, J.B. (1809) *Zoological Philosophy: an Exposition with Regard to the Natural History of Animals*, trans. H. Elliot (1984) Chicago IL: University of Chicago Press.

Larson, G., Dobney, K., Albarella, U., Fang, M., Matisoo-Smith, E., Robins, J., Lowden, S., Finlayson, H., Brand, T., Willerslev, E., Rowley-Conwy, P., Andersson,

L. and Cooper, A. (2005) "The World-wide Phylogeography of Wild Boar Reveals Multiple Centers of Pig Domestication," *Science* 307/5715: 1618–1621.

Lawrence, T.L.J. (ed.) (1980) *Growth in Animals*, London: Butterworth.

Legge, A.J. and Rowley-Conwy, P.A. (2000) "The Exploitation of Animals," in Moore *et al. Village on the Euphrates: From Foraging to Farming at Abu Hureyra*, Oxford: Oxford University Press.

Lev-Yadun, S., Gopher, A. and Abbo, A. (2000) "The Cradle of Agriculture," *Science* 288/5471, 1602–1603.

Lewin, R. and Foley, R.A. (2004) *Principles of Human Evolution*, 2nd edn, Malden MA: Blackwell.

Lewis-Williams, D. (2002) *The Mind in the Cave: Consciousness and the Origins of Art*, London: Thames & Hudson.

Linneaus, C. (1735) *Systema Naturae*, trans. M.S.J. Engle-Ledeboer and H. Engel (1964), Nieuwkoop: De Graff.

Malthus, T.R. (1798) *An Essay on the Principle of Population, or, A View of its Past and Present Effects on Human Happiness: with an Inquiry into our Prospects Respecting the Future Removal or Mitigation of the Evils which it Occasions*; reprinted (1992), Cambridge: Cambridge University Press.

McGee, H. (1997) *On Food and Cooking: The Science and Lore of the Kitchen*, New York: Fireside; originally published (1984), New York: Scribner.

McGovern, P.E. (2003) *Ancient Wine: In Search for the Origins of Viniculture*, Princeton NJ: Princeton University Press.

McGovern, P.E., Zhang, J., Tang, J., Zhang, Z., Hall, G., Moreau, R.A., Nuñez, A., Butrym, E.D., Richards, M.P., Wang, Chen-shan, Guangsheng, C., Zhao, Z. and Wang, Chen (2004) "Fermented Beverages of Pre- and Proto-historic China," *Proceedings of the National Academy of Sciences of the United States of America* 101/51: 17593–17598.

MacNeish, R. (1992) *The Origins of Agriculture and Settled Life*, Norman OK: University of Oklahoma Press.

Majerus, M. (1998) *Melanism: Evolution in Action*, Oxford: Oxford University Press.

Malone, C., Bonanno, A., Gouder, T., Stoddart, S. and Trump, D. (2005) "The Death Cults of Prehistoric Malta," *Scientific American* 15/1: 14–23.

Matson, F.R. (ed.) (1965) *Ceramics and Man*, Viking Fund Publications in Anthropology # 41, New York: Wenner-Gren Foundation for Anthropological Research.

Meadows, R.H. (1989) "Osteological Evidence for the Process of Animal Domestication," in J. Clutton-Brock (ed.) *The Walking Larder*, London: Unwin Hyman.

Meikeljohn, C., Schentag, C., Venema, A. and Key, P. (1984) "Socioeconomic Change and Patterns of Pathology and Variation in the Mesolithic and Neolithic of Western Europe: Some Suggestions," in N.M. Cohen and G.J. Armelagos (eds) *Paleopathology at the Origins of Agriculture*, New York: Academic Press.

Mellaart, J. (1965) *Earliest Civilizations of the Near East*, London: Thames & Hudson.

—— (1967) *Çatal Hüyük: A Neolithic Town in Anatolia*, London: Thames & Hudson.

—— (1970a) *Hacilar I*, Edinburgh: Edinburgh University Press.

—— (1970b) *Hacilar II*, Edinburgh: Edinburgh University Press.

—— (1975) *The Neolithic in the Near East*, London: Thames & Hudson.

Mellars, P. (1996) *The Neanderthal Legacy: An Archaeological Perspective from Western Europe*, Princeton NJ: Princeton University Press.

Mendel, G. (1865) "Versuche über Pflanzenhybriden," *VeRhandlungen des Naturforschenden Vereines in Brünn*; trans. R.A. Fisher and ed. J. H. Bennett (1965), Edinburgh: Oliver & Boyd.

Merlin, D.M. (1984) *On the Trail of the Ancient Opium Poppy*, Cranbury NJ: Associated University Presses.

Meurers-Balke, J. and Luning, J. (1999) "Some Aspects and Experiments Concerning the Processing of Glume Wheats," in P.C. Anderson (ed.) *Prehistory of Agriculture*, Institute of Archaeology Press Monograph 40, Los Angeles CA: UCLA Press.

Millet, M. (ed.) (1979) *Pottery and the Archaeologist*, Occasional Publication No. 4, London: London University Institute of Archaeology.

Mochizuki, A. (1997) Mochizuki Laboratory website. Online. Available HTTP: <http://www.busitu.numazu-ct.ac.jp/mochizuki/english/index/html> (accessed 3 August 2005).

Molleson, T.I. (2000) "The People of Abu Hureyra," in Moore *et al.*, *Village on the Euphrates: From Foraging to Farming at Abu Hureyra*, Oxford: Oxford University Press.

Moore, A.M.T. (1995) "The Inception of Potting in Western Asia and Its Impact on Economy and Society," in W.K. Barnett and J.W. Hoopes (eds) *The Emergence of Pottery: Technology and Innovation in Ancient Societies*, Washington DC: Smithsonian Institution Press.

Moore, A.M.T., Hillman, G.C. and Legge, A.J. (2000) *Village on the Euphrates: From Foraging to Farming at Abu Hureyra*, Oxford: Oxford University Press.

Moore, J. and Scott, E. (eds) (1997) *Invisible People and Processes: Writing Gender and Childhood into European Archaeology*, London: Leicester University Press.

Morris, D. (1986) *Cat Watching*, New York: Crown.

Moulins, D.D. (2000) "Abu Hureyra 2: Plant Remains from the Neolithic," in Moore *et al.*, *Village on the Euphrates: From Foraging to Farming at Abu Hureyra*, Oxford: Oxford University Press.

Nelson, S.M. (2004) *Gender in Archaeology: Analyzing Power and Prestige*, 2nd edn, Walnut Creek CA: AltaMira.

Nesbitt, M. (2002) "When and Where Did Domesticated Cereals First Occur in Southwest Asia?" in R.T.J. Cappers and S. Bottema (eds) *The Dawn of Farming in the Near East*, Studies in Early Near Eastern Production, Subsistence, and Environments 6, Berlin: ex oriente.

Neumann, K. (2003) "New Guinea: A Cradle of Agriculture," *Science* 301/5630: 180–181.

Newton, M.W. and Kuninholm, P.I. (1999) "Wiggles Worth Watching – Making Radiocarbon Work: The Case of Çatal Höyük," in P.P. Betancourt, V. Karageorghis, R. Laffineur and W.-D. Niemeier, MELETEMATA: *Studies in Aegean Archaeology Presented to Malcolm H. Weiner as He Enters His 65th Year*, Aegaeum 20: Liège: Université de Liège, and Austin TX: University of Texas.

Oates, D. and Oates, J. (1976) *The Rise of Civilization*, New York: E.P. Dutton.

Odell, G.H. (2000) "Stone Tool Research at the End of the Millennium: Procurement and Technology," *Journal of Archaeological Research* 8/4: 269–331.

Orrelle, E. and Gopher, A. (2000) "The Pottery Neolithic Period: Questions about Pottery Decoration, Symbolism, and Meaning," in I. Kujit (ed.) *Life in Neolithic*

Farming Communities: Social Organization, Identity, and Differentiation, New York: Kluwer Academic/Plenum.

Özdoğan, A. (1999) "Cayönü," in M. Özdoğan and N. Başgelen (eds) *Neolithic in Turkey, The Cradle of Civilization. New Discoveries*, Istanbul: Arkeoloji ve Sanat Yayınları.

Özdoğan, M. (2002) "Redefining the Neolithic of Anatolia: A Critical Overview," in R.T.J. Cappers and S. Bottema (eds) *The Dawn of Farming in the Near East*, Studies in Early Near Eastern Production, Subsistence, and Environments 6, Berlin: ex oriente.

Papathanasiou, A. (2005) "Health Status of the Neolithic Populations of Alepotrypa Cave," *American Journal of Physical Anthropology* 126/4: 377–390.

Payne, S. (1973) "Kill-off Patterns in Sheep and Goats: The Mandibles from Aşvan Kale," *Anatolian Studies* 23: 281–303.

—— (1985) "Morphological Distinctions between the Mandibular Teeth of Young Sheep, *Ovis*, and Goats, *Capra*," *Journal of Archaeological Science* 12: 139–147.

Payne, S. and Bull, G. (1988) "Components of Variation in Measurements of Pig Bones and Teeth, and the Use of Measurements to Distinguish Wild from Domestic Pig Remains," *Archaeozoologia* II/1, 2: 27–66.

Pearsall, D.M. (1999) "The Impact of Maize on Subsistence Systems in South America," in C. Gosden and J. Hather (eds) *The Prehistory of Food: Appetites for Change*, London: Routledge.

Perlès, C. (2001) *The Early Neolithic in Greece*, Cambridge: Cambridge University Press.

Perzigian, A.J., Tench, P.A. and Brawn, D.J. (1984) "Prehistoric Health in the Ohio River Valley," in N.M. Cohen and G.J. Armelagos (eds) *Paleopathology at the Origins of Agriculture*, New York: Academic Press.

Peterson, J. (2002) *Sexual Revolutions: Gender and Labor at the Dawn of Agriculture*, Walnut Creek CA: AltaMira.

Pickersgill, B. (1989) "Cytological and Genetical Evidence on the Domestication and Diffusion of Crops within the Americas," in D.R. Harris and G.C. Hillman (eds) *Foraging and Farming: The Evolution of Plant Exploitation*, London: Unwin Hyman.

Piperno, D.R. (2001) "On Maize and the Sunflower," *Science* 292/5525: 2260–2262.

Piperno, D.R. and Flannery, K.V. (2001) "The Earliest Archaeological Maize (zea mays L.) from Highland Mexico: New Accelerator Mass Spectrometry Dates and their Implications," *Proceedings of the National Academy of Sciences* 98(4): 2102–2103.

Possehl, G.L. (1990) "Revolution in the Urban Revolution: The Emergence of Indus Urbanization," *Annual Review of Anthropology* 19: 261–282.

Price, T.D. and Feinman, G.M. (2005) *Images of the Past*, 4th edn, New York: McGraw-Hill.

Price, T.D. and Gebauer, A.B. (eds) (1995) *Last Hunters – First Farmers*, Santa Fe NM: School of American Research Press.

Proffitt, F. (2004) "In Defense of Darwin and a Former Icon of Evolution," *Science* 304/5679: 1894–1895.

Rathbun, T.A. (1984) "Skeletal Pathology from the Paleolithic through the Metal Ages in Iran and Iraq," in N.M. Cohen and G.J. Armelagos (eds) *Paleopathology at the Origins of Agriculture*, New York: Academic Press.

Reed, C.A. (ed.) (1977) *The Origins of Agriculture*, The Hague: Mouton.

Renfrew, C. (1984) *Approaches to Social Archaeology*, Cambridge MA: Harvard University Press.

Renfrew, J. (1991) *New Light on Early Farming: Recent Developments in Palaeoethnobotany*, Edinburgh: Edinburgh University Press.

—— (2004) "Neo-thingness," in John Cherry *et al.* (eds) *Explaining Social Change: Studies in Honour of Colin Renfrew*, Cambridge: McDonald Institute for Archaeological Research.

Restelli, F.B. (2001) *Formation Processes of the First Developed Neolithic Societies in the Zagros and the Northern Mesopotamian Plain*, Studi di Preistoria Orientale, Vol. 1, Rome: Visceglia.

Rice, P.M. (ed.) (1988) *Pots and Potters: Current Approaches in Ceramic Archaeology*, Monograph XXIV, Institute of Archaeology, Los Angeles CA: UCLA Press.

Richards, M.P., Schulting, R.J. and Hedges, R.E.M. (2003) "Sharp Shift in Diet at Onset of Neolithic," *Nature* 425: 366.

Rindos, D. (1984) *The Origins of Agriculture: An Evolutionary Perspective*, London: Academic Press.

—— (1989) "Darwinism and its Role in the Explanation of Domestication," in D.R. Harris and G.C. Hillman (eds), *Foraging and Farming: the Evolution of Plant Exploitation*, London: Unwin Hyman.

Robb, J.E. and Farr, R.H. (2005) "Substances in Motion: Neolithic Mediterranean 'Trade'," in E. Blake and A.B. Knapp (eds) *The Archaeology of Mediterranean Prehistory*, Blackwell Studies in Global Archaeology Vol. 6, Oxford: Blackwell.

Rollefson, G.O. (2000) "Ritual and Social Structure at Neolithic 'Ain Ghazal," in I. Kuijt (ed.) *Life in Neolithic Farming Communities: Social Organization, Identity, and Differentiation*, New York: Kluwer Academic/Plenum.

Rose, J.C., Burnett, B.A., Blaeuer, M.W. and Nassaney, M.S. (1984) "Paleopathology and the Origins of Maize Agriculture in the Lower Mississippi Valley and Caddoan Culture Areas," in N.M. Cohen and G.J. Armelagos (eds) *Paleopathology at the Origins of Agriculture*, New York: Academic Press.

Rosen, S.A., Savinetsky, A.B., Plakht, Y., Kisseleva, N., Khassanov, B.F., Pereladov, A.M. and Haiman, M. (2005) "Dung in the Desert: Preliminary Results of the Negev Holocene Ecology Project," *Current Anthropology* 46/2: 317–327.

Rosenberg, M. and Redding, R.W. (2000) "Hallan Çemi and Early Village Organization in Eastern Anatolia," in I. Kuijt (ed.) *Life in Neolithic Farming Communities: Social Organization, Identity, and Differentiation*, New York: Kluwer Academic/Plenum.

Rowley-Conwy, P. (1969) "Milking Caprines, Hunting Pigs," in J. Ucko and G.W. Dimbleby (eds) *The Exploitation and Domestication of Plants and Animals*, Chicago IL: Aldine.

—— (ed.) (2000) *Animal Bones, Human Societies*, Oxford: Oxbow.

Rudofsky, B. (1964) *Architecture without Architects*, New York: Doubleday.

Sassaman, K.E. (1995) "The Social Contradictions of Traditional and Innovative Cooking Technologies in the Prehistoric American Southeast," in W.K. Barnett and J.W. Hoopes (eds) *The Emergence of Pottery: Technology and Innovation in Ancient Societies*, Washington DC: Smithsonian Institution Press.

Schäffer, J. (ed.) (1999) *Domestication of Animals: Interactions between Veterinary and Medical Sciences, Free Communications: Report of the 30th Congress of the WAHVM and the 6th Conference of the Historical Division of the DVG, 9–12 September 1998, Munich*, Giessen: Verlag der Deutschen Veterinärmedizinischen Gesellschaft.

Schmandt-Besserat, D. (1998) "'Ain Ghazal 'Monumental' Figures," *Bulletin of the American Schools of Oriental Research* 310: 1–17.

—— (ed.) (no date) "Symbols at 'Ain Ghazal," *'Ain Ghazal Excavation Reports* Vol. 1. Online. Available HTTP: <http://link.lanic.utexas.edu/menic/ghazal> (accessed 9 August 2006).

Schmidt, K. (2000) "Göbekli Tepe and the Early Neolithic Sites of the Urfa Region: A Synopsis of New Results and Current Views," *Neo-Lithics* 1/10: 9–11.

Settegast, M. (1986) *Plato Prehistorian*, Cambridge MA: Rotenberg.

Sharer, R. and Ashmore, W. (1993) *Archaeology: Discovering our Past*, 2nd edn, Mountain View CA: Mayview.

Shostak, M. (1981) *Nisa: The Life and Words of a !Kung Woman*, Cambridge MA: Harvard University Press.

Simms, S.R. and Russell, K.W. (1997) "Bedouin Hand Harvesting of Wheat and Barley: Implications for Early Cultivaion in Southwestern Asia," *Current Anthropology* 38: 696–702.

Smith, B. (1995) *The Emergence of Agriculture*, New York: Scientific American Library.

—— (1997) "The Initial Domestication of *Curcurbita pepo* in the Americas 10,000 years ago," *Science* 276/5319: 932–934.

—— (1998) "Between Foraging and Farming," *Science* 279/5351: 1651–1652.

Smith, P. (1972) *The Consequences of Food Production*, Reading: Addison-Wesley.

Smith, P., Bar-Yosef, O. and Sillen, A. (1984) "Archaeological and Skeletal Evidence for Dietary Change During the Late Pleistocene/Early Holocene in the Levant," in N.M. Cohen and G.J. Armelagos (eds) *Paleopathology at the Origins of Agriculture*, New York: Academic Press.

Sodestrom, T. (ed.) (1987) *Grass Systematics and Evolution*, Washington DC: Smithsonian Institution Press.

Sproul, B.C. (1979) *Primal Myths: Creation Myths Around the World*, New York: HarperCollins.

Stahl, A.B. (1989) "Plant-food processing: Implications for Dietary Quality," in D.R. Harris and G.C. Hillman (eds) *Foraging and Farming: The Evolution of Plant Exploitation*, London: Unwin Hyman.

Talalay, L.E. (2004) "Heady Business: Skulls, Heads, and Decapitation in Neolithic Anatolia and Greece," *Journal of Mediterranean Archaeology* 17/2: 139–163.

Thomas, J. (1991) *Rethinking the Neolithic*, Cambridge: Cambridge University Press.

Todd, I.A. (1976) *Çatal Hüyük in Perspective*, Menlo Park CA: Cummings.

Trachtenberg, M. and Hyman, I. (1986) *Architecture from Prehistory to Postmodernism/ The Western Tradition*, New York: Abrams.

Turnbaugh, W.A., Jurmain, R., Nelson, H. and Kilgore, L. (1999) *Understanding Physical Anthropology and Archaeology*, 7th edn, Belmont CA: Wadsworth.

Ucko, P.J. (1968) *Anthropomorphic Figurines of Predynastic Egypt and Neolithic Crete*, London: Royal Anthropological Institute.

Ucko, P.J. and Dimbleby, G.W. (eds) (1969) *The Exploitation and Domestication of Plants and Animals*, Chicago IL: Aldine.

Upham, S. (ed.) (1990) *The Evolution of Political Systems*, Cambridge: University of Cambridge Press.

Veth, P., Smith, M. and Hiscock, P. (eds) (2005) *Desert Peoples: Archaeological Perspectives*, Oxford: Blackwell.

Vigne, J.-D. and Guilaine, J. (2004) "Les Premiers Animaux de Compagnie, 8500 ans avant notre Ère? . . . Ou Comment J'ai Mangé mon Chat, mon Chien et mon Renard," *Anthropozoologica* 39/1: 249–273.

Vigne, J.-D., Guilaine, J., Debue, K., Haye, L. and Gérard, P. (2004) "Early Taming of the Cat in Cyprus," *Science* 304/5674: 259.

Vilà, C., Savolainen, P., Maldonado, J.E., Amorim, I.R., Rice, J.E., Honeycutt, R.I., Crandall, K.E., Lundberg, J. and Wayne, R.K. (1997) "Multiple and Ancient Origins of the Dog," *Science* 276/5319: 1687–1689.

Visser, M. (1986) *Much Depends on Dinner*, New York: Grove Press.

Vitelli, K.M. (1995) "Pots, Potters, and the Shaping of Greek Neolithic Society," in W.K. Barnett and J.W. Hoopes (eds) *The Emergence of Pottery: Technology and Innovation in Ancient Societies*, Washington DC: Smithsonian Institution Press.

Voigt, M.M. (1988) "Excavations at Neolithic Gritille," *Anatolica* 15: 215–232.

—— (2000) "Çatal Höyük in Context: Ritual at Early Neolithic Sites in Central and Eastern Turkey," in I. Kuijt (ed.) *Life in Neolithic Farming Communities: Social Organization, Identity, and Differentiation*, New York: Kluwer Academic/ Plenum.

Wailes, B. (ed.) (1996) *Craft Specialization and Social Evolution: In Memory of V. Gordon Childe*, University Museum Monograph 93, Philadelphia PA: University of Pennsylvania Museum.

Watson, J.D. (2003) *DNA: The Secret of Life*, New York: Knopf.

Watson, J.D. and Crick, F.H.C. (1953a) "A Structure for Deoxyribonucleic Acid," *Nature* 171: 737–738.

—— (1953b) "Genetical Implications of the Structure of Deoxyribonucleic Acid," *Nature* 171: 964–967.

Watson, P.J. (1995) "Explaining the Transition to Agriculture," in T.D. Price and A.B. Gebauer, (eds) *Last Hunters – First Farmers*, Santa Fe NM: School of American Research Press.

Weier, T.E., Stocking, C.R. and Barbour, M.G. (1982) *Botany: An Introduction to Plant Biology*, New York: Wiley.

Wheeler, M. (1956) *Still Digging*, New York: Dutton and Co.

Whittle, A. (1996) *Europe in the Neolithic: The Creation of New Worlds*, Cambridge: Cambridge University Press.

Widdowson, E.M. (1980) " Definitions of Growth," in T.L.J. Lawrence (ed.) *Growth in Animals*, London: Butterworth.

Wilford, J.N. (2007a) "Village May have Housed Builders of Stonehenge," *New York Times* online Available HTTP: <http://www.nytimes.com/2007/01/31/world/europe/31stonehenge.html?> (accessed 31 January 2007).

—— (2007b) "Traces of Ancient Village Found Near Stonehenge," *New York Times* online. Available HTTP: http://www.nytimes.com/2007/01/30/science/30cndstonehenge.html?> (accessed 30 January 2007).

Wilkes, G. (1989) "Maize: Domestication, Racial Evolution and Spread," in D.R. Harris and G.C. Hillman (eds) *Foraging and Farming: The Evolution of Plant Exploitation*, London: Unwin Hyman.

Zhang, J., Harbottle, G., Wang, C. and Kong, Z. (1999) "Oldest Playable Musical Instruments Found at Jiahu Early Neolithic Site in China," *Nature* 401: 366–368.

Zilhão, João (1993) "The Spread of Agro-Pastoral Economies Across Mediterranean Europe: A View from the Far West," *Journal of Mediterranean Archaeology* 6/1: 5–63.

Zohary, D. (1984) "Modes of Evolution of Plants under Domestication," in W.F. Grant (ed.) *Plant Biosystematics*, Montreal: Academic Press.

—— (1995) "Domestication of the Neolithic Near Eastern Crop Assemblage," in P.C. Anderson (ed.) *Prehistory of Agriculture*, Los Angeles CA: UCLA Institute of Archaeology Press Monograph 40.

—— (1996) "The Mode of Domestication of the Founder Crops of Southwest Asia," in D.R. Harris (ed.) *The Origins and Spread of Agriculture and Pastoralism in Eurasia*, London: UCL Press.

Zohary, D. and Hopf, M. (2000) *Domestication of Plants in the Old World*, 3rd edn, Oxford: Oxford University Press.

INDEX